The Wealth of the Elite

Stamatios Tsigos • Kevin Daly

The Wealth of the Elite

Toward a New Gilded Age

palgrave
macmillan

Stamatios Tsigos
Melbourne, Australia

Kevin Daly
Western Sydney University
Campbelltown, NSW, Australia

ISBN 978-981-15-2147-8 ISBN 978-981-15-2148-5 (eBook)
https://doi.org/10.1007/978-981-15-2148-5

This Palgrave Macmillan imprint is published by the registered company Springer Nature Singapore Pte Ltd.
The registered company address is: 152 Beach Road, #21-01/04 Gateway East, Singapore 189721, Singapore

Contents

Abbreviations

ABS	Australian Bureau of Statistics
ACP	Australian Consolidated Press
APC	average propensity to consume
ATO	Australian Taxation Office
CAPM	Capital Asset Pricing Model
CEO	Chief Executive Officer
CPPCC	Chinese People's Political Consultative Conference
CPU	central processing unit
DAX	Deutscher Aktienindex
DTC	double tax treaty
EDS	Electronic Data Systems
EU	European Union
G20	Group of Twenty
GDP	gross domestic product
GFC	Global Financial Crisis
GICS	Global Industry Classification System
HILDA	Household, Income and Labour Dynamics in Australia
HSD	honest significant difference
IBM	International Business Machines
IMF	International Monetary Fund
IPO	initial public offering
IT	information technology
LG	Lucky Goldstar
NSDAP	Nationalsozialistische Deutsche Arbeiterpartei
SNA	System of National Accounts

SOE	state-owned enterprise
TIEA	tax information exchange agreements
TMC	Toyota Motor Corporation
UK	United Kingdom
US	United States
WWID	World Wealth and Income Database

List of Figures

List of Tables

1

Introduction

Introduction

A key characteristic surrounding the wealth inequality debate is the extent to which personal initiative and productivity contribute to the amassment of vast fortunes. The associated debates have raged since the Gilded Age, which was characterised by the rise of vast wealth holdings amongst the few in the United States (US). Andrew Carnegie, for example, is often quoted as saying, 'People who are unable to motivate themselves must be content with mediocrity, no matter how impressive their other talents'. In stark contrast to the previous economic system of feudalism, in which feudal lords extracted rents from serfs through rights and privileges bestowed by kings, under the capitalist system any individual could pursue great fortune solely through success in commerce. This element of human agency, which anyone can attain great wealth through the successful application of their natural talents, has remained a central tenet in arguments against wealth redistribution. As Krugman (2014) states, 'implied in all this is that wealth is the reward for virtue, which makes it hard to argue for redistribution'. This centrality of the individual in the wealth story has persisted in mainstream economics. Contemporary economists such as Kaplan and Rauh (2013), for example, have sought to justify the existence of an ultra-rich class, as represented by the *Forbes* 400, along the lines of skill and entrepreneurial talent. This 'skill' is at the core of the extreme wealth levels of a few thousand individuals according to such narratives.

According to this viewpoint, Krugman (2014) argues, through hard work, along with a sprinkle of genius and luck, a vast accumulation of fortunes can arise. From a policy perspective, arguments that centralise and elevate

S. Tsigos, K. Daly, *The Wealth of the Elite*, https://doi.org/10.1007/978-981-15-2148-5_1

individuals' skills and talent above other factors in the wealth debate present a formidable challenge to any notion of wealth redistribution. Among business publications and the mass media, for example, one often encounters biographical portrayals of the wealthy containing 'rags-to-riches' stories. These stories simultaneously represent records of their success and the possibility that any individual, through sufficient application of productive hard work, can also attain the dizzying heights of extreme wealth (e.g. Baer, 2014; Giang & Goudreau, 2014; Stonington, 2010).

The wealthy and the concomitant wealth distribution skewed in their favour is gaining much focus among the contemporary media, policy makers and non-governmental organisations. In the wake of the financial system crisis in the US and the sovereign debt crisis that has engulfed Europe since 2008, there has been much renewed debate over the extent to which prevailing economic structures and institutions brought on the crises and, as a corollary, exacerbated the levels of wealth inequality observed across the world.

Indeed, the importance of the issue of the levels of wealth and income accumulation can be seen from the drastic policies recommended or considered when viewed through the prism of inequality. A report by the organisation Oxfam (2014) details the extent to which inequality has for the past decade increased substantially, as the wealth held by the top 1% now amounts to a staggering sum of USD110 trillion. In the US, home to the world's most *Forbes* billionaires, the top 1% captured 95% of the growth in wealth compared to the bottom 90%, who became poorer (Oxfam, 2014). To reverse the growing inequality, Oxfam (2014) recommended a number of policy initiatives. These policy recommendations ranged from reducing the incidence of tax evasion, enforce disclosure and transparency in all wealth holdings, the establishment of a living wage and, perhaps most controversially (depending on which side of the political spectrum one falls), the creation of progressive income and wealth tax regimes.

The International Monetary Fund (IMF) also explored the issue of income inequality, including its key drivers and its impact on economic growth (Dabla-Norris, Kochhar, Suphaphiphat, Ricka, & Tsounta, 2015). Dabla-Norris et al. (2015) find that significant income inequality decreases economic growth and that there is no 'trickle down' effect that represented the cornerstone of growth and development theories since the 1950s. They recommend investing more into education and training to develop the human capital for the poorest classes as well as implementing progressive tax regimes. The issue has already the entered political debate at the national government level. In 2012, for example, President Barack Obama raised the capital gains and dividend tax for couples with incomes above USD250,000 (Sanders, 2015). Of course, some countries have maintained a wealth tax for some time. France instituted the Solidarity Tax on Wealth in 1981, while a number of other western European nations have maintained wealth taxes throughout their respective histories, including Norway and Switzerland. Still, other countries have abandoned such an approach. Germany, for example, repealed a property tax law after it was found to be unconstitutional by the Federal Constitutional Court in Germany ("Umfairteilung" , 2012).

Recently, the Group of Twenty (G20) bloc has sought to reduce tax evasion via offshore financial centres by creating and enforcing a series of bilateral tax agreements and treaties (Lewis, 2014). More recently still, the Australian Taxation Office (ATO) has considered applying a 40% tax penalty, otherwise known as the 'Google tax', against multinationals with global incomes of $1bn AUD in a bid to address tax avoidance (Knaus, 2019).

The purpose of this book is to analyse the processes through which the modern forms of large fortunes are amassed. Despite the recent spate of governmental and non-governmental interest in inequality (be it wealth or income), the most privileged and fortunate have not generated much interest in mainstream economics. However, the publication of Piketty's (2014a) book, *Capital in the 21st Century*, has once again catapulted wealth into the focus of scholarly debate. As the issue of wealth is multifaceted, this book is not merely an exercise in business history but deals with the issue from multiple perspectives, accordingly, employing alternative research methods. Broadly, the trends and dynamics in high-tier wealth accumulation are coupled to the economic, political and social mechanisms that have been in play for at least half a century or more in some parts of the world. This approach leads to potential policy implications since much of the debate on wealth distribution centres on the extent to which wealth has been 'justly' attained.

Both world governments and non-government organisations are directing attention to the related issues of tax policy, wealth concentration and inequality. Piketty (2014a) forced a reconsideration on how economics and the social sciences at large tackle the issues driving wealth accumulation and concentration. By emphasising the importance of 'capital' in capitalism and the transition from an affluent society to a society based, potentially, on inheritance and patrimony, Piketty has revealed tremendous gaps and logic in how the latter is analysed.

Amongst mainstream economics, when the issues of high wealth concentration have been recognised and explored, the boundary of analysis has been restrictive. This body of research has typically focused on the returns to skills and education as an overriding aspect of the new economic elite. One of the most recent works in this strain, Kaplan and Rauh (2013), seeks to attribute the rise in US billionaires to the appearance of the 'tech' based billionaire where an education in computer science, preferably from an Ivy League university, is presumably a core requirement. Such sentiments echo Kalleberg (2011), where highly skilled workers reap enormous benefits in the 'modern' economy while the low-skilled miss out. Bonnet and Théry (2014) argue the elite themselves have adopted this view, believing that discourse that associates great fortunes with hard work in itself explains their privileged standing in society.

Such a discourse on the relation between economic elite and meritocracy negates much of the historical changes in both the political, social and economic realm that could potentially explain the existence of the new ultra-rich class. Meritocracy alone, for example, cannot explain the survival and prosperity of the German family dynasties throughout the past century which included two devastating world wars. Nor can a standard life cycle model account for its preponderance. Explanations in the realm of law and politics are better suited here.

Objectives of the Book

To date, the exploration of the ultra-rich has been limited and often beholden to restrictive precepts of neoclassical thought. The rise of the ultra-rich, and ever greater wealth concentration into their hands, are largely grounded in notions of winner-takes-all markets (Rosen, 1981), returns to education or human capital (Kaplan & Rauh, 2013) or the increasing scale of markets. Piketty's (2014a) focus on the rise of the patrimonial society heralds a transformation on how economists should explore these issues. The call for multidimensional studies into the dynamics of wealth accumulation (Bonnet & Théry, 2014; Piketty, 2014a, 2014b) to further understand the behaviour of the wealthy and their relation to broader economic, political and social forces is taken up in this book.

The primary objective of this book is to explore and analyse the evolution of wealth across time, space and the factors that play a critical role in any observed trends among the wealthiest sections of society, particularly in the advanced economies. This rests on the ability to amass and present statistical data on the world's wealthiest individuals with particular emphasis on examining the trends and relationships across important economic cycles and institutional developments. Further, the behaviour of wealthy households must be considered as consumption and savings, debt levels, the structure of income and taxation all have a role in either reducing the pace of accumulation or accelerating and accentuating it depending on the level of wealth held by households. In addition, an examination is made of the role of wealth in permitting enhanced risk taking. Given the increasing financialisation of household budgets, this seems an important channel through which wealth can further accrue rapidly to wealthier households. This has recently been recognised by Saez and Zucman (2014), who find that rising wealth inequality in the US is intimately intertwined not only with savings and consumption but also with rates of return to household portfolios.

Based on a review of the literature of wealth accumulation, the following research questions were formulated:

1. Which regions of the world have given rise to the greatest private fortunes?

   The first research question is explored in Chap. 3, where the general patterns of the rich are established at the regional level.

   This sets the global context by demonstrating how wealth accumulation is rapidly increasing at the highest wealth tier and establishing that this process is not just restricted to the developed world. Further, this research examines not only where today's wealth is generated, but also conducting an analysis that explores the generation of wealth across all sectors, such as information technology (IT) and pharmaceuticals, to more traditional commercial activities such as finance and retailing.
2. To what extent do various structural changes in economy and society impact upon wealth distribution and concentration across advanced economies?

   This question is examined in Chap. 3. The chapter seeks to establish a causal link, analytically, to historical trends in various factors associated with wealth dynamics. Significant emphasis is also placed on the changes in the structure of top income shares and the impact of tax policy on the dynamics of high wealth concentration, and the role of financialisation and consumerism in influencing the savings rates and the potential for household investment. Chapter 4 adopts an analytical approach in exploring how the above factors have played a role in increasing wealth concentration amongst the advanced economies.
3. Is inheritance concentrated in a few countries or regions, or does it manifest itself evenly across the globe, particularly in advanced, developed, capitalist societies?
4. What is the relationship between government policy and the creation and endurance of economic elites through succeeding generations of family dynasties?

5. For the great self-made fortunes, are there differences in the role of entrepreneurialism versus appropriation in the initial creation of wealth depending on a country's pattern of development?
6. Do entrepreneurs, depending on their budgetary constraints, specialise in 'low' budget risks or 'high' budget risks?

Questions 4, 5, 6 and 7 are explored in Chaps. 4 and 5. Chapter 5 is a cross-country study. This historical analysis focuses on the individual histories of extreme wealth holders and the historical context in which their wealth was made. Further, the relative importance of inheritance greatly varies across economies suggesting substantial divergence into the future. The analysis proceeds in the spirit of wealth historians (Rockoff, 2012; Rubinstein, 1980).

To address the questions raised above, the analysis is approached in a number of ways.

Firstly, the general trends in wealth across various countries and regions are analysed, utilising data from wealth lists between 1990 and 2013 and national wealth to income ratios. In total, the analysis consists of an unbalanced panel of 2609 individuals and families for a total sample size of 9426 across the 24-year sample period.[1] The wealth lists incorporate data on not only wealth size and demographic indicators but also the country of origin, age and date of birth, and the industrial or commercial sources of wealth.

Secondly, the study examines which regions appear to be producing the wealthiest individuals and whether these observations can be tied to changes in the economic environment, or if other forces more aligned with political, social or even personal circumstances are at work. This follows Watkins (1907) and Rockoff (2012), among others, who viewed the extreme wealth levels of the Gilded Age to be by-products of technological change in certain industries and the rise of financial capital. For these writers, individuals became wealthy due to fortuitous economic and technological circumstances. A century on, are the same forces still at work? In the Gilded Age, railroad growth fuelled the growth of newfound riches in finance and real estate. Has the World Wide Web revolution of the 1990s had a similar impact?

Thirdly, the study examines the world's most advanced economies to determine whether systematic differences in the patterns of wealth generation across economies and industries exist. Which common traits appear across countries that incubate and give rise to the largest fortunes observable? For example, Watkins (1907) argued that the rise of 'abstract property' was a

[1] Unbalanced panel refers to data in which observations for a group are missing across time.

necessary condition for wealth in the Gilded Age in the US. In contemporary times, Torgler and Piatti (2013) and Petras (2008) posit that corruption plays a major role in some countries, while Sanandaji and Leeson (2013) find that secure property rights are the most important element. Alternatively, do these forces differ depending on the associated historical developments of these countries, as Richard Jones (1831) once argued?

Generally, these issues are explored in an analytical and qualitative framework. The use of econometric analysis was rejected because the complexity of the micro data used in the study and its relationship to macro-wide or political factors does not readily lend itself to such an approach. Piketty (2014a), for example, argues that the use of a regression framework to explore the relationship between income and wealth inequality and $r>g$ (where, r = rate of return on capital and g = rate of national income growth) encounters a major impediment. The obstacle is that the growth of wealth stocks can be a very long process, often spanning generations, making it difficult to select an appropriate lag length. Indeed, the present study found numerous instances, for example, where an individual acquired wealth from their father's construction business that was built up before the Second World War. Subsequently, their progeny was catapulted into extreme wealth levels some two decades later. How does one choose an appropriate lag length in such an instance? In more extreme scenarios, some European dynasties span generations greater than three or four centuries, or greater than the existence of some nations. This book follows Piketty's (2014a) preferred approach, which relies 'on a mixture of careful case studies and structural theoretical models' (p. 77) and has been used previously in a number of economic history studies such as Rubinstein (1980) and Rockoff (2012).

Limitations of the Study

Throughout the process of data collection and collation for this research, a number of weaknesses and limitations were identified that limit the inferences and conclusions that can be made.

Firstly, the data on the ultra-rich is sourced from secondary data sources. Media lists on the ultra-rich are the most accessible data source on these individuals—but are plagued by errors or inaccuracies. This is particularly apparent when demarcating between fortunes that are inherited or self-made. In many instances, media publications appear to have moved to a flexible interpretation of what constitutes inheritance over the entirety of the sample period for any number of individuals. Given the longitudinal nature of the data and to ensure consistency across time, such instances were checked and validated from other primary sources including newspaper articles or biographical sources to ensure the coherence and consistency from period to period. Still, data accuracy represents a major caveat to the analysis of the data.

Secondly, the issue of gender is not explored. Some literature has identified this as an area demanding greater scholarship. For example, it would be instructive to observe the apportionment of wealth between siblings of different genders. Are these related to cultural norms or do the ultra-rich take a different approach? Such an issue could be explored in the primogeniture theoretical frameworks of Stiglitz (1969). Data on gender and inheritance is available in our database but the aforementioned research avenue is not explored here. In addition, the relationship between sector and gender is worthwhile exploring.

Thirdly, a major limitation of the study is not being able to expand the scope of certain sections to include more countries in the study. A primary obstacle is a lack of data availability in a longitudinal format. This is particularly in relation to distributional data on wealth, income and taxation. This limitation is particularly acute for this study focusing on the economic elite as many of these individuals come from Asia or Latin America for which relevant data is scarce. Even in the instances of advanced industrialised economies, significant data impediments were encountered despite great strides over the recent past toward this end. For example, wealth distribution data over a long time period, and without missing observations, for Canada, Germany or Japan is not available. Further, data on some variables may simply be missing or not directly comparable across countries due to definitional changes. In addition, much of the data that is available comes from household surveys undertaken on usually intermittent basis. These may only be produced once every ten years. These impediments ultimately limit the scope of what can be studied.

Organisation of the Book and Main Findings

The book is divided into six chapters. Chapter 2 reviews the literature on wealth and the ultra-rich. This research is relatively limited, given the importance of the ultra-rich in a capitalist system. The literature covers various aspects of wealth from different analytical frameworks. The chapter begins with historical notions of wealth and capital. Particular attention is paid to Piketty (2014a) and the associated framework for exploring the accumulation of wealth but a range of other empirical and theoretical works are considered.

These range from studies based on social science theories examining the emergence of economic elites in a society to the contemporary economics literature that has researched the issue of wealth from numerous areas, including from industry structure to corruption or stochastic accumulation models. The chapter also reviews how the definition of wealth has evolved over the ages and how it has been differentiated in economics from the definition of capital. Further, in a broader context, this chapter situates the book amongst the broader corpus of work associated with wealth accumulation models.

Chapter 3 presents an overview of the construction of the ultra-rich database including establishing age, industry and, where warranted, citizenship. Secondly, trends in aggregate wealth amassment are analysed in the form of wealth to income ratios and the amassment of wealth as exemplified by billionaire population and holdings. The chapter also discusses the impacts of economic crises, specifically the Asian Financial Crisis and the Global Financial Crisis (GFC) on these trends.

The main findings of Chap. 3 are as follows. Firstly, aggregate wealth, as measured by wealth to income ratios, has increased at a rapid rate across the advanced industrialised economies. At a micro level, the trends in accumulated wealth are reflected in the rise of the 'billionaire class' across the world with average increases in wealth of the class dwarfing income growth. The rise of this class is not restricted merely to the First World, but in all regions of the world. Here, Russia, China and South America are especially prominent. North America, however, remains the main engine of billionaire growth. Inheritance remains a significant force amongst the ultra-rich class in parts of Europe, Asia and South America contrary to the findings of studies that focus only on the US.

Chapter 4 discusses the rise of a dual economy among the world's advanced economies where wealth is concentrated in fewer hands proportionally. It follows the wealth accumulation model developed by Saez and Zucman (2014) and in the spirit of Meade (1964), as well as the work of Piketty and Zucman (2014) and Piketty (2014a), among others. The purpose of this chapter is twofold. Firstly, it illustrates the stark chasm that appears to be emerging between the wealthiest households and the rest of the population in certain advanced economies across several variables relevant to wealth holdings and concentration. Secondly, heavy emphasis is placed on situating these variables on the ever-increasing roles of financialisation and consumerism in both enhancing the position of the wealthy and suppressing the upward mobility of large sections of society. Taxation policy is also introduced in relation to labour and capital income, inheritances, and tax evasion.

The major findings of Chap. 4 are that various forces are increasingly becoming beneficial to the richest segments of society or economy. In each facet, consumerism, financialisation, income shares (wage and capital income) the rich are dominating. Further, the cross-country comparisons of taxation show again movement favouring the rich in all aspects of taxation. Taxes on labour incomes, capital incomes, estates and gifts, and wealth taxes all have moved in a direction that favour wealth concentration. Tax evasion itself is increasingly providing a further avenue of reducing the tax burden of the wealthy.

Chapter 5 delves much deeper into the high wealth accumulation trends by exploring the historical sources and processes for the creation of large fortunes across the world's advanced economies. Given the scope of the study, the focus here is to draw out the differing patterns of wealth accumulation, including the role of the entrepreneur and inheritance, where one group may dominate in a given region or country. The discussion ultimately rests on the prediction by Piketty (2014a) that the high rates of return of yesteryear are diminishing now and links this to prevailing institutional changes. In addition, the theoretical prediction of Shorrocks (1988) is considered. Shorrocks's model predicts that the dynamics associated with wealth accumulation vary substantially depending upon on the resources necessary to access certain entrepreneurial risks. Support for the theoretical predictions of both Shorrocks (1988) and Piketty (2014a) are found across the globe.

Finally, Chap. 6 provides the conclusion to the study. It summarises the main findings of the book in greater detail and provides avenues for future research.

Contributions

This study makes at least two major contributions to the extant literature of wealth accumulation and on the ultra-rich.

Firstly, this study contributes directly to the literature on the sources of great fortunes by showing that the riches observed today significantly differ across the globe depending on the countries' historical development. A recent trend in some literature, particularly that of a neoclassical economics standpoint, is to relate the rise of great fortunes to the human capital one possesses (Kaplan & Rauh, 2013). The results presented in Chap. 5 reveal that the wealth that has been amassed cannot be exclusively tied to such explanations.

Instead, the cross-country comparative study demonstrates the roles of government policy and institutions in governing the rise of fortunes. The impact of these varies region by region. The results complement recent studies by Piketty (2014a) and various empirical studies by scholars focusing on specific countries (Hazledine & Siegfried, 1997; Rockoff, 2012; Siegfried & Roberts, 1991; Siegfried & Round, 1994 and Stilwell & Ansari, 2003).

The second contribution is to show in a cross-country setting the dynamics of wealth accumulation through the prism of various socioeconomic factors. The work builds on the single country studies such as Saez and Zucman (2014), by using a convenient wealth accumulation model to decompose and to compare the process of accumulation across seven advanced economies. Unlike studies which purely focus on elements of inequality in isolation, this study seeks to combine the findings of a disparate set of studies into one uniform corpus of work.

References

Baer, D. (2014, September 30). 14 billionaires who started with nothing – Including Jack Ma and Larry Ellison. *Business Insider*. Retrieved from http://www.businessinsider.com.au/

Bonnet, F., & Théry, C. (2014). *Sociology and political science in the patrimonial society: Implications of Piketty's Capital*. Retrieved from https://halshs.archives-ouvertes.fr/halshs-01060570/document, <halshs-01060570>.

Dabla-Norris, E., Kochhar, K., Suphaphiphat, N., Ricka, F., & Tsounta, E. (2015). *Causes and consequences of income inequality: A global perspective* (No. 15/13). IMF Staff Discussion Notes. Retrieved from https://www.imf.org/

Giang, V., & Goudreau, J. (2014, February 21). 16 billionaires who started with nothing – Including WhatsApp's cofounder. *Business Insider*. Retrieved from http://www.businessinsider.com.au/

Hazledine, T., & Siegfried, J. J. (1997). How did the wealthiest New Zealanders get so rich? *New Zealand Economic Papers, 31*, 35–47.

Jones, R. (1831). *An essay on the distribution of wealth. Part 1: Rent*. London: John Murray.

Kalleberg, A. (2011). *Good jobs, bad jobs: The rise of polarized and precarious employment systems in the United, 1970s–2000s*. New York: Russell Sage Foundation, American Sociological Association Rose Series in Sociology.

Kaplan, S. N., & Rauh, J. D. (2013). Family, education, and sources of wealth among the richest Americans, 1982–2012. *The American Economic Review, 103*(3), 158–162.

Knaus, C. (2019). Tax office may apply 40% tax against multinationals for diverting profits. *The Guardian*. Retrieved from https://www.theguardian.com/australia-news/2019/apr/05/tax-office-may-apply-40-tax-against-multinationals-for-diverting-profits

Krugman, P. (2014, January 18). The myth of the deserving rich. *The New York Times*. Retrieved from http://krugman.blogs.nytimes.com/2014/01/18/the-myth-of-the-deserving-rich

Lewis, R. (2014, November 14). G20 to launch 'aggressive' attack on tax avoidance among multinationals. *The Australian*. Retrieved from http://www.theaustralian.com.au/

Meade, J. E. (1964). *Efficiency, equality, and the ownership of property*. London: George Allen & Unwin.

Oxfam. (2014). *Working for the few. Political capture and economic inequality* (No. 178). Oxfam Briefing Paper. Retrieved from http://www.oxfam.org/en/research/working-few

Petras, J. (2008). Global ruling class: Billionaires and how they "make it". *Journal of Contemporary Asia, 38*, 319–329.

Piketty, T. (2014a). *Capital in the twenty-first century*. Cambridge, MA: The Belknap Press of Harvard University Press.

Piketty, T. (2014b). Capital in the twenty-first century: A multidimensional approach to the history of capital and social classes. *The British Journal of Sociology, 65*, 736–747.

Piketty, T., & Zucman, G. (2014). Capital is back: Wealth-income ratios in rich countries 1700–2010. *The Quarterly Journal of Economics, 129*, 1155–1210.

Rockoff, H. (2012). The great fortunes of the Gilded Age and the crisis of 1893. *Research in Economic History, 28*, 233–262.

Rosen, S. (1981). The economics of superstars. *The American Economic Review, 71*, 845–858.

Rubinstein, W. D. (1980). Modern Britain. In W. D. Rubinstein (Ed.), *Wealth and the wealthy in the modern world* (pp. 46–89). London: Croom Helm.

Saez, E., & Zucman, G. (2014). *Wealth inequality in the United States Since 1913: Evidence from capitalized income tax data* (No. 20625). NBER Working Paper Series. Retrieved from http://www.nber.org/papers/w20625

Sanandaji, T., & Leeson, P. T. (2013). Billionaires. *Industrial and Corporate Change, 22*, 313–337.

Sanders, K. (2015, January 20). Obama wants higher tax rate on capital gains and tax rates. *Politifact*. Retrieved on 15 June, 2015, from http://www.politifact.com/

Shorrocks, A. F. (1988). Wealth holdings and entrepreneurial activity. In D. Kessler & A. Masson (Eds.), *Modelling the accumulation and distribution of wealth*. Oxford, UK: Clarendon Press.

Siegfried, J. J., & Roberts, A. (1991). How did the wealthiest Britons get so rich? *Review of Industrial Organization, 6*, 19–32.

Siegfried, J. J., & Round, D. K. (1994). How did the wealthiest Australians get so rich? *Review of Income and Wealth, 40*, 191–204.

Stiglitz, J. E. (1969). Distribution of income and wealth among individuals. *Econometrica, 37*, 382–397.

Stilwell, F., & Ansari, M. (2003). Wealthy Australians. *Journal of Australian Political Economy, 52*, 143–157.

Stonington, J. (2010, December 6). Twenty billionaires who started with nothing. *Bloomberg*. Retrieved from http://www.bloomberg.com/

Torgler, B., & Piatti, M. (2013). Extraordinary wealth, globalization, and corruption. *Review of Income and Wealth, 59*, 341–359.

Umfairteilung. (2012, September 8). *The Economist*. Retrieved from http://www.economist.com/

Watkins, G. P. (1907). The growth of large fortunes. *Publications of the American Economic Association, 8*(4), 1–170.

2

Literature Review: The Wealthy as a *Sui Generis*

This chapter provides a literature review of several of the works in the field of the ultra-rich and wealth accumulation. Specifically, the objectives of the chapter are:

- To discuss and define wealth and its close relative, capital.
- The relationship between wealth accumulation and capital accumulation models are discussed. The book focuses on models of wealth accumulation as its starting point rather than attempting to unify a theory of wealth distribution with an aggregate productivity theory of growth.
- A review of historical approaches to the issue of wealth accumulation is provided as it pertains to the ultra-rich specifically. This review is not solely limited to the discipline of economics but includes, aspects of elite theory from the social sciences. In addition, recent empirical analyses of the rich are reviewed, which have mostly focused on establishing the sources of great fortunes.

Introduction

Economic research on the ultra-wealthy is scarce, despite the attention they have received in the popular mind as discussed in Chap. 1. Academic discourse has typically examined the poverty-laden sections of society (Koh, Wissink, & Forrest, 2016, p. 18). However, such a focus may lead to the neglect of a class who play a pivotal role in economy and society in general. Economists who have researched the extremely wealthy such as Tuckman

S. Tsigos, K. Daly, *The Wealth of the Elite*, https://doi.org/10.1007/978-981-15-2148-5_2

(1973), argue that effectively taxing the rich would provide significant budget relief to the US government's finances. Attempting any such policy initiative, directed at the rich demands strong economic justification given their role as owners of capital and enterprise (Slemrod, 2000). From a general economic or commerce perspective, Hassler (1999) forcefully argues that this group of individuals makes decisions every day that affects the economic well-being of millions. Indeed, the subjects of this study either found or own many of the world's largest corporations that touch every aspect of our lives from food to computing, retailing to automobiles, and medicine to junk food.

The surprising lack of research on the wealthy, despite the recognition that wealth does 'make the world go around', could be related to how precisely the question of wealth accumulation is explored in orthodox economics.

Neoclassical economics with its focus on marginal productivity theories of capital and labour are limited in providing a sufficient analytical framework within which to investigate certain aspects of both wealth accumulation and distribution. Similarly, the post-Keynesian approach may not be sufficient either in exploring certain sections of the wealth distribution given its overall macroeconomic perspective. The lack of clear disciplinary demarcation lines has also perhaps deterred economists from exploring the topic, particularly in contemporary times, whereas social scientists and geographers are often more prepared to tackle the subject.

However, perhaps the biggest hurdle that confronts researchers, be they economists or social scientists, when seeking to grapple with the rich are the significant data limitations they encounter. Typically, economists approach the problem by employing tax records, deceased estate records or a rich list published by a major periodical. This data is then utilised in a typical econometric framework, employing regression analysis, to test various hypotheses. Tax records provide the most contemporary accurate records, but when dealing with the wealthiest of individuals, the issue of tax evasion becomes a consideration, as does reconciling tax measures across jurisdictions. Deceased estate records also provide a high degree of accuracy but can only be used for deceased individuals. Media lists provide a fruitful foundation for further exploration as long as one is mindful of their limitations, the most obvious being that of inaccurate wealth estimates. Numerous media lists exist across the world. In the US, the *Forbes* annual rankings are by far the most popular, focusing not just on the US but on regional and global wealth rankings. In Australia, there is the *Business Review Weekly's* Top 400 Rich List, while in the UK there is the *Sunday Times* Rich List. Despite these data limitations, some economists have developed a body of work that provides a foundation upon which this book can build.

In general terms, Chap. 2 is divided into two sections where there is a change in focus by moving from a general review of wealth accumulation to one focusing on just one aspect of the wealth distribution, the ultra-rich. The section entitled 'Conceptualising Wealth' principally focuses upon the concepts of wealth and the theoretical models that have considered the accumulation of wealth and the concomitant distributions of wealth. This section also incorporates a lengthy discussion on Piketty's (2014) concept of wealth and why his definition of wealth is employed throughout this book. A discussion on the link between capital accumulation and wealth accumulation models is also considered, particularly considering the theoretical contributions of Piketty (2014). Chapter 4 utilises a form of these models to examine the multifaceted nature of wealth accumulation. The section entitled 'Review of Scholarship on the Rich' deals exclusively with the ultra-rich and the literature which explores this small, but important, class. In contrast to the previous section, which is heavily focused on theoretical aspects, the focus here is on empirical works to this end. Some theoretical works are considered though from the history of ideas to more contemporary works that deal specifically with the ultra-rich. This section is particularly important for Chap. 5.

Conceptualising Wealth

The definition of wealth in economic or philosophical academic discourse has undergone significant variation since antiquity through to the contemporary era. In economics, the role of wealth has, to an extent, been supplanted by the concept of capital. The purpose of this section is to trace the historical evolution of the concept of wealth and how wealth and capital have become at once separated in the literature. The separation is often viewed as necessary as the two concepts may necessitate different conceptual frameworks in analysing their associated dynamics. The discussion then turns to the definition of wealth and capital that Piketty (2014) has proposed in which the two are viewed equivalently.

The publication of Piketty's (2014) book has generated significant scholastic debate. One aspect of Piketty (2014) upon which much criticism has centred is over his definition of wealth and capital (see e.g. Blume & Durlauf, 2015; Galbraith, 2014). In general, Piketty consistently equates wealth with capital. It will be argued that this approach is a by-product of Piketty (2014) attempting to reconcile macro observations (growth theory) with micro observations (the distribution of wealth and income).

Wealth and capital have undergone various definitional changes throughout history. In earlier times, the two concepts have been viewed as virtual synonyms, and in contemporary times they have emerged into distinct concepts.

Economic historian Robert Heilbroner (1987) emphasises that wealth represents the fundamental business of economics. Despite the ostensible centrality of wealth in economics, a precise consensus surrounding the definition of wealth has failed to emerge. The lack of consensus may be due to the various meanings of wealth spawned through the ages. The lack of definitional rigour potentially obfuscating the manner of how to debate and analyse wealth. At the core, the issues tend be as to the true purpose of wealth in an economy.

In antiquity, a consensus was absent. For some ancient Hellenic thinkers, the definition revolved around the ability to defy the need for work:

> A Greek was wealthy if he could live without having to work, poor if he did not have enough to live on without working. From this point of view, the majority of people in Greece were 'poor' since they had to work. (Austin & Vidal-Naquet, 1977, p. 16)

Applying such a definition from antiquity would suggest that some of the richest individuals in contemporary times are not wealthy, given that the majority continue to take a day-to-day managerial or entrepreneurial role in the operation of their business enterprises. Similarly, Carroll, Slacalek, and Tokuoka (2014) argue that wealth inequality emerges from those with low wealth-income ratios (high wealth and high income) and not from purely asset-rich households alone.

Distantly echoing concepts of modern capital rather than wealth, some ancient Hellenic thinkers emphasised the utility of wealth towards production. Xenophon (430–354 BC) viewed wealth as a resource that a person can use for some purpose. The use of wealth is not towards creating more wealth—but towards creating a household for the purposes of leisure and autarky. In other words, 'Xenophon ... gives no evidence of having considered wealth as anything but an instrument in the service of the good life' (Booth, 1993, p. 42). In some respects, this notion of wealth echoes those of modern neoclassical production functions in which capital (plant and machinery, land) is a core variable.

Pre-Enlightenment discourse adopted an appreciably unique concept of wealth. The role of money or *specie* in wealth was emphasised—to the detriment of 'real' goods. To some degree, these definitions were heavily informed, or aligned, with the machinations of the mercantilist international system and power politics that dominated international relations in the 1500s to 1600s. Negating the importance of production (unless it provided substantial trade surpluses), mercantilists elevated accumulated wealth as the primary means through which dominance in the international system could be attained. Large stocks of wealth were heavily tied to the amassment of *specie*, gold or silver from whatever source, including plunder or appropriation and not necessarily through an accumulation of national income. The massive reserves, representing a country's wealth, provided a surer foundation upon which to conduct wars or dominate neighbours before the advent of efficient tax regimes or modern central banks.

Equating only *specie* with wealth received considerable criticism, especially amongst the French laissez-faire thinkers and British Tories. Pierre de Boisguilbert vehemently rejected the amassment of *specie*, and instead emphasised that the essence of wealth was in goods. Spengler (1984) argues that the views of de Boisguilbert were highly influential on Adam Smith, though the latter never referenced the former. Similarly, the Tory, Dudley North, wrote that:

> he who is most diligent, and raiseth most Fruits, or maketh most of Manufactory, will abound most in what others make, or raise; and consequently be free from Want, and enjoy most Conveniences, which is truly to be Rich, altho' there were no such thing as Gold, Silver, or the like amongst them. (p. 14)

Amongst these thinkers, monetary holdings were not wealth; instead, the goods that one could produce and accumulate constituted wealth.

Enlightenment approaches to the problem of wealth significantly departed from pre-Enlightenment conceptions—by seeking to elaborate other aspects of wealth. Classical economists developed a significant point of departure from previous generations of philosophers with a much more narrowly bounded concept of wealth, namely capital (Hodgson 2014). Specifically, the idea of wealth largely transformed into the concept of capital and in doing so reduced the scope of economists' analysis of wealth. To a great extent, the primacy of the monetary holdings in wealth (or capital) was divested. For Adam Smith, the emergence of capitalism was synonymous with goods that were produced and reordered by labour. Adam Smith emphasised the importance of labour when elucidating what he viewed as the wealth of nations:

> The annual labor of every nation is the fund which originally supplies it with all the necessaries and conveniences of life which it annually consumes, and which consist always either in the immediate produce of that labor, or in what is purchased with that produce from other nations. (1952, p. 1)

The conflating of capital and wealth has led to much debate particularly in relation to Piketty's (2014) seminal treatise on wealth inequality. For Piketty (2014), the concept of wealth and capital represent virtual synonyms. Piketty's definition of capital makes explicit the role of market valuation for all forms of assets and goes beyond the concept of capital as defined in either neoclassical or post-Keynesian models of growth. The extent to which Piketty (2014), ostensibly, conflates the concepts of capital and wealth is apparent in the following passage of text which defines national 'capital' or 'wealth': 'the total market value of everything owned by the residents and government of a given country at a given point in time, provided that it can be traded on some market' (p. 48). Assets here go well beyond 'productive' assets and encompass land and housing and even consumer durables.

Numerous criticisms have been mounted about Piketty's (2014) definition of wealth and capital, from both Neoclassical and Marxist economists. Firstly, there is the issue of what can and cannot be included in the concept of 'capital'. Blume and Durlauf (2015) argue that Piketty's concept of capital is far too sensitive to changes in wealth holder preferences. 'Changes in tastes concerning impressionist paintings will change the wealth share of national output even though such changes leave the productivity of the capital component of wealth unchanged' (p. 752). Similarly, Kanbur and Stiglitz (2015) point out that a rise in property values will have a purely distributional effect but will not raise the productive capacity of a country.

Being faithful to the title of our book, we are concerned with wealth and not capital. Other contemporary definitions of wealth broadly encompass various assets and reflect more popular understanding of the word. Piketty and Saez (2014) are clear in their definition of wealth:

> Wealth (or capital) is a stock. It corresponds to the total wealth owned at a given point in time. This stock comes from the wealth appropriated or accumulated in the past.... [W]ealth is defined as nonhuman net worth, i.e., the sum of nonfinancial and financial assets, net of financial liabilities (debt). National wealth is the sum of private wealth (net worth owned by private individuals) and public wealth (net worth owned by the government and public agencies). (p. 842)

An explicit definition guided by the United Nations' System of National Accounts (SNA) is found in Piketty and Zucman (2014). Private wealth, they state:

> is the net wealth (assets minus liabilities) of households and non-profit institutions serving households. Following SNA guidelines, assets include all the non-financial assets – land, buildings, machines, etc. – and financial assets ... over which ownership rights can be enforced and that provide economic benefits to their owners. (Piketty & Zucman, 2014, p. 9)

Throughout this book, wealth is defined in the terms proposed by Piketty and Saez (2014). Analytically, the measure of wealth being proposed here is based on three key variables. These include real estate, corporate capital and financial assets. Real estate and corporate capital can be denoted as R and K, respectively, and let financial assets be denoted by F. Wealth, therefore, is $W = K + R + F$. *Wealth accumulates* through corporate 'capital' or real estate acquisition, accumulation or appropriation and/or growth in financial assets. Further, the measure of wealth is confined to marketable wealth. Non-marketable wealth such as pensions is excluded from the analysis. This definition of wealth falls within the definitions utilised in wealth accumulation models which are discussed below.

By adopting a broad definition of wealth, we are effectively able to study wealth accumulation and concentration beyond the traditional lines of neo-classical economic enquiry, to political economy and other schools that incorporate elements such as institutionalism or power. This has been recognised amongst critics of Piketty (2014). Galbraith (2014) states that 'private financial valuation measures power, including political power even if the holder plays no active economic role. Absentee landlords and the Koch brothers have power of this type'. In the very first chapter, Piketty (2014) strives to emphasise this when stating:

> The history of the distribution of wealth has always been deeply political, and it cannot be reduced to purely economic mechanisms. (...). It is shaped by the way economic, social, and political actors view what is just and what is not, as well as by the relative power of those actors and the collective choices that result. (p. 35)

The utility of conceptualising wealth along such plural or multidimensional lines becomes more evident when one attempts to analyse the impact of wealth accumulation on society at large. For example, given the potential re-emergence of inheritance as a source of great wealth, what will its impact be on societal relations? Alternatively, how does such a society and economy differ from an affluent society? The Affluent Society (Galbraith, 1958) largely coincides with a period when income growth was greater than the returns to wealth. Affluent societies tend to reward meritocracy and are plural in nature. Societies dominated by inherited wealth move to a paradigm characterised by the power and dominance of an elite (Bonnet & Théry, 2014). In contrast, according to Piketty (2014) the Affluent Society represents a historical anomaly. Instead, the domination of inherited wealth is the norm throughout recorded history, particularly when returns to capital are greater than national income growth. Bonnet and Théry (2014) argue that Piketty's approach to capital or wealth permits the detection of such societal transformations.

The multidimensional nature of wealth and the historical transformation it has undergone presents the opportunity to explore the issue of wealth accumulation and concentration from a plurality of dimensions. Aspects of modern-day wealth scholarship do already fall largely within this framework. Contemporary studies, which incorporate analysis of industrial sectors, are a case in point and discussed further on. We now turn to micro-founded wealth accumulation models. These models represent the body of scholarship to which this study is most closely aligned in spirit. These wealth accumulation models can be used to model wealth distributions, to fix ideas surrounding the decomposition of the constituent processes underlying wealth accumulation, and to provide a framework for examining the sources of great fortunes.

In a wide-ranging survey on the distribution of wealth, Davies and Shorrocks (2000) detail two broad empirical regularities that have been discovered in relation to the accumulation of wealth. Firstly, the distribution of wealth is positively skewed. Secondly, the extreme right of the wealth distribution tail is well approximated by a Pareto distribution. Further, when wealth is transformed by the logarithmic function, it approaches a log-normal distribution function.[1] Therefore, a stochastic process itself is sufficient to model wealth distributions as empirically observed. Feller (1971) describes the process of a coin tossing game in which the short-term winner gains momentum and indefinitely maintains the lead, contrary to the layperson's prediction that the lead would change roughly evenly. It is not difficult to see how a stochastic process can lead to situations where a winner-takes-all market emerges. Thurow's (1975) theory of wealth inequality in the US is based upon notions of luck where prudence only takes one so far. Echoing modern theories of financial economics, Thurow (1975) argues that coupled with luck, modern financial markets provide the means for rapid capitalisation and, consequently, the path to large fortunes. In other words, adopting a financial economics perspective, the Efficient Market Hypothesis (Fama, 1970) provides a sufficient explanation for a given wealth distribution observed in a market.

[1] A lognormal process suggests a random walk model, $ln W_t = ln W_{t-1} + u_t$

Although the Efficient Market Hypothesis can provide a clear framework for thinking about extreme wealth, testing whether observed extreme wealth accumulation is down to luck may prove exceedingly difficult (Canterbery & Nosari, 1985). The concept of 'long leads' initially filtered into the industrial organisation literature with Scherer's (1980) simulation model in which without market frictions such as economies of scale or entry barriers, some firms managed to grow well above average and capture up to 30% market share. Furthermore, once in front, these firms maintained this lead.

However, a simple random-walk model of wealth accumulation possesses a significant drawback when taken to a real-world context. Davies and Shorrocks (2000) point out there are no upper-bound to these models—therefore, they provide no explanatory power when confronted by decreasing wealth inequality. Empirically, the deficiency of these models is apparent when one considers the immediate post-Second World War era where a decrease in wealth inequality was observed.

An alternative to the stochastic process framework is to introduce a myriad of mechanisms which can either accelerate or decelerate wealth accumulation. These models are micro-founded in their approach. Meade (1975) provides an accounting identity for analysing the distribution of household wealth distribution:

$$W_t = W_{t-1} + E_t + r_t W_{t-1} - C_t + I_t \tag{2.1}$$

where W_t is wealth at time t, r_t is the rate of return on investments, E_t is earned income, $C_t$is consumption and I_t are gifts and bequests received. Meade's formulation can be rewritten to encapsulate an individual's or family's total lifetime experience (Davies & Shorrocks, 2000). Assuming zero wealth at age 0, the dynamics of wealth accumulation in Eq. 2.1 can be rewritten as follows:

$$W_t = \sum_{k=1}^{t} \left(E_k - C_k + I_k\right) \prod_{j=k+1}^{t} \left(1 + r_j\right) \tag{2.2}$$

Therefore, per Meade (1975), a family's wealth is determined by its age and history of:

(i) earnings
(ii) savings rates
(iii) rates of returns
(iv) inheritances

In Chap. 4, a model developed by Saez and Zucman (2014) is used to decompose wealth accumulation across similar variables. An advantage of both models is the capacity to cover different classes of individuals, and not just bifurcate classes to worker and the rentier capitalist. On a smaller incidental point, an advantage of the Saez and Zucman (2014) model is the incorporation of taxation as a mechanism for equalising or lowering the rate of wealth accumulation—but this can be easily accommodated in the Meade process.

Equations 2.1 and 2.2 identify general contributors to the process of wealth accumulation and are by no means representative of a gener*al theory of wealth distribution*. Attempts at constructing a general theory of wealth distribution have typically adopted either a life-cycle approach or a dynastic modelling approach. The Lifecycle Model (LCM) of Modigliani and Brumberg (1954) postulates that individuals save and accumulate wealth for financing consumption in retirement. From a wealth distribution perspective, this has two implications. Firstly, the relationship between age and wealth is humped shaped, with the peak of wealth accumulation near retirement. Secondly, and most importantly, wealth inequality is wholly an age-based phenomenon. The richest members of society are the ones near retirement, and the poorest those just entering the workforce. In the LCM approach, no allowance is made for the possibility of bequest motives but for which casual empiricism suggests becomes more important at the upper tail of the wealth distribution. Further, the wealth distribution produced by the LCM predicts too little wealth inequality, and simply reflects income distribution. This despite empirical evidence indicating that wealth is distributed more unequally than income. In addition, the LCM class of models are incapable of explaining the rise of extreme wealth holders as exemplified by modern-day billionaires.

In opposition to the LCM, are models that emphasise wholly the intergenerational transmission of stocks of wealth. Such models assume that individuals seek to maximise dynastic utility functions with infinite time horizons. In contrast to the LCM, age, retirement and death are irrelevant; therefore, individuals' wealth accumulation undertakes substantially different paths depending on initial inheritance (Piketty & Zucman, 2015). Empirically, the importance of inheritance in the distribution of wealth has received considerable attention. These debates have centred upon the level of inheritance. In the US, for example, the level of inheritance as a proportion of wealth has been estimated as low as 20% to a high of 80% (see e.g. Davies & Shorrocks, 2000). The lower bound estimates used as empirical support of the LCM whilst the higher bound estimates are used as evidence supporting intergenerational dynastic models.

A theoretical compromise between the two approaches can be found in random shock type models. These differ from simple random walk models through the incorporation of shocks which have multiplicative effects and propagate through time. Piketty and Saez (2014) adopt a dynamic wealth accumulation model to explain the dynamics of wealth accumulation, and in doing so provide a micro context for the relation between the returns to capital and income growth. Depending upon the structure of shocks, these models amplify the effect of the Piketty (2014) inequality, $r-g$. Further, a dynamic wealth accumulation model can be proven to give rise to wealth distributions with fat Pareto tails, thereby approximating empirical observations in the higher spectrum of wealth distribution (Piketty & Zucman, 2015). Piketty and Saez (2014) propose a simple dynamic model of wealth accumulation with multiplicative shocks to the distribution of wealth with the form:

$$\mathrm{n}_{it+1} = \omega_{it}\mathrm{n}_{it} + \varepsilon_{it} \tag{2.3}$$

where n_{it} is the position of individual i in the wealth distribution, ω_{it} is a multiplicative random shock and ε_{it} is an additive random shock.

According to Piketty and Saez (2014), the random shocks of Eq. 2.3 can manifest in a wide variety of ways. What precisely these phenomena represent is not made explicit in the formulation. However, various forms can be speculated. These include, but are not limited to, Stiglitz's (1969) primogeniture model to investment shocks and impact on the rates of return (Benhabib, Bisin, & Zhu, 2013). Alternatively, the structure of shocks can relate to changes in the share of labour or capital income or growth, or to shocks in the preferences of savings rates. These shocks ultimately emanating from broader socioeconomic forces, such as war or a major economic recession. The point here is that the models are wide enough to capture a variety of phenomena.

It is argued in Chap. 4, that the manner of how these shocks manifest themselves and propagate through time, is through wealth accumulation models of the sort shown in Eqs. 2.1 and 2.2. These models provide a useful means of conceptualising the process of wealth accumulation to capture relevant shocks through different channels over time when analysing relevant empirical phenomena.

A primary objective of this book is to study the emergence of individuals and family dynasties that have amassed great fortunes, embedding them at the very apex of the wealth distribution. However, the aforementioned theories fail to account well for the phenomenon of the self-made ultra-rich (Davies & Shorrocks, 2000). These drawbacks manifest themselves in two ways. Firstly, bequest motives go beyond utility for terminal wealth or even for the survival of a dynasty for which current dynastic models and LCMs are inadequately equipped to analyse. Secondly, current theories cannot point to why large fortunes arise in the first place. Davies and Shorrocks (2000) argue that such an explanation must contain elements that incorporate entrepreneurial risk, dynastic considerations and institutional influences.

The section below devotes considerable space and attention to both early theoretical studies directed at understanding great fortunes and contemporary empirics in this domain. In the spirit of Piketty's (2014) call for a broader sociological attempt at understanding wealth from the wider domain of the social sciences and political economy are also considered. For example, the ideas proposed by elite theory are reviewed as they can potentially shed some like on issues of wealth, power and economic policy in general.

Review of Scholarship on the Rich

Theoretical Studies of the Rich

The absence of easily accessible data was not a deterrent to the classical political economists. Perhaps the first to focus purely on the rich or wealthy as a *sui generis* was Richard Jones' (1831) *An Essay on the Distribution of Wealth.* Jones' study systematically sought to establish and categorise the system of rent or profit and how it differed across the globe during the early 1800s. Its significance for this book resides in the application of an inductive approach to understanding the interdependence of economy and society in producing the prevailing wealth distribution. In this approach, as described by Rashid (1979), the 'primary concern was to try and extract some generally valid proposition from a study of facts, and then try and extrapolate, however cautiously, into the future' (p. 166). Jones (1831) developed several key insights, including the centrality of both technological progress and the dissemination of knowledge in guiding wealth accumulation in some circumstances. Further, Jones (1831) made clear distinctions between social groups that would point to significant differentiation between the organisation of societies and the way wealth is ultimately distributed according to law or custom.

At the core of Jones' (1831) approach was the accumulation of facts and observations from which universal or general propositions could be developed. This was very much in the tradition of Bacon's inductionism that was found useful in biology and astronomy. Induction is defined as a process whereby one can 'construct general propositions themselves from the contemplation of particulars, and attribute to them a universality which experience is incapable of warranting' (Herschel, 1841, p. 193). Although Jones (1831) was not wholly against deduction in economics, often applying concepts such as diminishing returns and selfish man to analyse rent and wealth associated with British capitalism, he attributed more influence to institutional forces, particularly among despotic-type regimes that dominated the international system at the time (Rashid, 1979).

In today's parlance, Jones (1831) could be classified as an institutionalist or of the historical school. The institutionalist school of economics has typically been most open to examining the rich and wealthy. An early American institutionalist, Commons (1893), sought to construct a theory of wealth distribution based upon the integration of legal and economic theory. Much like Jones (1831), Commons' (1893) work suffered a legacy of scholarly neglect, largely due to the socialist radical tendencies perceived in his thesis by his peers (Häring & Douglas, 2012).

Another work that has been neglected by both past and contemporary scholars is that of Watkins (1907), who drew upon legal, technological and even geographical concepts as the defining characteristics that gave rise to the great fortunes of the Gilded Age during the late 1800s and early 1900s. Watkins's (1907) thesis remains highly relevant in its analysis and effectively foreshadows many of the key forces that are in play today. Watkins (1907) was concerned with the rise in the wealth of the Gilded Age entrepreneurs, or the Robber Barons, as they were later labelled by Josephson (2013), who presided over vast fortunes in an era not dissimilar to today in terms of both the rate of accumulation and the prevalence of technological development and economic shocks. Rockoff (2012) argues that many of the large infrastructure and energy changes (rail and oil) reflect the technological revolutions of today in transportation, communications and energy.

Further, much like our era, Watkins (1907) viewed four primary forces as fostering the growth of great fortunes during the Gilded Age. Firstly, technological advancements in manufacturing ensured that corporations achieved unprecedented economies of scale. Secondly, the logistics behind commerce were revolutionised with the expansion of a vast railway network straddling the US, which created a market scale hitherto unattainable. For example, large meatworks in Chicago could quickly transport their cargo to the eastern US, leading to the emergence of the meat tycoons (Rockoff, 2012). The wealth of the oil tycoons John D. Rockefeller and his brother William Rockefeller, at Standard Oil, was only achieved by the vast railroad infrastructure built by the likes of Jay Gould, Jim Fisk and Russell Sage (Rockoff, 2012).

Similarly, the fortune established by Henry Ford required the efficiency of the combustion engine that relied on oil for the automobiles, the transportation of vast materials to the Highland Park Ford Plant and the implementation of other nascent engineering technologies to enable the functioning of the first mass assembly plant (Bradley, 1999). Thirdly, the rise of what Watkins (1907, p. 15) terms 'abstract property', such as equities and bonds, facilitated the rapid capitalisation of entrepreneurs. For some modern scholars, this is the primary mechanism for rapid wealth accumulation (Thurow, 1975). Fourthly, Watkins (1907) viewed the process of urbanisation in the US as a further catalyst to rapid and large wealth accumulation, creating larger markets and the growth of property barons. The second and fourth points echo the theoretical and deductive argument by Rosen (1981) that the sheer scale of large cities results in a greater probability that extraordinary wealth will be created, given the ability to reach a large audience in a geographically concentrated area.

Ultimately, however, Watkins (1907) appears to explain the rise of an ultra-rich economic class based on an underlying belief in institutions and the limited role of individual agency. That is, there is little room for either personal talent or natural endowment in explaining the existence of large wealth stocks into few hands. Behavioural or personality explanations are rejected for their lack of precision, as Watkins (1907) argues:

> A postulate of any scientific theory of the causes of large fortunes is that those causes are impersonal. That is, they must be such as permit of being made the basis of generalisations. 'Pull' and privilege are not such. Neither can the causes of the change in the degree of development of riches lie in human nature or in inequality of natural endowment. (p. 5)

This rejection of the 'inequality of natural endowment' as an explanation for great fortunes stands in contrast to contemporary economic literature that has sought to explain wealth accumulation and inequality through a 'plethora of capitals' (Hodgson, 2014, p. 12).

Although Watkins (1907) identified many relevant elements of wealth accumulation amongst the wealthy, his approach neglected or dismissed many key aspects of wealth accumulation. Of note is the rejection of privilege in sustaining large fortunes in the afore quoted passage from Watkins (1907, p. 5). The dismissal of inheritance or privilege may not be tenable in many parts of the world today and particularly not during Watkins's (1907) own era, with, for example, inheritance playing a major role in wealth accumulation in the 1800s' France (Daumard, 1980). Further, Watkins (1907) missed the potential of entrepreneurs to create markets in goods and services for which there was no pre-existing requirement. For example, Rubinstein (1980) points out that Rockefeller rose to great fortune by creating market demand for his oil in China by providing oil lanterns to the Chinese. Nevertheless, Watkins's (1907) overall thesis remains highly relevant today.

Contemporary Theoretical Approaches to the Ultra-rich

Although there has been a tremendous amount of theoretical modelling regarding life cycle considerations or dynastic considerations, there is little that deals with large wealth holdings and entrepreneurial activity. Two important but contrasting works that do consider these issues are those of Rosen (1981) and Shorrocks (1988). Rosen (1981) sought to determine how a small number of individuals can come to dominate the distribution of wealth given small differences in 'talent' or 'ability' in their chosen fields of enterprise. A central prediction of Rosen is that the relative minor variation in the distribution of talent at the top of a given sector will translate into substantial differences in revenues. Empirically, Kaplan and Rauh (2013) base their explanation for the rise of the US *Forbes* 400 on the basis of Rosen's (1981) theoretical framework.

An alternative approach is one that incorporates notions of risk, initial wealth and entrepreneurial activity. Shorrocks (1988) develops a model in which two kinds of entrepreneurs are considered, who both face different entrepreneurial opportunities depending on their respective initial stocks of wealth. Firstly, there are those entrepreneurs who need not possess significant initial wealth; only time is required to search out for opportunities that can provide significant rewards. The second class of entrepreneur is already a highly successful entrepreneur and also searches out opportunities for large rewards. However, these opportunities require substantial access to both time and substantial wealth holdings to access due to markedly different risk profiles of the opportunities presented. Shorrocks model predicts two results. Firstly, entrepreneurs with little initial wealth will target or specialise in 'single' risk opportunities. Secondly, entrepreneurs possessing high budgets will instead seek to engage in projects where risks can be diversified as much as possible and in conjunction with other wealthy individuals. Targeting such projects ensures the perpetuation of wealth and one's status. According to Shorrocks (1988), 'the model developed in this paper bears little resemblance to any previous study of wealth holdings' (p. 242). In Chap. 5, Shorrocks' predictions are considered in the context of self-made entrepreneurs.

A potentially interesting extension of Shorrocks (1988) theory is the implication of inheritance for the type of commercial and financial activities estate beneficiaries will engage in. A logical extension of Shorrocks (1988) is to argue that inheritance beneficiaries (in relation to billionaires) will also diversify their risks as much as possible just like self-made entrepreneurs with high wealth stocks. This might have macroeconomic implications. Standard financial economic theory would posit that with greater diversification, the risk premium would reduce. Piketty (2014) and Piketty and Saez (2014) have shown that returns have fallen since the 1960s. In Chaps. 4 and 5 the linkages between entrepreneurialism, risk and returns and inheritance are all considered.

Sociological Explorations of the Ultra-rich

Throughout the 1960s, several scholars tackled the issue of extreme wealth holdings from a sociological perspective. Lundberg (1969), in an eclectic exploration, argues that the rise of the ultra-rich in an economy is best viewed through the prism of a sociological theory such as elite theory. Following Lorenzian thought, Lundberg (1969) argues that society always produces and endures an elite class who maintains substantial control over society's resources and culture. Interestingly, he argues that the rich of the 1960s in the capitalist world were largely an evolution of the barons of the feudal system of the Middle Ages, who lorded over both land and peasants. This was a major departure from classical economists such as Jones (1831), Marx (1981) and Watkins (1907), who viewed capitalist wealth as distinct in both nature and source and possessing substantially different dynamics from the landed feudalist system that dominated Europe's economic system prior to the Industrial Revolution. Moreover, Lundberg (1969) also argues that the existence of an economic elite is a natural outcome in any economic system not just observed in a capitalist system. Indeed, in the Soviet Union the emergence of the *nomenklatura* from the Stalinist era could be viewed as being the equivalent of Western elite establishments (Hosking, 1985).

The issue of whether the emergence of economic elites is a natural outcome of any economic system has received attention in contemporary writings. Figueroa (2008) develops a simple model of how the economic elite maintains their position at the apex of society. The theory proposed by Figueroa predicts that, as the social equivalent of the economic monopolist that erects barriers to entry into an industry, the economic elite restrict entry to the highest echelons of the social *milieu* where economic power is held and wielded with considerable influence. How such barriers are erected is not made clear, but Figueroa (2008) uncovers empirical evidence that the Peruvian economic elite maintains a degree of control over who is admitted into their ranks. To an extent, Figueroa's (2008) thesis echoes Shorrocks (1988) who argues that there are investments or projects that an economic elite are only able to access given the risks associated with those projects.

Bodley (1999) argues, from an anthropological perspective, that economic growth is an elite-directed process. The elite undertakes economic growth only so long as it provides continuously increasing returns to them. The fundamental assumption of elite theorists is that with increasing scale in any setting (e.g. market size, population or government), economic power tends to become more and more concentrated in the hands of the elite. The emergence of the elite is a natural outcome in any type of economic system, no matter how objectionable such a conclusion is. For example, Bodley (1999) refers to how property owners in the US assume greater roles in municipal governments, which encourages further growth and inevitably results in greater wealth for the elite, and the cycle continues.

It is worthwhile to emphasise at this juncture as to what is meant by an elite and elite theory in general. 'Elites' can be defined as individuals who control real or symbolic resources, occupying key positions and 'operating in networks of influence' (Yamokoski & Dubrow, 2008, p. 319). Thus, power represents the central element of elite theory. López (2013) argues that this is not very distant from Marxist conceptions of the capitalist class. Indeed, numerous Marxists have utilised elite theory themselves, including Mills (1956) and Domhoff (1967). However, it should be noted that elite theory is opposed very much to social class theory. The divergence in the two schools of thought was exemplified in the debates between structural Marxism and instrumental Marxism surrounding the nature of the state (Poulantzas & Miliband, 1972).

Contemporary Empirical Studies of Wealth

The lack of a well-developed theoretical framework has not precluded a fruitful empirical study on the issue of where and how great wealth is generated.

Canterbery and Nosari (1985) explore the determinants of 'super wealth' among America's *Forbes* 400, employing a cross-sectional regression framework to construct a model with various personal and economic variables. At the personal level, they find that age and inheritance are positively correlated with larger wealth levels in agreement with both dynastic models and the LCM. In terms of the industrial sources of great fortunes, they find that wealth is typically made in oil and shipping (Canterbery & Nosari, 1985). Contrary to previous eras (see Rockoff, 2012; Watkins, 1907) in the US, they do not find any significant wealth being generated in real estate. However, Canterbery and Nosari's (1985) study just focuses on one year, 1982, which means their model cannot capture by construction the dynamics of the economy over time and where a different time period may yield different findings as Piketty (2014) emphasises. For example, Blitz and Siegfried (1992) examine the *Forbes* 400 for 1986 and find that most wealth is generated in oil, wholesale trade *and* property. Given the small time difference between these two studies, it is surprising to see how much of a greater role real estate has in generating wealth as observed in Blitz and Siegfried's (1992) study, which highlights the importance of adopting a panel framework when exploring issues related to extreme wealth. Studies on the Gilded Age, however, have also found a significant surge of wealth generation in real estate during relatively short time frames (Watkins, 1907).

Similar studies have been conducted for the rest of the Anglo-Saxon world. Siegfried and Round (1994) explore the sources of great wealth in Australia using the *Business Review Weekly's* rich list, and find that new wealth was largely made and concentrated in finance, property development, and retail and wholesale trade in the 1980s. Australia's rich typically have reflected the areas in which the country has been able to gain the greatest scale. For example, most of the 'old wealth' was generated in agriculture and manufacturing. They also find that the majority of new wealth appears to be generated in competitive industries. On this basis, they argue that risk and uncertainty, returns to business acumen and strategic resources, and market dis-equilibria are the main drivers of great wealth generation, a finding that reflects Thurow's (1975) thesis of the centrality of efficient markets.

Stilwell and Ansari (2003) also examine Australia's wealthy utilising the *Business Review Weekly's* rich list for the years 1993–2003. They focus on three questions: to what extent has wealth at the pinnacle of the wealth pyramid increased; to what extent has the entry into the ranks of the wealthy been elevated; and what are the economic activities that have permitted the concomitant concentration of wealth? Much like Siegfried and Round (1994), Stilwell and Ansari (2003) find that retail, investments and property are the greatest wealth generators. Significantly, mining and resources are not listed in their study. This provides a striking juxtaposition with the results in Chap. 5 of this book, where mining magnates dominate the total wealth share and further illustrates the dynamic and stochastic nature of the creation and destruction of wealth. In addition, Stilwell and Ansari (2003) highlight the increased patrimonial nature of wealth accumulation at the time, observing that '6 out of the 10 wealthiest people in 2003 attained a substantial basis for their affluence through inheritance: the comparable figure in 1993 was 4 out of 10' (p. 151). Foreshadowing recent scholarship, Stilwell and Ansari (2003) also emphasise the role of financial assets in wealth accumulation, as 'share ownership is much more concentrated, with a staggering 86% being held by the wealthiest 10 per cent of families' (pp. 154–155). Ownership of other assets (cash, business assets and rental properties) are also high, averaging in the 50-percentile range (Ansari & Stilwell, p. 155).

The centrality of real estate and/or banking and finance is further reflected in the UK, where Siegfried and Roberts (1991) find that these sectors provided the greatest source of extreme wealth. Furthermore, they observe that where great wealth is found, most of it is concentrated in competitive industries and not in industries that can be classified as either oligopolistic or monopolistic by economists. Siegfried and Roberts (1991) find this surprising, as they assert that in the absence of barriers, new entrants should rapidly remove any dis-equilibria and restrict the number of wealthy individuals.

Hazledine and Siegfried (1997), who examine how New Zealand's wealthy became so rich, also establish an empirical regularity: most wealth is made in property and finance. They also find the appearance of great wealth in industries that are characterised by intense competition which they concluded represents a paradox, as the greatest wealth was expected to exist in monopoly industries. However, the extent to which this is an empirical paradox has been challenged by, for example, Waldman (1991), who contends that, if anything, such extreme wealth is a natural consequence of capitalism and its associated stochastic nature. Indeed, the notion of long leads in probability theory illuminates Waldman's point well.

Other works have adopted a purely historical perspective but also consider the sources of wealth in a similar vein to the contemporary studies reviewed above. These historically focused studies analyse the 1800s in Europe or the Gilded Age of the US and utilising contemporary estate data, journalistic wealth lists or news media sources to analyse the sources of great fortunes. Rubinstein (1980) explores the social and demographic characteristics of the rich in Britain at the turn of the eighteenth century, utilising estate data. For Rubinstein (1980), the defining characteristic of British wealth was the concentration of the rich in finance and property, and the absence of inheritance beneficiaries. Furthermore, there was a lack of wealthy industrialists in Britain, despite the technological, economic and social changes wrought by the Industrial Revolution. Rockoff (2012) explores the sources of wealth in the US during the late 1800s and discovers that finance and property again were the main engines of wealth growth. In contrast to the Anglo countries of the US and the UK, Daumard (1980) explores the wealth distribution of France in the 1800s and finds that wealth typically was patrimonial in nature.

Summary

To summarise, the nature of wealth and how it has been approached in economic discourse has changed substantially. The definition of wealth as proposed by Piketty (2014) recognises the monetary and marketable value of all assets. This significantly differs from economists who have sought to focus on a limited notion of productive capital.

Although contemporary mainstream economists have largely ignored the study of wealth, there is a small strand from the early political economists to today that have tackled the issue from various frameworks and perspectives. Modern scholarship has developed wealth accumulation models which can be used to model (a) the process of wealth accumulation across all individuals; and (b) to produce a predicted distribution of wealth which have shown to closely mimic Pareto distributions observed in reality. Broadly, these wealth accumulation models fall into three broad categories, the Life Cycle Models, the dynastic models of wealth accumulation and the dynamic multiplicative random shock models. The latter provide the most applicability but are bereft in content as to what shocks are necessary to model wealth accumulation. The models stand in contrast to capital accumulation models that are macroeconomic in their focus and have typically been concerned with the distribution of income on economic growth. Despite the divergence in theoretical approaches, it was posited that Piketty (2014) largely represents an attempt to bridge the different conceptual frameworks.

Studies that focus on the ultra-rich rather than the whole distribution have considered different questions and adopted different approaches to the deductive methods. An inductive approach was often utilised, seeking to situate the rise of great fortunes in sociological, political or technological change and transformation. For early political economists, such as Jones (1831), Commons (1893) and Watkins (1907), the main elements giving rise to great wealth included:

- Social ordering and customs (Commons, 1893; Jones, 1831)
- Rise of finance and the separation of management and control (Watkins, 1907)
- Technological shocks (Jones, 1831; Watkins, 1907)
- The rise of the capitalist system over the feudal system (Watkins, 1907)

Elite theory, which emerged in the 1950s and 1960s significantly departed from the classical political economy in two ways. Firstly, the emergence of an economic elite is a given in any economic system, with little differentiation between the feudal era and modern capitalism. The rise of an elite can be subsumed under a stochastic process hypothesis. Secondly, the economic elite direct economic growth only as far as it benefits them.

Modern empiricism has focused on the sources of contemporary fortunes. Various explanations have been proposed for the rise of great fortunes. At the core of these studies though is the view that the industrial sources of great fortunes have an important explanatory role in understanding why the ultra-rich exist. These approaches echo Piketty's (2014) view that the history of capital or wealth is not homogenous in nature. Rather, it is a history of alternative forms of wealth, manifested in different industries or sectors of the economy, be it financial wealth, property or oil capital. Further, modern empiricism views market efficiency and abnormal returns to risk as important elements in the attainment of vast fortunes. Society, law and custom have little role in the growth of large fortunes in most modern empirical literature *sans* Piketty (2014).

References

Austin, M. M., & Vidal-Naquet, P. V. (1977). *Economic and social history of ancient Greece: An introduction*. Berkeley, CA: University of California Press.

Benhabib, J., Bisin, A., & Zhu, S. (2013). *The wealth distribution in Bewley models with investment risk*. Working Paper, New York University, New York.

Blitz, R. C., & Siegfried, J. J. (1992). How did the wealthiest Americans get so rich? *The Quarterly Review of Economics and Finance, 32*, 5–26.

Blume, L. E., & Durlauf, S. N. (2015). Capital in the twenty-first century: A review essay. *Journal of Political Economy, 123*, 749–777.

Bodley, J. H. (1999). Socioeconomic growth, culture scale, and household well-being: A test of the power-elite hypothesis. *Current Anthropology, 40*, 595–620.

Bonnet, F., & Théry, C. (2014). *Sociology and political science in the patrimonial society: Implications of Piketty's Capital*. Retrieved from https://halshs.archives-ouvertes.fr/halshs-01060570/document, <halshs-01060570>.

Booth, W. J. (1993). *Households: On the moral architecture of the economy*. New York: Cornell University Press.

Bradley, B. H. (1999). *The works: The industrial architecture of the United States*. New York: Oxford University Press.

Canterbery, E. R., & Nosari, E. J. (1985). The Forbes four hundred: The determinants of super-wealth. *Southern Economic Journal, 5*, 1073–1083.

Carroll, C. D., Slacalek, J., & Tokuoka, K. (2014). *The distribution of wealth and the marginal propensity to consume* (No. 1655). European Central Bank Working Paper Series. Retrieved from https://www.ecb.europa.eu/

Commons, J. R. (1893). *The distribution of wealth*. New York: Macmillan and Co..
Daumard, A. (1980). Wealth and affluence in France since the beginning of the nineteenth century. In W. D. Rubinstein (Ed.), *Wealth and the wealthy in the modern world* (pp. 90–121). London: Croom Helm.
Davies, J. B., & Shorrocks, A. F. (2000). The distribution of wealth. In A. B. Atkinson & F. Bourguignon (Eds.), *Handbook of income distribution* (Vol. 1, pp. 605–675). Amsterdam: North-Holland.
Domhoff, G. W. (1967). *Who rules America?* Englewood Cliffs, NJ: Prentice Hall.
Fama, E. F. (1970). Efficient capital markets: A review of theory and empirical work. *The Journal of Finance, 25*, 383–417.
Feller, W. (1971). *An introduction to probability theory and its applications 2*. New York: Wiley.
Figueroa, A. (2008). Competition and circulation of economic elites: Theory and application to the case of Peru. *The Quarterly Review of Economics and Finance, 48*, 263–273.
Galbraith, J. K. (1958). *The affluent society*. New York: Houghton Mifflin Company.
Galbraith, J. K. (2014). Kapital for the twenty-first century?. *Dissent*. Retrieved on 15 September, 2015, from https://www.dissentmagazine.org/
Häring, N., & Douglas, N. (2012). *Economists and the powerful: Convenient theories, distorted facts, ample rewards*. London: Anthem Press.
Hassler, S. (1999). *The super-rich*. London: Macmillan.
Hazledine, T., & Siegfried, J. J. (1997). How did the wealthiest New Zealanders get so rich? *New Zealand Economic Papers, 31*, 35–47.
Heilbroner, R. L. (1987). Wealth. In J. Eatwell, M. Milgate, & P. Newman (Eds.), *The new Palgrave: A dictionary of economics* (1st ed.). London: Macmillan.
Herschel, J. F. (1841). Review of Whewell's history of the inductive sciences from the earliest to the present times (1837) and the philosophy of the inductive sciences founded upon their history. *The London Quarterly Review, 68*, 177–238.
Hodgson, G. M. (2014). What is capital? Economists and sociologists have changed its meaning: Should it be changed back? *Cambridge Journal of Economics, 38*, 1063–1086.
Hosking, G. (1985). *A history of the Soviet Union*. London: Fontana Press.
Jones, R. (1831). *An essay on the distribution of wealth. Part 1: Rent*. London: John Murray.
Josephson, M. (2013). *The robber barons*. Piscataway, NY: Transaction Publishers.
Kanbur, R., & Stiglitz, J. (2015). *Wealth and income distribution: New theories needed for a new era*. VOX CEPR Policy Portal. Retrieved from http://voxeu.org/article/wealth-and-income-distribution-new-theories-needed-new-era
Kaplan, S. N., & Rauh, J. D. (2013). Family, education, and sources of wealth among the richest Americans, 1982–2012. *The American Economic Review, 103*(3), 158–162.
Koh, S. Y., Wissink, B., & Forrest, R. (2016). Reconsidering the super-rich: Variations, structural conditions and urban consequences. In I. Hay & J. V. Beaverstock (Eds.),

Handbook on wealth and the super-rich (pp. 18–42). Cheltenham: Cheltenham Edward Elgar Publishing.

López, M. (2013). Elite theory. *Sociopedia.isa.*https://doi.org/10.1177/2056846013112.

Lundberg, F. (1969). *The rich & the super rich: A study in the power of money today.* London: Nelson.

Marx, K. (1981). *Capital, vol. 3.* Harmondsworth, UK: Pelican.

Meade, J. E. (1975). *The just economy.* London: George Allen & Unwin.

Mills, C. W. (1956). *The power elite.* New York: Oxford University Press.

Modigliani, F., & Brumberg, R. (1954). Utility analysis and the consumption function: An interpretation of cross-section data. In K. K. Kurihara (Ed.), *Post Keynesian economics.* New York: Rutgers University Press.

Piketty, T. (2014). *Capital in the twenty-first century.* Cambridge, MA: The Belknap Press of Harvard University Press.

Piketty, T., & Saez, E. (2014). Inequality in the long run. *Science, 344*, 838–843.

Piketty, T., & Zucman, G. (2014). Capital is back: Wealth-income ratios in rich countries 1700–2010. *The Quarterly Journal of Economics, 129*, 1155–1210.

Piketty, T., & Zucman, G. (2015). Wealth and inheritance in the long run. In A. B. Atkinson & F. Bourguignon (Eds.), *Handbook of income distribution* (pp. 1303–1368). Oxford, UK: Elsevier.

Poulantzas, N., & Miliband, R. (1972). The problem of the capitalist state. In R. Blackburn (Ed.), *Ideology in social science: Readings in critical social theory* (pp. 238–262). New York: Pantheon Books.

Rashid, S. (1979). Richard Jones and Baconian historicism at Cambridge. *Journal of Economic Issues, 13*, 159–173.

Rockoff, H. (2012). The great fortunes of the Gilded Age and the crisis of 1893. *Research in Economic History, 28*, 233–262.

Rosen, S. (1981). The economics of superstars. *The American Economic Review, 71*, 845–858.

Rubinstein, W. D. (1980). Modern Britain. In W. D. Rubinstein (Ed.), *Wealth and the wealthy in the modern world* (pp. 46–89). London: Croom Helm.

Saez, E., & Zucman, G. (2014). *Wealth inequality in the United States Since 1913: Evidence from capitalized income tax data* (No. 20625). NBER Working Paper Series. Retrieved from http://www.nber.org/papers/w20625

Scherer, F. M. (1980). *Industrial market structure and economic performance.* Boston: Houghton Mifflin Company.

Shorrocks, A. F. (1988). Wealth holdings and entrepreneurial activity. In D. Kessler & A. Masson (Eds.), *Modelling the accumulation and distribution of wealth.* Oxford, UK: Clarendon Press.

Siegfried, J. J., & Roberts, A. (1991). How did the wealthiest Britons get so rich? *Review of Industrial Organization, 6*, 19–32.

Siegfried, J. J., & Round, D. K. (1994). How did the wealthiest Australians get so rich? *Review of Income and Wealth, 40*, 191–204.

Slemrod, J. (2000). The economics of taxing the rich. In J. Slemrod (Ed.), *Does atlas shrug? The economic consequences of taxing the rich* (pp. 2–28). Cambridge, MA: Harvard University Press.

Smith, A. (1952). *An inquiry into the nature and causes of the wealth of nations*. Chicago: William Benton.

Spengler, J. J. (1984). Boisguilbert's economic views vis-à-vis those of contemporary *reformateurs*. *History of Political Economy, 16*, 69–88.

Stiglitz, J. E. (1969). Distribution of income and wealth among individuals. *Econometrica, 37*, 382–397.

Stilwell, F., & Ansari, M. (2003). Wealthy Australians. *Journal of Australian Political Economy, 52*, 143–157.

Thurow, L. (1975). *Generating inequality*. New York: Basic Books, Inc..

Tuckman, E. (1973). *The economics of the rich*. New York: Random House.

Waldman, D. E. (1991). How did the wealthiest Britons get so rich?: A comment. *Review of Industrial Organization, 6*, 291–294.

Watkins, G. P. (1907). The growth of large fortunes. *Publications of the American Economic Association, 8*(4), 1–170.

Yamokoski, A., & Dubrow, J. K. (2008). How do elites define influence? Personality and respect as sources of social power. *Sociological Focus, 41*(4), 319–336.

3

Trends in Wealth and the Rise of the Elite

The purpose of this chapter is to provide an analysis of the trends in high wealth accumulation by exploring primary data used to study the ultra-rich in the contemporary world. To this end, the key elements of the chapter include:

- Providing a preliminary overview of the data sources employed in the construction of a global billionaire database. The use of other primary and secondary data sources is discussed. We emphasise the limitations regarding the data sources employed.
- Secondly, a general overview of the contemporary trends and patterns in the globe's billionaire population is presented. These trends and patterns are viewed through the prism of various characteristics at a global and regional level and at the sectoral and demographic intersection.
- Ultra-rich trends are discussed in the context of aggregate wealth-income ratios for several advanced economies for which data is available.

Introduction

This chapter examines the trends in the accumulation of vast fortunes over the period 1990–2013, focusing on individuals or families with an estimated net worth of USD1 billion. As the title of the book suggests, many have claimed that the rise of great fortunes in our epoch reflects the process that was observed in the late 1800s and early 1900s in the US. Much like our era, the Gilded Age was characterised by rapid income growth, rising inequality and the sudden onset of vast fortunes, and economic crises (Rockoff, 2012).

S. Tsigos, K. Daly, *The Wealth of the Elite*, https://doi.org/10.1007/978-981-15-2148-5_3

This chapter details the rise of vast contemporary fortunes across the globe, hypothesises why some nations have been the more prolific in wealth creation, discusses the impact of the Global Financial Crisis on wealth creation and finally examines the extent to which inheritance represents a source of great fortune amongst the world's economic elite.

The analysis is based on lists of the world's billionaires published between 1990 and 2013. This is by no means the first study to use these lists, with recent examples including Saez and Zucman (2014), Cagetti and De Nardi (2006), Kopczuk and Saez (2004), and Klevmarken, Lupton and Stafford (2003). The present chapter builds on these works by extending the sample range and adding detailed information on the sectoral sources, by the application of the GICS classifications, of wealth and the extent of inheritance pervading the data.

This chapter is divided into six sections. The first discusses the methodology and database construction. The second analyses the aggregate trends in wealth accumulation, including wealth to income ratios and the concomitant rise of the billionaires. The third presents a regional breakdown of wealth accumulation in both developed and developing regions of the world. The fourth presents data on the evolution of inheritance versus self-made wealth across time and space.

Methodology and Data

Analysing Trends and Assigning Causality

Both Chaps. 4 and 5 explore where current wealth came from and how it is being sustained among the advanced economies of the world. The *Forbes* data provides a starting point for establishing names, ages, industries and countries to construct a historical typology of the economic and political forces at play. Enumeration plays an important role for detecting or signalling areas of systematic difference within a region or across regions, while the personal business histories provide the framework for developing generalisations across time and space. This approach is aligned with the works of Rockoff (2012) and Kaplan and Rauh (2013). Similarly, Jones (1831) argues that careful accumulation of historical facts is essential before the production of generalisations with regard to wealth can be made. In general, econometric analysis is kept to a minimum and utilised only to establish inter- and intra-regional differences based on various underlying drivers throughout Chaps. 3, 4 and 5.

A major problem with using such historical data is the risk of generalising from intuition (Jaher, 1980). To address this problem, the collective biography attempted here is guided by theoretical or conceptual rationales from past literature. Conceptually, the framework to analyse wealth borrows heavily from Piketty (2014a), Jones (1831), Watkins (1907), Rubinstein (1980) and Shorrocks (1988). For example, technological shocks, government fiscal policy, rules on corporate governance and the benefits of diversification are sound economic ideas and theories utilised in this study to establish the key markers of differentiation in wealth generation across the globe, including how is wealth made? Where was it made? When were the large fortunes first amassed? Is wealth creation being sustained?

Constructing the Billionaires Database

An immediate impediment encountered by any study of the state of extreme wealth is the scarcity of accessible and relevant sources. Broadly, the researcher has four sources from which to examine the upper tail of the wealth distribution: (1) journalistic lists of the rich, (2) wealth tax data, (3) estate data and (4) investment income data. Of these, Davies and Shorrocks (2000) conclude 'estate and wealth tax data probably yield more reliable information on the upper tail of the distribution' (p. 605). This presents two problems for this study. Firstly, this study is concerned with the distribution of extreme wealth across both geography and industries. Wealth data is limited to those nations that have a wealth tax, and those with wealth taxes do not necessarily have the same definition of what constitutes wealth for taxable purposes (Atkinson, 2006). In addition, tax evasion or avoidance substantially plagues this type of data set (Atkinson, 2006; Spånt, 1987). Secondly, estate data does not reflect the contemporaneous evolution of industry dynamics in the present epoch analysed here. For example, to capture the source and evolution of Mark Zuckerberg's or Sergey Brin's net worth, one would have to wait until after their deaths. An impractical solution given the ages of these two Internet entrepreneurs. Furthermore, estate data typically neglects wealth tied up in large trust funds, which are often the favoured investment vehicle of the super-rich for concealing their net worth from the tax system (Lundberg, 1969).

In this chapter, we employ the *Forbes* World Rich List to generate a time and geographical distribution of wealth. Here we are mainly interested in the qualitative aspects of wealthy individuals rather than the recorded wealth figures per se.[1] The study incorporates data on individuals from 1990 through to 2013, although the *Forbes* data only started including point estimates on individual wealth from 1996, which is when most quantitative studies begin (see von Neumayer, 2006; Sanandaji & Leeson, 2013; Torgler & Piatti, 2013). Journalistic 'rich lists' have been utilised by a few prior studies. For Australia, Siegfried and Round (1994) utilise the *Business Review Weekly* Rich List, and for the UK, Siegfried and Roberts (1991) use the *Sunday Times* Rich List. Von Neumayer's (2006) sample is restricted to a three-year period (2001, 2002 and 2003), while Torgler and Piatti's (2013) sample covers 1996 through to 2003. In both instances, the lists were used in an econometric exercise where the number of billionaires recorded in each country was the dependent variable.

The first *Forbes* world billionaire list was published on 5 October 1987, listing 140 billionaires with an aggregate net worth of USD295 billion. The wealthiest person recorded on this list was Yoshiaki Tsutsumi, with an estimated net worth of USD20 billion. His wealth was generated by inheriting the control of his father's industrial conglomerate, Seibu Corporation, which had various business interests in tourism, railroads and finance (Downer, 1994). As of 2013, there were over 1400 individuals on the list from across the globe. *Forbes* sources its data from both public and private sources some of which remain anonymous. This data is then used to construct a picture of individual wealth holdings. Although *Forbes* may go directly to the source, anonymous lawyers, financial advisors and accountants close to the listed individuals are often contacted (Kroll, 2014).

Despite having access to the rich and their close associates, *Forbes* is compelled to follow certain valuation rules in instances where sources are not forthcoming (Canterbery & Nosari, 1985). Valuation of privately listed companies, which is often the case with the individuals in these lists, proves problematic. In the case of privately held business concerns, the firms are valued by estimating revenues and combining them with price-to-earnings ratios of similar public companies (Kroll, 2014). For oil and gas companies, *Forbes* will often settle for placing a 'fair estimate' on oil reserves, for example. The worth of television networks or stations, which are not listed on a stock exchange, 'is evaluated by reputable media brokers' (Canterbery & Nosari, 1985, p. 1056).

Although this data set has been used successfully in the past, there are limitations associated with its use. Atkinson (2006) argues that liabilities often are

[1] Estimates of wealth are intermittently utilised throughout Chaps. 3, 4 and 5. However, a significant caveat in the use of media sourced data is the accuracy of journalists' wealth estimates. It is for this reason that reliance on these wealth figures are kept to a minimum.

not discovered, which artificially raises the net worth of some individuals. For example, the UK publishing mogul Robert Maxwell revealed extraordinary debts in the early 1990s that, in real terms, transformed him from a billionaire into a penniless pauper (Cohen, 1991; Wearing, 2005).

A further problem with the *Forbes* list is in dealings with wealthy dynastic families such as the Rothschild and Rockefeller families. Although aggregate family wealth is often large, the *Forbes* lists focus mainly on individuals and, at most, the nuclear family. When business interests diverge significantly, as in the case of two siblings, they are counted as separate wealth holdings. For example, the brothers Karl and Theo Albrecht own and operate ALDI Sud and ALDI Nord, respectively. Due to the independence of the two business operations, *Forbes* maintains a separate listing, despite both inheriting their wealth from their father. In contrast, the French fashion billionaires, Alain and Gerard Wertheimer, who maintain a controlling interest in Chanel, are listed jointly by *Forbes* and would be counted as one individual and not two. Further, in the case of large, wealthy dynasties, the wealth is often far too diffused among the extended family, and this diffusion leads to substantial opaqueness making it difficult to arrive at an overall valuation or, more importantly for this study's purpose, individual enumeration (Goff, 2010; Kroll, 2014). Rather than recode and aggregate family dynasties to individuals, this study strictly follows the *Forbes* approach and does not make any changes.

A further complication is the treatment of location. *Forbes* magazine records, at times, both the citizenship and the residence of the individual. Given that billionaires encounter few if any liquidity constraints to consumption, they typically leave their country of origin and find an abode in one of the cosmopolitan centres of the world. Roman Abramovich, for example, made his fortune in Russia via its vast gas resources but is listed as a resident of the UK. While it may seem logical to code citizenship as the home state of an individual, this would be disingenuous in the instance of billionaires as location confers substantial advantages to the billionaire. Watkins (1907) argued that the wealthy of his era who moved to New York City possessed significant commercial advantages over the older agrarian wealthy, for example. In contemporary times, Beaverstock, Hubbard and Short (2004) document the rise of a trans-global rich elite who cluster in a few globalised cities and their subsequent enormous impact on the local populations, both in terms of generating economic activity as well as exacerbating inequalities. To simplify the analysis, the place of primary business interests is assumed to be the primary geographical identifier. In the case of large diversified holdings with income sources across the world, citizenship is assumed here as the identifier.

Further problems present themselves in relation to the coding of inheritances. Firstly, *Forbes* has on occasion changed the source of wealth of an individual from inherited to self-made, without explanation. Secondly, there is the issue of whether one should encode the degree of inheritance received per some prespecified relative level. Kaplan and Rauh (2013) attempt this by applying a weighted inheritance score across a range of scales. For example, if individuals inherited a small business and built it into a larger enterprise then they would provide a weighting of 1.5 compared to 1, which indicates the wealthy individual founded the business. A score of 2 would then equate to inheriting a large enterprise and so on. The problem with this approach is judging what constitutes a small or large inherited business. Given that many of these business span generations, and the international nature of the database would require subjectively determining what constituted a relatively small business in, for example, immediate post-war ravaged Germany compared to the US. Under this approach, the Koch brothers are not considered to have come from a privileged background, according to Kaplan and Rauh (2013). Regarding the first point, the *Forbes* data is used in this study only as a starting point in determining whether to classify an individual's source of wealth as inherited or self-made. Where feasible, individuals' biographical information was examined to ensure accuracy. Regarding the second point, this study maintains a simple dichotomy between the two groups, following past scholarship (Canterbery & Nosari, 1985; Rockoff, 2012).

Lastly, a major undertaking in constructing the billionaire database was to assign each individual over time a relevant GICS identifier code. The GICS system of industry codes provides a convenient and consistent means of assigning individual billionaires to various industries or sectors over time. This is extremely important for two reasons. Firstly, Chap. 5 requires detailed records of the industrial sources of great wealth. The *Forbes* data does provide similar such information but in a far from rigorous and consistent fashion. There were numerous instances in the data where *Forbes* would, for example, in one-year list an individual's industry as 'diversified investments' and in subsequent years switch this to 'diversified conglomerate'. To ensure an accurate allocation of individuals to GICS sectors, each individual's personal business history was examined over time and allocated a GICS sector accordingly. In total, the sample consisted of more than 1400 individuals over 30 years and covers 1990–2013.

In addition to the journalistic rich lists that play a critical role in quantifying and enumerating the billionaires of the world, the nature and approach of the study requires substantial use of both primary and secondary sources of information on individuals. Historical news articles, media interviews and, where available, government reports, provide much of the evidence and context for developing the key themes throughout Chaps. 4 and 5. For example, although the *Forbes* list demonstrates a high proportion of inheritances in each region, it does not and cannot provide context as to why inheritance should constitute the main source of wealth in a given region.

Macroeconomic Data on Wealth and Income Distribution

In Chap. 4, the amassment of great fortunes is analysed in the broader context of the wealth accumulation dynamics. Adopting such an approach requires the use of various data sources from various advanced economies. These data sources are varied, but include data on income shares, after-tax incomes shares, the structure of income (capital versus labour) and savings and consumption data.

The main data source relied upon to this end is the World Wealth and Income Database (WWID). The WWID is a database constructed from an accumulation and synthesis of several succeeding studies. The utility of the database is particularly apparent regarding the use of estimates in relation to income shares. In general, the income statistics are based upon income tax data rather than household surveys which are used by, for example, the Luxembourg Income Study (n.d.). The advantage of income tax approach of WWID is in furnishing the researcher with longer estimates of income shares. In contrast, household surveys may only be undertaken every few years.

The database is significant in scope and scale covering 31 countries. Despite the scale of the database, the analysis using this data is restricted to seven countries: Australia, Canada, France, Germany, Japan, the UK and the US. In addition, some countries may simply be missing from the WWID. Brazil is one such example despite some recent studies appearing. The analysis is largely restricted due to the length of time series available and the availability of data for various percentiles and the structure of income. Despite having the most coverage, there are numerous gaps in what data is available for these countries.

In addition to the income statistics, a wealth of data on taxation, consumption, savings and debt were gathered from various statistical bodies across the globe. An inherent problem in this data gathering process is that the data is not strictly comparable across countries due to substantial variation in what is recorded. For example, wealth may be defined differently. Alternatively, a common base such as wealth or income data on a given percentile might be missing, making direct comparisons on a certain factor, such as debt, across countries problematic.

An Initial Exploration of Wealth and the Global Rich

This subsection develops the empirical context for the subsequent chapters. It seeks to emphasise the growth of the number of billionaires within the context of a 'wealthier' world. The reasons for the rise of accumulated wealth and the wealthy is then considered in subsequent chapters.

Comparison of Wealth-Income Ratios Across Advanced Economies

To set the context and differentiate the 1990s and 2000s versus the 1960s and 1970s, a broad overview of wealth accumulation is presented across advanced economies. Table 3.1 presents the aggregate ratio of wealth to national income across the major industrialised economies between 1960 and 2010, as estimated by Piketty and Zucman (2014a). The wealth to income ratio is a measure of the extent that wealth has accumulated relative to income and in effect represents a measure of wealth deepening. In addition, it provides the means to directly measure the extent to which the accumulation of wealth has increased over time and across countries (Piketty & Saez, 2014).

In aggregate, there is an overall upward trend in wealth to income ratios since the 1960s. Overall, the mean wealth-income ratio is 3.729× ($\sigma = 0.995$), although there has been substantial variation across decades. Throughout the 1960s and 1970s, the mean wealth to income ratio was averaging 3.011× to 3.068×, but a marked increase is observed during the 1990s when it rose by over 32.4% from the 1970s to 4.064× in the 1990s. In the subsequent decade, 2000 to 2010, the wealth to income ratio further increased to 4.676×.

Which countries have driven the substantial increases in the wealth to income ratio? Figure 3.1 illustrates the trends across the seven industrialised countries of interest. The highest observed wealth-income ratio is observed in Japan in 1990, which coincides with that country's property boom high. It is

Table 3.1 Mean wealth to income ratios of advanced economies by decade

Decade	Wealth-income ratio
1960–1969	3.011×
1970–1979	3.068×
1980–1989	3.528×
1990–1999	4.064×
2000–2010	4.670×

Source: Piketty and Zucman (2014b)

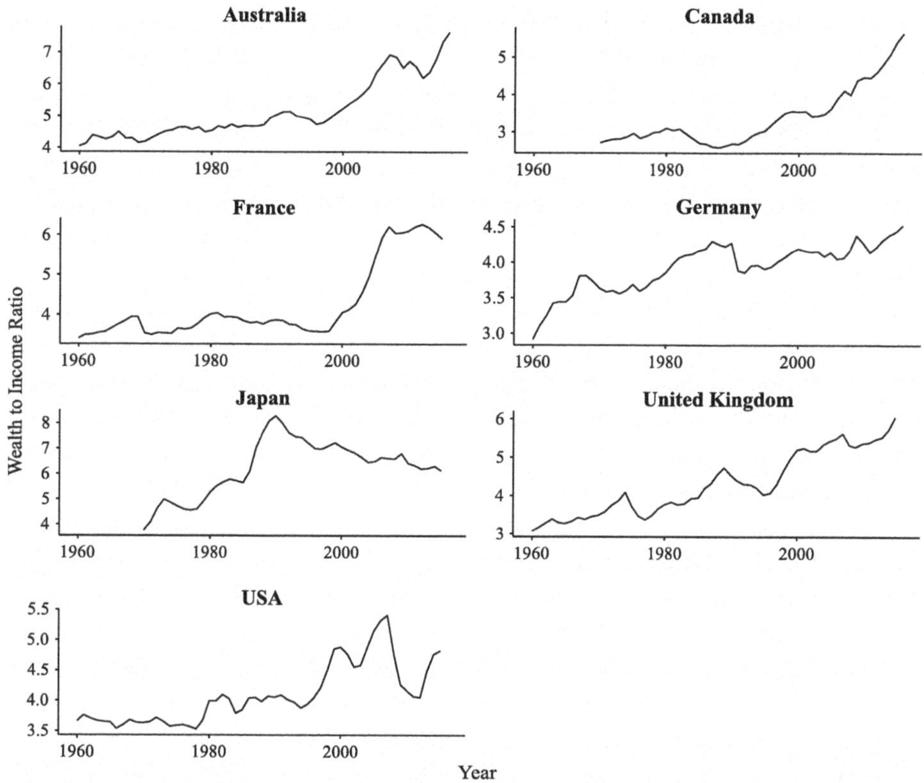

Fig. 3.1 Wealth to income ratios of advanced economies, 1960–2010. (*Source*: Data from World Inequality Database, http://wid.world/)

also the year when Japan dominated the global rich lists, with the two richest men of 1990 being Yoshiaki Tsutsumi (net worth of USD16 billion) and Taikichiro Mori (net worth of USD14.6 billion). This follows a precipitous increase throughout the 1980s in Japan's wealth to income ratio. In 1979, Japan's wealth to income ratio was 4.057×, the highest in the world at the time. However, by 1985 it reached 4.864× and peaked at 6.985× in 1990, an increase of approximately 72.2%. It then decreased to 6.073× in the 1990s and to 5.876× from 2000 to 2010. The rapid wealth accumulation in the 1980s in Japan is not observed in every country. In Germany, a much more stable and slow growth pattern is observed. Its lowest wealth to income ratio was 1.723× in 1960, averaging 2.093× over the 1960s compared to the global average of 3.011×. It then grew at an average of 1.79% to 3.135× in the 1990s, converging with global averages, and reaching 3.798× over 2000 to 2010.

The striking differences between the two former Axis powers after the Second World War reflect the dynamics of wealth accumulation in this era. It can be argued that the high values of wealth observed in Japan are tied to its real estate boom in the 1980s, and the subsequent collapse in property values reflects the trend observed in Fig. 3.1. However, notwithstanding the decline in its wealth to income ratios in the 1990s and 2000s, Japan still averages far above the ratios estimated for Germany. Germany did not experience a property boom during this period, but the divergence between the two nations may attest to substantial industrial or institutional differentiation affecting the manner and rate through which wealth might be accumulated. For example, Germany's high rates of housing rent and rental price controls may have significantly reduced the degree of wealth accumulation. Moreover, the variance in the wealth to income ratios may partly be attributable to systematic differences in the policies of the Allied occupying forces towards commercial and industrial interests in the immediate post-war period. This is further explored and discussed in Chap. 5.

The heterogeneity in wealth to income ratios is not restricted to vast physical or cultural distances, as demonstrated by the experience across the Rhine River, where France differs substantially from Germany. Starting from a relatively low mean of 2.7973× for the 1960s, France's wealth to income ratio barely averaged beyond 3 (mean of 3.039× over 1960 to 1989). Only in the late 1990s is a precipitous increase observed. By 2000, the ratio was 3.757× and by 2010 it had increased exponentially to 5.746× (compared to 3.798× in Germany), equating to an annual growth rate of 4.38% compared to −0.0948% between 1960 and 1999.

In contrast to the significant heterogeneity observed between the continental European powerhouses of Germany and France, and that of Japan, the economies of the Anglo- Saxon world tend to exhibit similar trends in their wealth to income ratios. By far the largest economy, the US, exhibits the most variation in the 50-year sample. Overall, the US mean wealth to income ratio is 3.785× ($\sigma = 0.4364$). Figure 3.1 shows that it exhibits a J-shaped path over the sample. The trough arises in the 1970s, where the mean wealth-income ratio decreased to 3.320× from 3.615× in the 1960s. By the 1990s, the ratio had increased to 3.571×. The increase in wealth accumulation coincides with an explosion in great fortunes in the US during the 2000s. The influx of new wealth is captured in the macro data, with the wealth to income ratio averaging 4.190× over the 2000 to 2010 period, with the peak observed in 2007 at 4.940×. Although the ratio decreased after 2007, if the general trends in billionaire individuals are to be viewed as a barometer of wealth accumulation, the US wealth to income ratio would be expected to increase again soon. Finance, IT and retail are the key drivers of this wealth creation and accumulation at the micro level in the US, which will be discussed in depth in Chap. 5.

Amongst the other Anglo-Saxon economies, the highest observed ratios are in Australia and the UK. In Australia, the highest wealth to income ratio was 5.552× in 2007, compared to the overall country mean (1960–2010) of 3.911× (σ = 0.6596). The history of this increase in wealth accumulation could be traced to any number of sources. One could point to the economic rationalisation programmes of successive Labor and Coalition Governments. Alternatively, the mining and property booms of the last 20 years have had a clear impact on Australian household wealth. Prior to the 1990s, Australia's wealth to income ratio averaged approximately 3.500×, which may have reflected the strong agricultural sector that dominated economic output in this period but was never a major producer of wealth. Similarly, the mean wealth to income ratio of the UK was 3.1 over the 1960s to 1970s. By the mid-1980s, an upward trend was established, increasing to over four in the 1990s and to the low fives by the 2000–2010 period. Similar to Australia's experience, the increase in the wealth to income ratio of the UK tend to coincide with the implementation of increasingly pro-market government policies. The rise of London as a global centre for finance also acted as a strong catalyst in the rapid rise of wealth in the UK, particularly for self-made entrepreneurs. Indeed, as Chap. 5 demonstrates, peerage plays a minor role in modern Britain's extreme wealth ranks, with only two notable names appearing in the property sector. Instead, in the UK, self-made financiers dominate the wealth rankings.

The Return on Wealth and National Income Growth

The trend towards very high wealth to income ratios or high wealth intensity does not necessarily say anything about the dynamics behind wealth concentration in and of itself. A useful consideration here is to examine Piketty's (2014a) view that the high wealth to income ratios have been associated with the inequality between the return on capital or wealth and national income growth. As Pressman (2015) states, if there is one definitive manner of summarising Piketty's (2014b) *Capital in the Twenty-First Century*, it is the inequality $r > g$. Here, r is the return on wealth[2] and g is the growth in national income.

Empirically, the evidence does suggest that returns to wealth have tended to exceed income growth. The real rate of return to capital has, since the 1960s, tended to remain above the national incomes of the seven

[2] Piketty (2014a) defines and wealth and capital equivalently. The definition of wealth is discussed in Chap. 2.

industrialised countries discussed here. Figure 3.2 plots their national income growth and real rates of return based on Piketty and Zucman (2014b), although the authors do not provide real return data for the 1960s for the US, the UK, Japan or Canada. The figure reveals that the rate of return on capital, across all countries, is on average above contemporaneous national income growth rates. From the 1970s, the highest rates of returns are observed in Canada (9.03%) and Germany (8.44%). In contrast, the lowest returns are observed in Japan (5.62%) and Australia (6.14%), followed by France (6.53%), the UK (6.55%) and the US (6.89%).

In contrast to the relatively high rates of return to capital, income growth rates are less than real returns, and exhibit more volatility. Australia's mean income growth has averaged 3.21%, which is the highest observed with the least variability (σ = 1.86%). France (2.26%), Germany (2.19%) and the UK (2.19%) all registered the lowest growth rate overall. Germany's average growth shows a significant increase in income growth in 1991 at 12.7%, which was no doubt spurred by the enlarged population of the newly unified German state.

From Fig. 3.2, it is observable that most countries have experienced decreasing or flat real returns. Japan and Germany both exhibit the greatest negative gradient. For Germany, the real rate of return averaged 10.4% during the 1960s and 1970s, before falling to 8.25% for subsequent decades. The decline in Japan's real rate of return traces out a more precipitous decline. During the

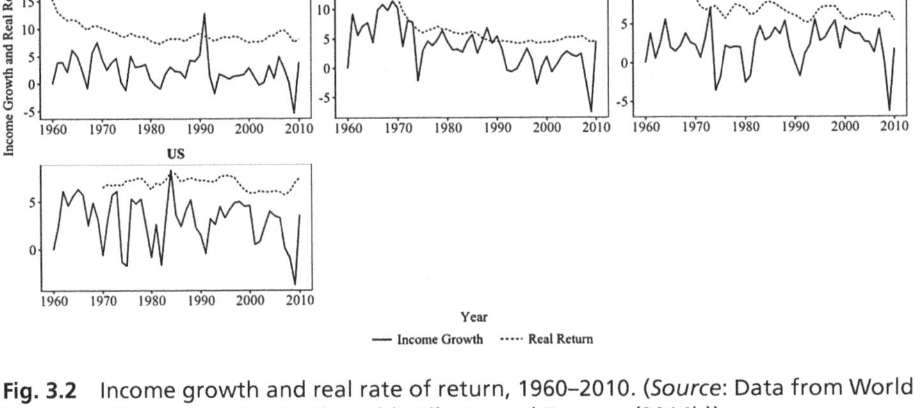

Fig. 3.2 Income growth and real rate of return, 1960–2010. (*Source*: Data from World Inequality Database, http://wid.world/, Piketty and Zucman (2014b))

1970s, Japan averaged 7.67%, one of the highest in the world. In subsequent decades, it had decreased to 4.96%, falling further to 4.85% from 2001 to 2010. Conversely, France demonstrated considerable variability in r, with no clear trend early in the sample. During the 1960s and 1970s, the French mean r was 7.15%. Between 1975 and 1985, a large decrease is observed corresponding to a mean of 5.43%, followed by a reversion to levels above 7% from 1986 to 2001. In 2001, there is a dramatic decrease once again, and from 2001 to 2010, the mean real return to French capital was 5.21%.

The Anglo-Saxon economies tend to exhibit decreasing real returns over the sample period. In the case of the US and the UK, this is not highly perceptible but it is there, as they have mean real rates of return of 6.89% and 6.55%, respectively. Between 1970 and 1989, the average rate of return in the US was 7.12%, and from 1990 to 2010 it was 6.67%. The UK's experience was very similar. Between 1970 and 1989, the mean r was 7.00% and by the 1990 to 2010 period it fell to 6.12%. Both Australia and Canada exhibit similar behaviour, although Canada had one of the highest rates in the Anglo-Saxon world. Between 1970 and 1989, Australia's and Canada's mean r was 6.68% and 9.85%, respectively. By the subsequent sample period, 1990 to 2010, a fall is once again observed to 5.63% for Australia and 8.35% for Canada.

An interesting exercise is to consider the relation between returns to capital and the wealth to income ratios depicted in Fig. 3.1. This exercise is relevant from one significant perspective. High returns to capital may be related to high risk factors such as high entrepreneurial risk. Conversely, lower returns may be indicative of a move from entrepreneurial activity in generating wealth to one based on diversification and/or inheritance. The inheritor may prefer to diversify their portfolios thereby reducing overall returns and risk. Piketty (2014a) predicts that increases in β (wealth to income ratio) would ultimately be driven by falls in the realised real rates of return. Figure 3.3 presents the relationship between β and r over time, with the coloured shapes depicting the sample decades in Piketty and Zucman's (2014b) data.

The negative relationship between β and r largely holds across the sample and is strongest among countries that demonstrate both the greatest changes in β and large changes in the annual real rate of return. The pattern tends to be repeated across the majority countries. In the latest decade, returns tend to be clustered at the lower end of the spectrum, whereas in the 1960s and, where applicable, the 1970s, they are typically clustered at lower levels of β. The only major exception to this general pattern is France, where the negative relationship between r and β does not hold over the 1980s and the US during the 1970s and 1980s. However, the 2000s largely confirms the observations across the general sample. Overall, the correlation of the relation is quite high for most countries: Australia −0.7849, Canada −0.7514, France −0.6139, Germany −0.6344, Japan −0.8582, the UK −0.5508 and the US −0.6629. The question that naturally arises is what relevance such a negative relationship has for inequality.

The negative relationship between returns and wealth-income ratios might be indicative of a transformation of capitalism in some economies from one based on entrepreneurial activity to one in which inheritor or rentier plays a greater role. Piketty (2014a) argues that any number of reasons can be provided for this relationship, but the preferred one resides in linking the amount of entrepreneurial effort expended during periods of high income growth and returns, as substantial entrepreneurial labour effort and energy are exerted to allocate capital. In contrast, during periods of low growth, the entrepreneur moves back and the rentier approach gains dominance as the latter requires less effort in allocating capital (Piketty, 2014a). Watkins (1907) also recognises the effect of a low-interest income on entrepreneurial effort. Examining the impact of falling returns for the rich, Watkins (1907) argues:

> For them further accumulation is still easy and the low rate of interest puts others at a disadvantage, so long as the large incomes from property are much larger than the large incomes from personal effect. Family pride will sustain the effort of those already rich to keep their relative position in the face of a falling interest rate. (p. 125)

This basic argument, along with the data on rates of return presented in Fig. 3.3, provides an initial motivation for seeking to establish the origins of extreme wealth across the advanced economies. For example, many of the observations for the US in the 1990s are clustered in the high percentage return range (over 7%), with the recorded years coinciding with the influx of new wealth from internet start-ups and new finance industries (e.g. hedge funds) where relatively more youthful entrepreneurs dominate. The UK, too, experienced an influx of the new rich in the 1990s, which was associated with the emergence of a new elite financial. In contrast, Japan's entrepreneurial renaissance in the immediate post-war era tapered off in the 1990s and 2000s with many of the wealthiest and their estate beneficiaries diversifying away from their dynasty's traditional locus of entrepreneurial activity. Many of the wealthiest entrepreneurs in these countries found initial success during the 1960s–1980s. This is further explored in a historical framework in Chap. 5.

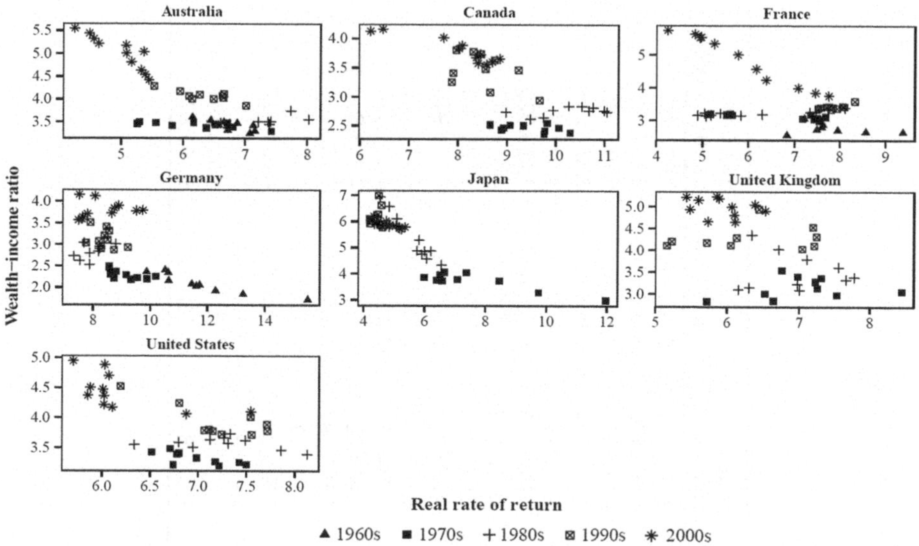

Fig. 3.3 Real rates of return and wealth to income ratios, 1960–2010. (*Source*: Data from World Inequality Database, http://wid.world/, Piketty and Zucman (2014b))

Trends in Billionaire Wealth Holdings

Moving from the general macro wealth context, we now turn to another aspect of wealth for which this book is principally concerned; the rise of individuals with extreme wealth holdings. The enumerated list of billionaires covers a 24-year period from 1990 through to 2013. As mentioned previously, the *Forbes* global billionaire list only provides point estimates of net worth from 1996 and beyond. Although this study is ultimately interested in the historical processes and sources associated with large fortunes, it is still useful to examine the general trends in the actual monetary wealth levels as reported by *Forbes*. Table 3.2 presents the descriptive statistics on the aggregate sample for both the number of billionaires and the average wealth of those listed on the *Forbes* global billionaire list. As Table 3.2 indicates, there has been a 511% increase in the number of billionaires from 232 in 1990 to 1417 in 2013. On a per annum basis, the growth rate in billionaires equates to an average 10% growth rate in the billionaire ranks, although this varies considerably from year to year. Certain periods show little growth or a reversal in the fortunes of the rich. Between 1997 and 2000, there was little growth in the numbers, with 1998 showing the lowest number of billionaires of the past 24 years at 203.

The middle of the last decade saw a substantial increase in the ranks of the world's billionaires. From 2003 to 2008 an average 19% growth rate in the

Table 3.2 Global aggregate billionaire wealth (USD), 1996–2013

Year	No. of countries	No. of individuals	Sample growth rate	Total wealth ($'000)	Median ($'000)	Mean ($'000)	Max ($'000)	Standard deviation ($'000)
1996	39	414		1,028,000,000	1,950,000	2,483,092	18,500,000	2,037,720
1997	39	221	−46.6%	965,590,000	2,900,000	4,369,186	36,400,000	4,377,129
1998	38	203	−8.1%	1,007,900,000	3,300,000	4,965,025	51,999,999	5,935,095
1999	39	294	44.8%	1,252,800,000	2,900,000	4,261,224	90,000,000	6,367,236
2000	39	319	8.5%	1,379,199,999	2,900,000	4,323,197	60,000,000	5,527,475
2001	42	531	66.5%	1,710,200,000	1,800,000	3,220,716	58,700,000	4,459,070
2002	41	468	−11.9%	1,503,300,000	1,700,000	3,212,179	52,800,000	4,464,847
2003	41	472	0.9%	1,392,300,000	1,900,000	2,949,788	40,700,000	3,726,738
2004	42	582	23.3%	1,902,600,000	2,000,000	3,269,072	46,600,000	4,171,913
2005	45	686	17.9%	2,222,000,000	2,000,000	3,239,067	46,500,000	4,108,015
2006	48	790	15.2%	2,634,600,000	2,100,000	3,334,937	50,000,000	4,111,956
2007	51	942	19.2%	3,438,000,000	2,200,000	3,649,682	56,000,000	4,783,892
2008	53	1122	19.1%	4,370,400,000	1,800,000	3,895,187	62,000,000	5,437,303
2009	51	790	−29.6%	2,407,900,000	2,000,000	3,047,975	40,000,000	3,761,497
2010	51	1000	26.6%	3,520,300,000	2,000,000	3,520,300	53,500,000	4,691,937
2011	52	1205	20.5%	4,483,100,000	2,000,000	3,720,415	64,000,000	5,206,276
2012	55	1220	1.2%	4,559,000,000	2,100,000	3,736,885	69,000,000	5,120,191
2013	59	1417	16.1%	5,411,260,000	2,100,000	3,818,814	73,000,000	5,392,871

Source: Forbes (1990–2013)

number of billionaires is observed. In 2008, the billionaires list exceeded 1000 individuals for the first time, an extraordinary increase considering that only ten years prior the number of billionaires languished at 203. The rapid rise is partly explained by the influx of *nouveau riche* from Russia, China and South America, with the new entrants' impact being captured by the increase in the number of countries being represented in the *Forbes* list. In 1996, 39 countries were represented, increasing to 59 by 2013.

It would be highly premature to draw inferences from these trends, and there is a potential problem in using journalistic lists without delving more deeply into the personal histories of these individuals. For example, it can be argued that the fall in billionaires observed between 1997 and 2000 is due to the economic downturn associated with the Asian Financial Crisis, as they perfectly coincide. However, there are problems in establishing such a causal relation regarding Western Europe, for example. Although the number of Western European billionaires fell from 84 in 1996 to 48 in 1997 and to 40 in 1998, Western European policy makers and the markets were both much more sanguine about Europe's economic position during 1998 despite the Asian Financial Crisis. In fact:

> European Commission President Jacques Santer could argue that the direct effect on the European economies of the Asian Pacific economic turmoil would be 'slight' and that he saw no need to revise downward growth projections for the European Union (EU) for 1998. (Bridge, 1999, p. 458)

Market indicators were also quite healthy and did not signal any cause for concern for the rich of Europe. If the *Deutscher Aktienindex* (DAX), for example, is assumed to be a gauge for the financial health of Western Europe's economic elite,[3] the DAX closed at 2473.60 in February 1996, 3259.60 in February 1997 and at 4693.50 in February 1998. Taking another European index, the Euro STOXX 50 closed at 2077.22 in February 1997 and at 2878.04 in February 1998. Given the relative health of Europe's financial markets, one is either left to conclude that the European economic elite made terrible investments *en masse* compared to the rest of the market, or there were other factors at play. This might be explained by the data gathering process of *Forbes*, or substantial changes in wealth holdings through intergenerational transfers or divorce.

[3] As will be shown below, Germany produces the bulk of Western Europe's billionaire economic elite, followed by the UK and France.

Although the number of billionaires may have plummeted in the late 1990s, the mean wealth of billionaires fortunate enough to maintain their position on the list reached the highest-ever observed levels at USD4.965 billion in 1999, compared to USD3.564 billion over the entire sample. It is possible that the mean is influenced by extreme valuations. In 1999 the highest-ever recorded valuation by *Forbes* was made for Bill Gates at USD90 billion. To put this into perspective, Gates's wealth exceeded the combined wealth of the next top three (all from the US and two from Microsoft): Warren Buffet (USD36 billion), Paul Allen (USD30 billion) and Steven Ballmer (USD19.5 billion). The greatest dispersion of wealth was also observed, with a standard deviation of USD6.367 billion during 1999. Given the sample incorporates extreme values, the median may provide a better measure of the central tendency of extreme wealth. Between 1998 and 2000, the median value ranged between USD2.9 billion and USD3.3 billion, compared to USD2.1 billion in subsequent years. Overall, the total wealth owned has seen a fivefold increase from 1996 to 2013. In 1996, the total estimated net worth of the billionaires was USD1.028 trillion. In 2000, it had increased to 1.379 trillion. Finally, by 2013, it had almost quadrupled to USD5.411 trillion. On an annual basis, this equates to a wealth growth rate of 9.76% per annum and in excess of the average returns and national income growth rates outlined shown in Fig. 3.2.

The global industrial segmentation reveals that most industries have produced billionaires. Table 3.3 presents a sectoral breakdown of billionaires over time. Reflecting on all sectors, there is a rapid increase in the number of billionaires throughout the life of the sample. Globally, both consumer discretionary and financials produced the bulk of billionaires and have also demonstrated the most growth. The growth is most pronounced after the year 2000. Next are industrials and consumer staples. Despite the media popularity of individuals in the sector, the number of billionaires in IT is far below these industries and had produced 90 billionaires by 2013. Perhaps even more interesting is the lack of representation of the telecommunications industry, with the number of billionaires barely reaching 20 in 2013, and typically averaging 15 throughout the period 2000–2010. At least on a global basis, the findings of Kaplan and Rauh (2013) that the ultra-rich will be typically found in industries requiring a high education premium does not, on casual observance, fit the global data.

Although the energy industry is often viewed as a constant stream of wealth generation in popular discourse, it is surprisingly under-represented in the sample. Just under 61 energy billionaires appear in 2013 albeit showing an upward trend compared to previous years. Health care also exhibited a similarly

Table 3.3 Global distribution of billionaires by industry, 1990–2013

Year	Misc.	Energy	Materials	Industrials	Con. discretionary	Con. staples	Health care	Financials	Info. tech.	Comm. services	Utilities
1996	8	13	19	83	120	48	13	88	21	6	
1997	7	12	10	42	59	25	7	41	15	4	
1998	6	11	9	31	61	21	4	49	12	4	
1999	7	6	15	63	85	31	6	56	22	7	
2000	8	8	16	68	85	33	7	52	34	11	
2001	9	27	17	89	156	40	16	122	45	17	
2002	6	22	16	77	144	41	12	108	32	14	
2003	2	27	21	66	152	45	13	110	31	8	
2004	4	30	29	81	185	54	16	132	42	13	
2005	3	28	43	90	214	65	21	170	45	11	
2006	5	33	47	115	224	77	24	204	50	14	
2007	5	40	67	145	249	83	27	254	58	18	
2008	5	52	79	177	264	90	33	335	67	23	
2009	4	36	53	114	205	81	25	211	49	15	
2010	5	42	78	153	246	93	36	276	65	17	
2011	5	50	113	198	289	101	54	301	82	17	
2012	4	51	111	197	293	105	47	315	86	16	1
2013	7	56	130	230	343	135	63	357	86	16	3

Source: Forbes (1990–2013), authors' compilation from various secondary sources

consistent and relatively smooth upward trend. Utility billionaires only made an appearance in 2012 and 2013, a far cry from the Gilded Age when 27 super rich were associated with this industry (Rockoff, 2012). Except for telecommunication services, most industries exhibit very low volatility in billionaire numbers.

The creation of much of the wealth in these industries, however, has a history stretching farther back than the figures would lead one to believe. Although Thurow (1975) and Hirsch (1911) argue that rapid capitalisation is an essential element of wealth creation (examples of which abound today), typically the road to extreme wealth spans decades. Indeed, for many in the billionaire rankings, the source of their wealth may appear in family histories spanning well over a century. These accounts are examined on a region-by-region basis focused on individuals in Chap. 5.

The Impact of the GFC on Billionaire Numbers

How did billionaires fare during the GFC? On a superficial level, not exceptionally well. In early 2009, world markets hit their lowest point. In 2009, there were 790 billionaires across the globe, a decrease of 30% from 1122 in 2008. *Forbes* records asset prices as at 14 February annually. Global equity returns in February 2009 had the worst recorded year-to-year returns since 2003, with yields falling by approximately 60% from 2008. Once again, however, a degree of scepticism should be maintained when seeking a correlation between aggregate macro statistics and rise or fall of billionaires. There is some evidence that the decline is not entirely attributable to the economic crisis. Table 3.4 presents data on the estimated dropouts from 2008 to 2009, and those who managed to reappear in the wealth list in subsequent years.

At the *global* level, the fall was more dramatic than that revealed by the 332 decrease. Table 3.4 shows that of the 332 net recorded decreases, 374 were from dropouts and 42 were additions. The greatest number of dropouts came from North America (142), followed by Eastern Europe (61) and Western Europe (33). Of the 374 global dropouts, 208 managed to re-emerge in subsequent years (2010 to 2013), while 166 have not reappeared at all. The absence could be due to any number of factors, including business and investment misfortune, death, prison or divorce.

An examination of the regional dynamics suggests at first glance that other factors are at work not purely associated with the economic crisis. The number or proportion of dropouts adheres to the general contribution of a region to the overall global number of billionaires. For example, in 2009, the Middle

Table 3.4 Impact of the GFC on billionaire population

	2008	Dropouts	Additions	Net additions	2009	Survived	Did not reappear	Additions/Dropouts
Global	*1122*	*−374*	*42*	*−332*	*790*	*208*	*166*	*−0.11*
North America	500	142	23	−119	381	76	66	0.16
Western Europe	159	33	6	−27	132	18	15	0.18
Eastern Europe	96	61	0	−61	35	19	42	0.00
Middle East	78	30	4	−26	52	16	14	0.13
East Asia	70	24	3	−21	49	8	16	0.13
South Asia	53	29	0	−29	24	11	18	0.00
China	46	23	4	−19	27	5	18	0.17
Southern Europe	37	14	1	−13	24	9	5	0.07
South America	26	7	0	−7	19	2	5	0.00
South East Asia	26	5	0	−5	21	0	5	0.00
Oceania	17	5	0	−5	12	3	2	0.00
Central Asia	7	4	1	−3	4	0	4	0.25
Sub-Saharan Africa	6	1	2	1	5	1	0	2.00

Source: Forbes (1990–2013), authors' compilation from various secondary sources

East contributed 6.6% of the world's billionaires and 8% to the proportion of dropouts. Similarly, Australia contributed 1.5% of total billionaires and 1.3% to the share of dropouts. The correlation between dropouts and contribution to the wealth lists is very high at 0.92. However, three regions deviate from this trend in terms of both dropouts and additions. While both the US and Western Europe played significant roles in the GFC, the proportion of dropouts from this billionaire list is relatively less than in other regions. However, they contributed more additions during 2009 while still reeling from the economic crisis. The US contributed 44.6% to the global billionaire ranks and 38% to the number of dropouts, while Europe only contributed 8.8% to dropouts and 14.2% to the overall population in 2009. Further, both regions contributed the bulk (US 54.8% and Western Europe 14.3%) of new billionaire additions in 2009, despite their respective populations suffering through a protracted economic contraction.

Table 3.4 also lists the ratio of additions to dropouts for every region for 2008–2009. Apart from China (0.17), both North America and Western Europe appeared to have performed above the global average of 0.11.[4] The only region that seemed to experience from substantial losses in the ranks of the ultra-rich was Eastern Europe, with 61 dropouts throughout the course of 2008–2009, decreasing the absolute number of billionaires from 96 in 2008 to 35 in 2009. In relative terms, Eastern Europe contributed 4.43% to the population of ultra-rich in 2009 but constituted a disproportionate 16.3% of its dropouts.

What is most significant is that for many individuals, 2009 was a momentary blip with many reappearing in 2010 and beyond to the status of wealth elite. The regional decomposition shows that for the US (76 survived and 66 disappeared) and Western Europe (18 survived and 15 disappeared), many billionaires managed to rapidly re-establish their wealth above the one billion USD threshold. The personal circumstances of these individuals, health or the wellbeing of their marriages even, can have an impact on the number of representative individuals. Of the 166 who have remained absent from the list in subsequent years, 21 died in 2008, and 11 died sometime between 2009 and 2013, with the majority being in North America or Western Europe. A few fell from wealth's grace due to divorce (Robert Johnson) or criminal activities (Timothy Blixseth and Robert Allen Stanford). The rest still appear to be in relatively good financial health despite not appearing in the ultra-rich lists mainly due to the truncated nature of the *Forbes* list.

[4] Both Sub-Saharan Africa and Central Asia actually performed the best, although their absolute numbers are insignificant.

Another major element shaping the number of billionaires has been the influx of individuals from developing economies. The emergence of a new super-rich group from Russia and the People's Republic of China as well as parts of Eastern Europe and South America, appear to be the primary drivers, although the Russian contribution has been reduced since 2009. Also, the rise of new industries in well-established economies has also continued to be an active contributor, with the US, for example, maintaining the mantle of the world's factory for producing the most billionaires, far outstripping the numbers from both Russia and China due to new sectors of the economy emerging. Although new wealth from the developing world has played a significant role in many parts of the world, privilege and old wealth continue to increase both the number of billionaires and their absolute wealth. For both continental Europe and South Korea, inherited wealth forms the primary source of new billionaires. These points are developed further below.

To summarise, a basic review of the data suggests that except for the late 1990s and 2009, the world's billionaires have managed to both increase their total wealth while also enlarging the club of the economic elite. In addition, the data suggests that distribution of wealth at these extreme levels is extraordinarily wide as evidenced by the large standard deviations listed in Table 3.3. During periods of expansion or recovery, more individuals attained high wealth status with large influxes swelling the number of global billionaires. The extent to which different regions contribute to this growth is explored below.

Regional Trends

This section discusses the regional trends in ultra-wealth. The relevance of such a geographical exercise has long been recognised in the literature relating to the rich. John Stuart Mill (1929), for example, once argued that the distribution of wealth is largely contingent upon the prevailing laws and social customs in a state. Further, the pace of economic development and the strength of prevailing market institutions can have an impact on any regional variations in the number of billionaires. Given the sheer heterogeneity in the regions and industries represented in the billionaire database, only an overview of the various regions is provided here. Chapter 5 provides a more detailed exploration and sectoral analysis of these regions of the globe.

Determining how to allocate individuals to countries and regions is complicated by the global nature of the data. Briefly, the process followed is to allocate an individual billionaire according to their residency. For individuals that hold significant commercial interests spanning the globe, this may be an

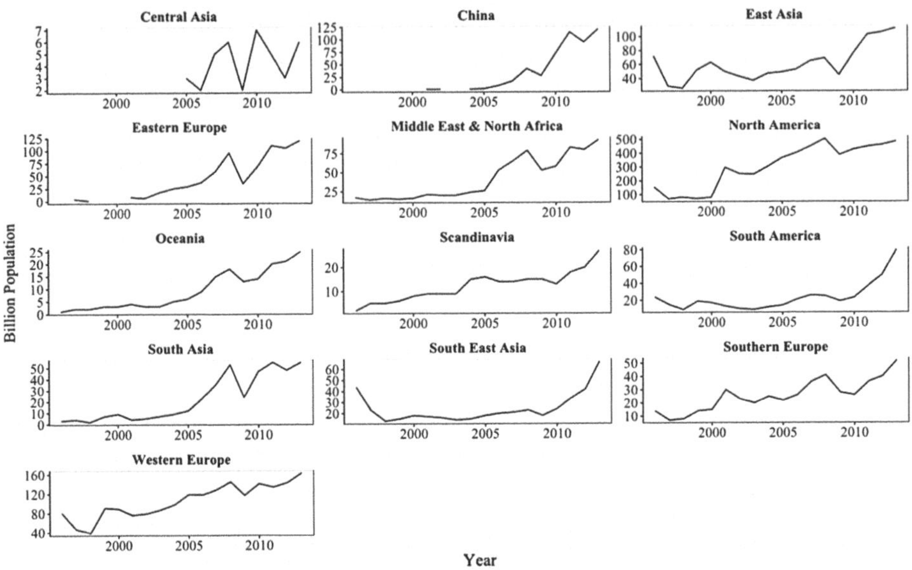

Fig. 3.4 Billionaire population, geographical distribution, 1990–2013. (*Source*: Forbes (1990–2013), authors' compilation from various secondary sources)

issue due to the high mobility. In these situations, the residency of the individual billionaire is assumed to be, for this study, the headquarters of their business empires.

The extent to which geography matters to the distribution of large fortunes can be inferred by charting the regional trends over the 24-year sample. Figure 3.4 presents the evolution across time and space in the number of billionaires on the *Forbes* list from 1990 to 2013. What is immediately apparent is the extent to which all regions (except Central Asia and, to a lesser extent, South East Asia) exhibit the same upward trend in the number of billionaires observed at the global level in Table 3.2 and for the wealth to income ratios in Fig. 3.1. This pattern is tied not only to the developed world but also to the emerging regions of the world, with both contributing heavily to the increase of the billionaire group.

In the developed world, the largest cohort of billionaires lives in North America where a significant increase in numbers is observed. From 1990 to 2013, the number of billionaires increased from 73 to 485, an increase of 664%, or an annual growth rate of 27% compared to 10% for the global statistics. Although North America has seen the biggest increase in absolute numbers, the relative magnitudes and growth rates are just as impressive in other regions of the developed world. In Western Europe, the absolute numbers of billionaires have lagged behind those of North America, with little substantial growth from the late 1990s to 2003. However, a large rise in the number of ultra-rich individuals is observed in Western Europe, from 93 in 2003 to 190 by 2013, with an associated annual growth rate of approximately 7.8%. The GFC appears to have had only a small transitory impact on wealth creation in Western Europe, with a fall to just 132 in 2009, but had largely stabilised to pre-GFC levels by 2010.

The other great region of advanced capitalism, the Japanese-dominated East Asia, had an anaemic rise in the number of billionaires in the previous few years. From a low of 21 in 2009, the number of billionaires has more than doubled in 2013 to reach 47. This growth, however, represents a marginal increase during the 1990s. Throughout the 1990s and much of the 2000s, the region showed barely any growth in the number of billionaires, typically averaging 31. The mean growth rate throughout the sample is 7.4% closely aligned to that of Western Europe, though well below what is observed in North America. The bulk of the growth post-2008 is mainly tied to South Korea, where the fortunes of a few family dynasties have dramatically increased through inter vivos gifts or bequests. In contrast, Japan has not seen any dramatic increase during the sample period.

Among the least-populated areas of the advanced industrialised world, there has been an impressive growth in numbers. In Oceania, the mining and property booms have seen the number of billionaires increase from only 1 in 1996, the Australian media mogul, the late Kerry Packer, to 25 by 2013. In southern Europe, which has endured protracted economic issues and recession since 2009, a similar upward trend can be observed in the number of billionaires, recording its highest number in 2013. Much of this growth came from Spain (20 billionaires in 2013) with an annual growth rate of 10% and Italy (23 billionaires in 2013) with a 5.8% growth rate.

Next, Fig. 3.5 depicts the mean wealth level across the 15 regions. Average net worth is within similar ranges across the globe. In North America, mean net worth peaked at $7 billion in 1998 and 2000 before settling between $3 and $4.5 billion between 2001 and 2013. When read in conjunction with Fig. 3.5, the drop is more likely due to an influx of new billionaires rather than a systematic decline in wealth levels. The Middle East has shown similar trends in mean net dropping from $8 billion to $3 billion by 2013. In East Asia and South East Asia, mean net worth peaked at approximately $4.5 billion in 1997 before encountering a precipitous decline.

Manifestly, contemporaneous market developments immediately present themselves as candidates for the substantial decreases observed in the data. The falls recorded in North America closely parallel the falls in equity market valuations in 2001. In the *Forbes* data, a drop in mean net worth is recorded

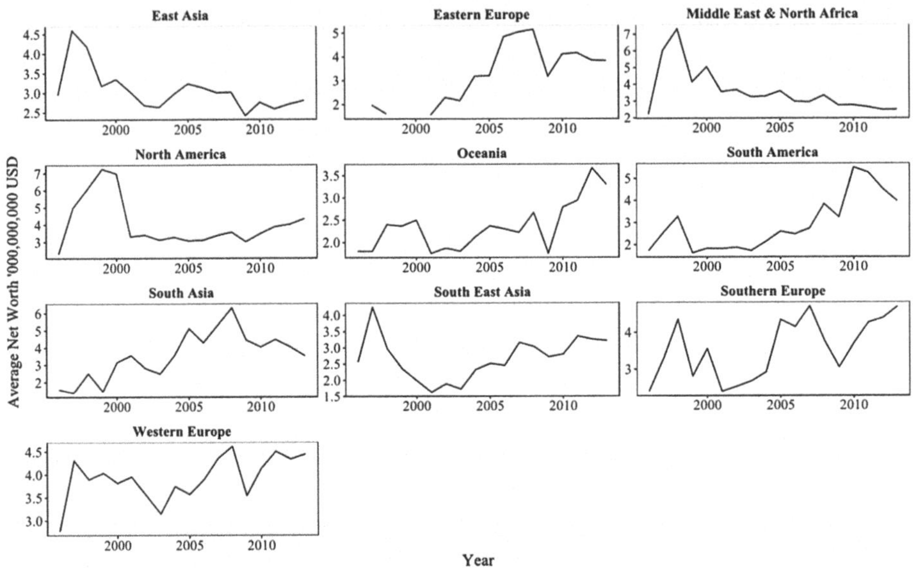

Fig. 3.5 Mean net worth (USD) by region, 1996–2013. (*Source*: Forbes (1990–2013), authors' compilation from various secondary sources)

in 2002, a full year after the bursting of the US equity markets. As the *Forbes* measurements take place in February for a given year, it is to be expected that a fall would become evident a year after the event. For Asia, the obvious candidate is the Asian Financial Crisis, which affected the region over 1997 and 1998.

Returning to the number of billionaires, in emerging markets a similar upward trend is detected, with the exception that growth was delayed between the years 2005 and 2010 in many regions. However, for the People's Republic of China, the number of billionaires has grown from just 1 in 2001 to 125 by 2013. The loosening of central government controls on ownership clearly had a dramatic but not surprising impact in China's wealth landscape. A dramatic increase in the number of billionaires in Eastern Europe is also observed, peaking in 2013 at 120. The peak reflects the precipitous increase observed in China, with the first four Eastern European billionaires only appearing in 1997. The only depression in the trend was the GFC in 2009, which caused some billionaires to fall from the rich lists and not to reappear. Southern Asia, dominated by India, also shows substantial growth, albeit less than China or Eastern Europe. In the 1990s, the mean number of billionaires was 2.4, and between 2000 to 2013 it had increased to 27.6, with the highest recorded number being 55 in 2011 and 2013.

Significant increases are observed in South America, where the mean number of billionaires throughout the 1990s was 11, before more than doubling to an average of 25 throughout the 2000s. The biggest increase is observed in 2013 when the population of billionaires reached 76, an increase of 204% on the average. Similarly, in South East Asia, the mean in the 1990s was 15, increasing to 25 for 2000 to 2013. Following global trends, the most growth occurred between 2008 and 2013. In 2008, the number of South East Asian billionaires was 18, and by 2013 it had increased to 64, an increase of 255%.

What has caused the general upward trend across the developing regions of the world, particularly among former heavily centrally planned economies (India) and communist states (China and Russia)? Any explanation may be found in legal and political changes, technological developments, or access to large markets. As Chap. 2 discussed, older studies of wealth have typically fixated on these three avenues through which wealth can rapidly accumulate and develop into substantial concentrations. Although their degree of influence will vary, all can be seen to be at play. Indeed, any discussion needs to highlight the dramatic changes in the economic and geopolitical sphere that have arisen not only since the early 1990s but also from far earlier across these regions. When considering China, Russia and India, the interplay between politics and law have had just as much an impact as pure economics in elevating certain individuals to the status of economic elite. In legal terms, the primary concern is to what extent private ownership of modes of production would be distributed among the population. Each of these regions has experienced monumental changes to private ownership and policy-maker discretion over directing commerce since the unravelling of the socialist state economy in the early 1990s. These issues are analysed in Chap. 5.

Inheritance and Self-Made Wealth

In studies of the wealthy, inheritance and, by extension, liberal inheritance laws have long been recognised as having an important role in the prevailing distribution of wealth and on the economy in general. Some authors have argued from the view that it promotes an environment that stifles initiative, particularly among the beneficiaries. Andrew Carnegie (1900) argued that inheritance has a distortionary impact upon the incentives of a market economy, as 'the parent who leaves his son enormous wealth generally deadens the talents and energies of the son and tempts him to lead a less useful and less worthy life than he otherwise would' (p. 56). Similarly, Rubinstein (1980) finds that for the UK in the late 1800s, the lack of inherited wealth in the rich lists perhaps had to do with the lack of motivation on the part of beneficiaries who squandered their fortunes. Other authors have focused on the impact of inheritance laws and corporate laws that enable massive, intergenerational wealth transfers from generation to generation. Tuckman (1973) argues that death taxes would be an effective 'tool in the implementation of policies designed to limit the concentration of wealth' (p. 56). Lundberg (1969) argues that inheritance issues go beyond taxes and include the ability of family dynasties to maintain and expand their sphere of ownership and influence through holding companies and foundations, citing the Ford Foundation as an example.

Typically, estate beneficiaries occupy positions of ownership at the very top of the wealth tables. For example, the Walton family is by far the wealthiest family dynasty at a global level, with an estimated combined wealth of USD125 billion in 2013. In South Korea, the Lee family possesses enormous economic power through its ownership of Samsung. In Europe, there are older family dynasties, such as the Grosvenors in the UK, the von Siemens and Quandt families in Germany, and the Dassault family in France, all of which often dominate the top of the wealth tables. In Australia, when measured by personal wealth, mining is dominated by Gina Rinehart, and media and gaming by the Packer family.

When taking a regional view of the world's ultra-rich, detection of systematic differences between the proportions of inherited versus self-made wealth across regions may point to underlying differences in either legal or cultural attitudes towards the intergenerational transfer of wealth. Table 3.5 presents data on inherited and self-made fortunes as the sources of wealth. Overall, the proportion of individuals inheriting their wealth between 1990 and 2013 has averaged 45.1% (54.9% self-made). Dividing the sample into two periods, 1990–2001 and 2002–2013, reveals the trends clearly. Throughout the first half of the sample, there were more inherited billionaires, averaging 53.4%. Between 2000 and 2013, the mean proportion of inherited wealth had decreased to 36.8%.

A regional decomposition, however, reveals substantial variation in the relative share of inheritance during different periods. Firstly, the regional breakdown of estate beneficiaries points to the influx of new wealth from the former centrally commanded economies. The share of inheritances has languished at a mean of 2.0% in China and 1.6% in Eastern Europe. Similarly, in South Asia (India and Sri Lanka), the mean proportion of inheritances decreased from 92.3% throughout the 1990s to 59.2% between 2002 and 2013, following India's dismantling of the License Raj system. Secondly, the fall in the frequency of the inherited billionaire is also in evidence in developed regions. In North

Table 3.5 Proportion of billionaires receiving inheritances—regional decomposition 1990–2013

	Global		Central Asia		China		East Asia		Eastern Europe		Middle East and North Africa		North America	
	No	*Yes*	*No*	*Yes*	*No*	*Yes*	*No*	*Yes*	*No*	*Yes*	*No*	*Yes*	*No*	*Yes*
1990	48.1%	51.9%					67.2%	32.8%			35.7%	64.3%	50.7%	49.3%
1991	45.6%	54.4%					69.5%	30.5%			33.3%	66.7%	47.4%	52.6%
1992	37.1%	62.9%					52.9%	47.1%			36.4%	63.6%	37.7%	62.3%
1993	36.4%	63.6%					49.1%	50.9%			23.1%	76.9%	39.1%	60.9%
1994	39.7%	60.3%					57.4%	42.6%			30.8%	69.2%	40.4%	59.6%
1995	43.7%	56.3%					68.2%	31.8%			30.8%	69.2%	39.8%	59.0%
1996	49.0%	51.0%					65.3%	34.7%			47.1%	52.9%	51.9%	48.1%
1997	49.8%	50.2%					65.5%	34.5%	100.0%	0.0%	28.6%	71.4%	62.3%	37.7%
1998	52.7%	47.3%					61.5%	38.5%	100.0%	0.0%	31.3%	68.8%	59.3%	40.7%
1999	49.0%	51.0%					63.5%	36.5%			46.7%	53.3%	64.3%	35.7%
2000	50.8%	49.2%					66.7%	33.3%			50.0%	50.0%	60.0%	40.0%
2001	57.6%	42.4%			100.0%	0.0%	66.0%	34.0%	100.0%	0.0%	52.4%	47.6%	62.0%	38.0%
2002	56.4%	43.6%			100.0%	0.0%	62.8%	37.2%	100.0%	0.0%	50.0%	50.0%	62.2%	37.8%
2003	56.4%	43.6%					67.6%	32.4%	100.0%	0.0%	45.0%	55.0%	62.8%	37.2%
2004	58.4%	41.6%			100.0%	0.0%	70.2%	29.8%	100.0%	0.0%	54.2%	45.8%	62.8%	37.2%
2005	59.5%	40.5%	100.0%	0.0%	100.0%	0.0%	69.4%	30.6%	100.0%	0.0%	53.8%	46.2%	61.0%	39.0%
2006	60.6%	39.4%	100.0%	0.0%	100.0%	0.0%	66.0%	34.0%	97.3%	2.7%	45.3%	54.7%	62.8%	37.2%
2007	64.3%	35.7%	80.0%	20.0%	100.0%	0.0%	60.0%	40.0%	96.6%	3.4%	47.7%	52.3%	66.5%	33.5%
2008	67.3%	32.7%	83.3%	16.7%	97.6%	2.4%	62.3%	37.7%	97.9%	2.1%	44.3%	55.7%	68.8%	31.2%
2009	64.4%	35.6%	100.0%	0.0%	96.4%	3.6%	68.9%	31.1%	97.1%	2.9%	52.8%	47.2%	66.2%	33.8%
2010	66.8%	33.2%	85.7%	14.3%	90.3%	9.7%	64.5%	35.5%	97.1%	2.9%	41.4%	58.6%	68.6%	31.4%
2011	68.8%	31.2%	80.0%	20.0%	98.3%	1.7%	65.0%	35.0%	98.2%	1.8%	47.0%	53.0%	69.0%	31.0%
2012	68.3%	31.7%	100.0%	0.0%	97.9%	2.1%	62.3%	37.7%	98.1%	1.9%	46.3%	53.8%	70.6%	29.4%
2013	67.0%	33.0%	66.7%	33.3%	97.5%	2.5%	61.6%	38.4%	98.3%	1.7%	44.1%	55.9%	70.1%	29.9%
μ	54.9%	45.1%	88.4%	11.6%	98.2%	1.8%	63.9%	36.1%	98.7%	1.3%	42.4%	57.6%	58.6%	41.3%
σ	10.1%	10.1%	12.2%	12.2%	2.8%	2.8%	5.1%	5.1%	1.3%	1.3%	9.0%	9.0%	10.6%	10.5%
μ ('90 – '01)	46.6%	53.4%			100.0%	0.0%	62.7%	37.3%	100.0%	0.0%	37.2%	62.8%	51.2%	48.7%
μ ('02 – '13)	63.2%	36.8%	88.4%	11.6%	98.0%	2.0%	65.0%	35.0%	98.4%	1.6%	47.7%	52.3%	66.0%	34.0%

(continued)

Table 3.5 (continued)

	Oceania		South America		South Asia		South East Asia		Southern Europe		Sub-Saharan Africa		Western Europe	
	No	*Yes*	*No*	*Yes*	*No*	*Yes*	*No*	*Yes*	*No*	*Yes*	*No*	*Yes*	*No*	*Yes*
1990	0.0%	100.0%	75.0%	25.0%	0.0%	100.0%	60.0%	40.0%	54.5%	45.5%			28.8%	71.2%
1991	0.0%	100.0%	50.0%	50.0%	0.0%	100.0%	44.4%	55.6%	50.0%	50.0%			23.8%	76.2%
1992	0.0%	100.0%	53.8%	46.2%	0.0%	100.0%	37.5%	62.5%	46.2%	53.8%			20.6%	79.4%
1993	0.0%	100.0%	52.9%	47.1%	0.0%	100.0%	50.0%	50.0%	42.9%	57.1%			19.5%	80.5%
1994	0.0%	100.0%	55.0%	45.0%	0.0%	100.0%	43.5%	56.5%	53.3%	46.7%	100.0%	0.0%	20.0%	80.0%
1995	0.0%	100.0%	52.2%	47.8%	0.0%	100.0%	54.8%	45.2%	53.3%	46.7%	100.0%	0.0%	24.7%	75.3%
1996	0.0%	100.0%	41.7%	58.3%	0.0%	100.0%	59.1%	40.9%	50.0%	50.0%	100.0%	0.0%	27.7%	72.3%
1997	50.0%	50.0%	53.3%	46.7%	0.0%	100.0%	47.8%	52.2%	71.4%	28.6%	50.0%	50.0%	26.9%	73.1%
1998	50.0%	50.0%	66.7%	33.3%	0.0%	100.0%	53.8%	46.2%	75.0%	25.0%	100.0%	0.0%	36.4%	63.6%
1999	33.3%	66.7%	52.6%	47.4%	16.7%	85.7%	40.0%	60.0%	64.3%	35.7%	50.0%	50.0%	32.0%	68.0%
2000	33.3%	66.7%	41.2%	58.8%	50.0%	66.7%	50.0%	50.0%	73.3%	26.7%	100.0%	0.0%	33.0%	67.0%
2001	25.0%	75.0%	38.5%	61.5%	33.3%	75.0%	52.9%	47.1%	70.0%	30.0%	50.0%	50.0%	36.9%	63.1%
2002	66.7%	33.3%	40.0%	60.0%	25.0%	80.0%	50.0%	50.0%	65.2%	34.8%	50.0%	50.0%	37.5%	62.5%
2003	33.3%	66.7%	55.6%	44.4%	16.7%	85.7%	50.0%	50.0%	70.0%	30.0%	0.0%	100.0%	33.3%	66.7%
2004	40.0%	60.0%	58.3%	41.7%	50.0%	66.7%	53.3%	46.7%	68.0%	32.0%	0.0%	100.0%	35.4%	64.6%
2005	50.0%	50.0%	64.3%	35.7%	100.0%	50.0%	55.6%	44.4%	72.7%	27.3%	33.3%	66.7%	42.2%	57.8%
2006	55.6%	44.4%	61.9%	38.1%	76.9%	56.5%	55.0%	45.0%	76.9%	23.1%	33.3%	66.7%	46.2%	53.8%
2007	60.0%	40.0%	69.2%	30.8%	89.5%	52.8%	61.9%	38.1%	77.8%	22.2%	33.3%	66.7%	50.3%	49.7%
2008	66.7%	33.3%	65.4%	34.6%	103.8%	49.1%	69.6%	30.4%	75.6%	24.4%	60.0%	40.0%	52.5%	47.5%
2009	53.8%	46.2%	68.4%	31.6%	71.4%	58.3%	66.7%	33.3%	75.0%	25.0%	60.0%	40.0%	48.5%	51.5%
2010	57.1%	42.9%	65.2%	34.8%	80.8%	55.3%	70.8%	29.2%	73.1%	26.9%	50.0%	50.0%	53.9%	46.1%
2011	75.0%	25.0%	52.6%	47.4%	77.4%	56.4%	61.8%	38.2%	63.9%	36.1%	66.7%	33.3%	53.9%	46.1%
2012	71.4%	28.6%	52.9%	47.1%	65.5%	60.4%	61.9%	38.1%	62.5%	37.5%	66.7%	33.3%	55.5%	44.5%
2013	76.0%	24.0%	50.6%	49.4%	66.7%	60.0%	61.2%	38.8%	59.6%	40.4%	60.0%	40.0%	52.6%	47.4%
μ	39.0%	61.0%	54.9%	45.1%	40.2%	76.5%	54.4%	45.6%	64.8%	35.2%	58.2%	41.8%	37.5%	62.5%
σ	27.8%	27.8%	9.8%	9.8%	37.8%	20.3%	8.7%	8.7%	10.7%	10.7%	30.7%	30.7%	12.0%	12.0%
μ ('90 – '01)	21.5%	78.5%	49.8%	50.2%	10.4%	92.3%	48.7%	51.3%	59.6%	40.4%	77.8%	22.2%	28.2%	71.8%
μ ('02 – '13)	58.1%	41.9%	60.4%	39.6%	72.6%	59.2%	60.7%	39.3%	70.5%	29.5%	42.1%	57.9%	47.7%	52.3%

America, despite the prominence of family dynasties such as the Waltons, du Ponts, Fords and Kochs, the mean proportion of inheritances has decreased in the 24-year sample, falling from 48.7% in the 1990s to 34.0% in the second half. Only Western Europe and Oceania record a mean proportion of greater inheritance than self-made wealth. In Western Europe, the mean proportion of inheritance across the entire sample's time length is 62.5%. A large fall from 71.8% between 1990 and 2001 to 52.3% between 2002 and 2013 is registered, but this result may be driven by substantial variation at the sub-regional level, where inheritance appears to dominate in continental Europe. For Oceania, a similar dramatic fall is recorded with the number of inheritances falling from 78.5% to 41.9%, though the overall mean proportion of inheritances is 61.0%.

It would be premature based on the preceding summary of inheritance trends to conclude that the data shows some convergence globally to lower inheritance levels. A one-way ANOVA test between subjects found a significant regional effect on the proportion of observed inheritance at the $p < 0.05$ level across all 12 regions [$F(12, 259) = 302.16$, $p = 0.000$]. Post-hoc comparisons indicated that the mean score for advanced economies systematically differed, particularly when comparing North America ($\mu = 41.3\%$, $\sigma = 10.4\%$), Western Europe ($\mu = 62.5\%$, $\sigma = 12.02\%$), East Asia ($\mu = 36.1\%$, $\sigma = 5.13\%$) and Oceania ($\mu = 61.00\%$, $\sigma = 27.8\%$) in terms of their impact on the proportion of inheritances. Rather, the results strongly point to the fact that the observed levels of inheritance are ultimately determined at a country or regional level wherein substantial heterogeneity is observed. Whether these are due to legal, cultural or economic factors is determined through an intra-regional analysis presented in Chap. 5.

The relationship between age and inheritance is worth examining, too. Individuals may inherit their wealth at relatively young age; for example, Prince Albert von Thurn and Taxis appeared in the rich list at age 7 in 1991. Alternatively, inheritance between marital partners can occur and is often the most sizeable among the older individuals in the sample. Alternatively, inter vivos gifts may constitute an important channel through which inheritance flows. The age at which one inherits wealth can have a dramatic impact on one's future success. As mentioned above, Rubinstein (1980) does not find much evidence for inheritance in British society despite the country's peerage system and suggests that many who inherit an estate squander their fortunes. Table 3.6 provides some data on this issue. At a superficial level, there appears to be a slight inheritance effect. Although both subsamples follow very similar trends in the cohort perspective, the inheritance group tends to be slightly younger than the self-made group. Between 1990 and 2003, the average age of the inheritance group ranged between 60 and 63, whereas the self-made billionaire, the average age ranged between 62 and 67.

Table 3.6 Age and cohort trends, 1990–2013

	Overall		Self-made individuals			Inherited		
	Age	*Birth year*	*Age*	*Birth year*	*Number*	*Age*	*Birth year*	*Number*
1990	64	1925	67	1923	112	61	1930	121
1991	64	1915	67	1923	109	60	1905	130
1992	64	1928	67	1925	101	62	1930	172
1993	64	1918	67	1926	111	62	1910	195
1994	64	1921	67	1927	136	60	1913	211
1995	63	1924	66	1928	180	60	1919	233
1996	62	1933	64	1931	203	60	1936	211
1997	62	1935	63	1934	110	61	1936	111
1998	63	1935	64	1934	107	62	1936	96
1999	63	1936	64	1935	144	61	1937	150
2000	61	1939	62	1938	162	61	1939	157
2001	62	1939	62	1939	306	61	1939	225
2002	64	1938	64	1938	264	63	1939	204
2003	64	1939	64	1939	266	63	1940	206
2004	67	1940	70	1940	340	64	1940	242
2005	64	1941	64	1941	408	63	1941	278
2006	63	1943	63	1943	479	63	1942	311
2007	62	1945	62	1945	606	63	1944	336
2008	61	1947	61	1947	755	63	1945	367
2009	64	1945	63	1946	509	64	1945	281
2010	63	1947	62	1948	668	64	1946	332
2011	62	1949	61	1950	829	64	1947	376
2012	63	1949	62	1950	833	64	1948	387
2013	63	1950	62	1951	950	64	1949	467

Source: Forbes (1990–2013), authors' compilation from various secondary sources

Summary

This chapter presented several findings on global and regional trends among billionaires and wealth in general. The following salient facts were established. Firstly, the secular trend in billionaire population has demonstrated a precipitous increase since approximately 2000. By 2013, the number of billionaires was at 1417 with an estimated combined net worth of $5 trillion. The growth in the super rich has to some degree arisen from a concomitant influx of billionaires from more countries, particularly from emerging markets. However, the advanced regions of the world, particularly North America, continue to represent the bulk of both the growth and proportion of billionaires.

Significant economic events such as the GFC had, at most, a transitory impact on billionaire numbers. Even in the US, many who had lost their position in the rich lists in 2008 were back by 2009 or 2010. In Asia too, the late 1990s' crisis appeared to have had only a temporary impact on the growth of the mega rich. Indeed, death or personal circumstances had just as a meaningful impact as transient fluctuation in asset prices.

Significantly, financial services and consumer discretionary are the two sectors producing the most growth in billionaires. Innovative industries such as IT are still relatively minor in terms of their relative numbers on the global scale despite their recognition in the general population's mind. These results foreshadow the potential for alternative explanations to the human capital or skill-based ones that have been typically advanced (e.g. Kaplan & Rauh, 2013).

Interestingly, the proportion of inheritance has diminished globally, particularly compared to the late 1990s, where inherited wealth represented the greater proportion of the super-rich. On initial review, this appears to contradict Piketty (2014a) who argues that capitalism is in the midst of a transformation towards a system based on patrimony. Closer inspection suggests that the trend towards self-made wealth may be transient in nature. Indeed, the influx of *nouveau riche* from China and Russia, and the rise of financiers amongst Western economies largely explains the declining share of inherited wealth in the present. A fuller exploration of the issues behind the structure of wealth, in terms of inherited and self-made, is provided in Chap. 5.

References

Atkinson, A. B. (2006). *Concentration among the rich.* World Institute for Development Economic Research RP2006/151. Retrieved from http://www.wider.unu.edu/sites/default/files/rp2006-151.pdf

Beaverstock, J. V., Hubbard, P., & Short, J. R. (2004). Getting away with it? (Exposing) the geographies of the super-rich. *Geoforum, 35*, 401–407.

Bridge, B. (1999). Europe and the Asian financial crisis: Coping with contagion. *Asian Survey, 39*, 456–467.

Cagetti, M., & De Nardi, M. (2006). Entrepreneurship, frictions, and wealth. *Journal of Political Economy, 114*, 835–870.

Canterbery, E. R., & Nosari, E. J. (1985). The Forbes four hundred: The determinants of super-wealth. *Southern Economic Journal, 5*, 1073–1083.

Carnegie, A. (1900). *The gospel of wealth and other timely essays.* New York: Century.

Cohen, R. (1991, 20 December). Maxwell's empire: How it grew, how it fell – A special report; Charming the Big Bankers Out of Billions. *The New York Times.* Retrieved from http://www.nytimes.com/

Davies, J. B., & Shorrocks, A. F. (2000). The distribution of wealth. In A. B. Atkinson & F. Bourguignon (Eds.), *Handbook of income distribution* (Vol. 1, pp. 605–675). Amsterdam: North-Holland.

Downer, L. (1994). *The brothers: The hidden world of Japan's richest family*. New York: Random House.
Forbes. (1990–2013). *The world's billionaires*. Retrieved from http://www.forbes.com/lists
Goff, S. (2010, March 25). The Rothschilds' family fortune. *Financial Times*. Retrieved from http://www.ft.com/
Hirsch, M. (1911). *The problem of wealth (an open letter to Andrew Carnegie) and other essays*. Melbourne, VIC: Renwick, Pride, Nuttall Pty. Ltd..
Jaher, F. C. (1980). The gilded elite: American multimillionaires, 1865 to the present. In W. D. Rubinstein (Ed.), *Wealth and the wealthy in the modern world*. London: Croom Helm.
Jones, R. (1831). *An essay on the distribution of wealth. Part 1: Rent*. London: John Murray.
Kaplan, S. N., & Rauh, J. D. (2013). Family, education, and sources of wealth among the richest Americans, 1982–2012. *The American Economic Review, 103*(3), 158–162.
Klevmarken, N. A., Lupton, J. P., & Stafford, F. P. (2003). Wealth dynamics in the 1980s and 1990s: Sweden and the United States. *The Journal of Human Resources, 38*, 322–353.
Kopczuk, W., & Saez, E. (2004). Top wealth shares in the United States, 1916–2000: Evidence from estate tax returns. *National Tax Journal, 57*(2), 445–487.
Kroll, L. (2014, September). Methodology. *Forbes*. Retrieved 30 September, 2014, from http://www.forbes.com/sites/luisakroll/2014/03/03/inside-the-2014-forbes-billionaires-list-facts-and-figures/
Lundberg, F. (1969). *The rich & the super rich: A study in the power of money today*. London: Nelson.
Mill, J. S. (1929). *Principles of economics*. London: Longman Company.
Piketty, T. (2014a). *Capital in the twenty-first century*. Cambridge, MA: The Belknap Press of Harvard University Press.
Piketty, T. (2014b). Capital in the twenty-first century: A multidimensional approach to the history of capital and social classes. *The British Journal of Sociology, 65*, 736–747.
Piketty, T., & Saez, E. (2014). Inequality in the long run. *Science, 344*(6186), 838–843.
Piketty, T., & Zucman, G. (2014a). Capital is back: Wealth-income ratios in rich countries 1700–2010. *The Quarterly Journal of Economics, 129*, 1155–1210.
Piketty, T., & Zucman, G. (2014b). *Appendix of Capital is back: Wealth-income ratios in rich countries 1700–2010*. Retrieved on 10 June, 2015, from http://gabriel-zucman.eu/files/PikettyZucman2013Data.zip
Pressman, S. (2015). *Understanding Piketty's capital in the twenty-first century*. London: Routledge.
Rockoff, H. (2012). The great fortunes of the Gilded Age and the crisis of 1893. *Research in Economic History, 28*, 233–262.

Rubinstein, W. D. (1980). Modern Britain. In W. D. Rubinstein (Ed.), *Wealth and the wealthy in the modern world* (pp. 46–89). London: Croom Helm.

Saez, E., & Zucman, G. (2014). *Wealth inequality in the United States Since 1913: Evidence from capitalized income tax data* (No. 20625). NBER Working Paper Series. Retrieved from http://www.nber.org/papers/w20625

Sanandaji, T., & Leeson, P. T. (2013). Billionaires. *Industrial and Corporate Change, 22*, 313–337.

Shorrocks, A. F. (1988). Wealth holdings and entrepreneurial activity. In D. Kessler & A. Masson (Eds.), *Modelling the accumulation and distribution of wealth*. Oxford, UK: Clarendon Press.

Siegfried, J. J., & Roberts, A. (1991). How did the wealthiest Britons get so rich? *Review of Industrial Organization, 6*, 19–32.

Siegfried, J. J., & Round, D. K. (1994). How did the wealthiest Australians get so rich? *Review of Income and Wealth, 40*, 191–204.

Spånt, R. (1987). Wealth distribution in Sweden: 1920–1983. In E. Wolff (Ed.), *International comparisons of the distribution of household wealth*. Oxford, UK: Oxford University Press.

Thurow, L. (1975). *Generating inequality*. New York: Basic Books, Inc..

Torgler, B., & Piatti, M. (2013). Extraordinary wealth, globalization, and corruption. *Review of Income and Wealth, 59*, 341–359.

Tuckman, E. (1973). *The economics of the rich*. New York: Random House.

von Neumayer, E. (2006). The super-rich in global perspective: a quantitative analysis of the Forbes list of billionaires. *Applied Economics Letters, 11*(13), 793–796.

Watkins, G. P. (1907). The growth of large fortunes. *Publications of the American Economic Association, 8*(4), 1–170.

Wearing, R. (2005). *Cases in corporate governance*. London: Sage Publications.

4

The Rise of the Dual Economy: Wealth Accumulation and Inequality

The purpose of Chap. 4 is to study the determinants of wealth accumulation and inequality in the modern world. The conceptual framework adopted borrows heavily from Meade (1964, 1975) and Saez and Zucman (2014), but contextualises their framework in a grander socioeconomic context. To this end, the key objectives of Chap. 4 are as follows:

- To explain the key aggregate trends raised in Chap. 3 against the backdrop of significant historical changes in the economic systems of the advanced economies.
- Adopting an analytical approach, then focuses on the respective roles of consumerism, the financialisation of household balance sheets (both liabilities and assets), the role of capital income and taxation policy in fuelling the rise of vast fortunes whilst concurrently ensuring the detachment of the fortunate few from the rest of society.

Introduction

This chapter explores the general changes and underlying forces associated with the accumulation of wealth and wealth inequality. It has become a well-established empirical regularity that both income and wealth exhibit increasing levels of inequality in contemporary times (one of the most recent studies from the International Monetary Fund; see Dabla-Norris, Kochhar, Suphaphiphat, Ricka, & Tsounta, 2015; also Alvaredo, Atkinson, Piketty, & Saez, 2013). Although income inequality has received considerable attention,

S. Tsigos, K. Daly, *The Wealth of the Elite*, https://doi.org/10.1007/978-981-15-2148-5_4

wealth inequality has only recently received the same level of research interest. The emergence of wealth inequality, or as a corollary, the amassment of great fortunes into few hands does represent a significant departure from the experience of the post-Second World War era. This era, roughly coinciding with the conclusion of the Second World War and the early to mid-1970s in the developed world, had ushered in a golden age of unprecedented wealth and income equality, driven by robust income growth across the working and middle classes (Alvaredo et al., 2013; Piketty, 2014a).

The 1940s had the most impact on income and established the egalitarian distribution of wealth for the next three decades. Goldin and Margo (1992) labelled this period 'The Great Compression", a term used to contrast with the Great Depression of the 1930s. The 'Great Compression' had produced a wage structure endowed with significant equality beyond any period before or experienced since. Scholars writing in the immediacy of this era recognised this positive and socially progressive anomaly. Thurow (1975), for example, observed:

> After the wage differentials of the Great Depression and World War II had become embedded in the labour market for a number of years, they became the new standard of relative deprivation and were regarded as 'just' even after the egalitarian pressures of World War II had disappeared. Basically, the same differentials exist to this day, thirty years later. (p. 111)

Contemporary studies, at both national and international levels, confirmed that the post-war era was unique from an (income and wealth) equality perspective. In contrast, Alvaredo et al. (2013) document, for example, that since the 'great compression' the share of the top 1% has increased, but their growth has not been uniform across the advanced industrialised economies of the world. Although they do not find evidence that the wealth concentration, at least in the US, has significantly increased over the same period, they do find a significant relationship between the rise of the share of the top 1% and the growth in capital incomes, an area that has been under-explored.

However, recent studies emphasise that wealth inequality has also re-emerged. Saez and Zucman (2014) document that in the US, just like the share of top incomes, the level of wealth concentration has followed a U-shaped path since the early 1900s to 2012. Saez and Zucman (2014) challenge the view that wealth concentration has not increased in the US, finding that the top wealth holders now accumulate wealth at a more rapid rate than the rest of the populace, particularly over the last three decades. Significantly, the richest families increased their share of wealth from 7% in 1978 to 22%

in 2012 (Saez & Zucman, 2014, p. 1). Interestingly, they find that their estimates of wealth accumulation by this group of the US population are consistent with other sources, including the *Forbes* billionaire wealth estimates. The question here is what forces have driven this process and not just in the US but across other First World economies?

The purpose of this chapter is to go beyond *singular* explanations and to find the potential causes for modern-day wealth concentration in forces found in the socioeconomic changes that have transpired since the Second World War. Clearly, the immediate post-war period was different. Although capital destruction in Europe effectively reset the wealth counter to zero, it can only represent part of the explanation (Piketty, 2014a). Therefore, this chapter pursues several alternative explanations within the context of a wealth accumulation model. The changes associated with wealth accumulation are discussed within the context of larger societal changes and how society engages in economic activity, including consumerism and financialisation. Analytically, it examines these broad changes within a wealth accumulation framework in the spirit of Meade (1975) and Saez and Zucman (2014). In both, the growth of wealth is decomposed into the main constituent elements of savings, returns, investments, earnings, consumption and taxation. These elements being considered within their respective historical contexts.

Broadly, the chapter comprises two sections. The first discusses the general conceptual framework that is followed throughout this chapter. The second examines the role of consumerism, financialisation, the structure of income and taxation policy as possible channels through which inequality has eventuated.

Conceptual Framework

Of primary interest are the dynamics associated with wealth, income, savings and taxation policy across the entire wealth distribution encompassing seven advanced economies. These seven economies include Australia, Canada, France, Germany, Japan, the UK and the US. The four forces provide the channels through which the process of wealth accumulation can initially be considered in a simple accounting identity. Further, they can act as a proxy for a number of explanatory variables to this end including consumerism, financialisation, investment behaviour, income structure and taxation policy.

In Chap. 2, the existence of models possessing dynamic random multiplicative shocks was considered. Piketty and Saez (2014) point out that for a given structure of shocks, such models best approximate the distribution of wealth in a given economy. As was argued in Chap. 2 too, what constitutes these shocks is not determined by theory but through historical enquiry. Piketty and Saez (2014), for example, point to labour income shocks in the aftermath of the Second World War that enabled the propagation of low wealth inequality through to the early 1970s in Europe and the US.

Determining what shocks to consider as relevant to the dynamics of wealth accumulation requires adopting a formalised structure. Accounting identities of wealth accumulation were used by Meade (1964, 1975) and more recently Saez and Zucman (2014). These models provide a convenient means of decomposing the constituent elements of wealth into basic components. Saez and Zucman's (2014) model of wealth accumulation consists of five essential elements—current labour income, saving rates, rate of return, tax on labour and capital and consumption—formally written as:

$$W_{t+1}^{i} = W_{t}^{i} \mathrm{n}\left[1 + r_{t}^{i} \mathrm{n}\left(1 - \tau_{K}^{i}\right) + q_{t}^{i}\right] + Y_{Lt}^{i} \mathrm{n}\left(1 - t_{L}^{i}\right) - C_{t}^{i} \tag{4.1}$$

where W_t^i is initial household wealth, r_t^i is the real rate of return, τ_K^i is the corporate tax rate, q_t^i is the asset price effect, Y_{Lt}^i is labour income, t_L^i is the tax rate on labour income and C_t^i is household consumption. The potential for wealth concentration arises first from the existence of labour income inequality. The greater wealth accruing to higher incomes leads to greater capital income, assuming households elect to save more. In addition, 'for a given distribution of income, wealth inequality will tend to grow if consumption C_t^i of poor households becomes larger and larger compared to their income while rich households keep saving' (Saez & Zucman, 2014, p. 27). This emphasis on consumption and saving behaviour is one key element to understanding the dynamics of wealth accumulation. Equation 4.1 does not explicitly model for savings. To do so, savings, S_t^i, are assumed to represent increases in net wealth *prior* to changes in asset prices:

$$W_{t+1}^{i} = \left(1 + q_{t}^{i}\right) \mathrm{n}\left(W_{t}^{i} + S_{t}^{i}\right) \tag{4.2}$$

Savings, S_t^i, are assumed to be capitalised, and are equal to net capital income and labour income:

$$\left(1 + q_{t}^{i}\right) S_{t}^{i} = r_{t}^{i} \mathrm{n}\left(1 - \tau_{K}^{i}\right) \mathrm{n} W_{t}^{i} + Y_{Lt}^{i} \mathrm{n}\left(1 - \tau_{L}^{i}\right) - C_{t}^{i} \tag{4.3}$$

An advantage of the Saez and Zucman (2014) models is that it permits the distribution to be decomposed into percentiles or quintiles as it makes no a priori assumption as to how a given class receives its income (capital or labour) or how it spends and saves. It does not, for example, rigidly assume a two-class society of workers and rentiers or capitalists as in capital accumulation models such as those of Kaldor (1960) or Pasinetti (1962). The general framework above captures the primary elements associated with wealth accumulation.

The Socioeconomic Context

The Role of Consumerism and Savings

To begin, the role of consumerism in wealth accumulation is considered. In Eq. 4.1, the last element C represents a proxy for consumerism. In reality, the full impact of consumerism can also manifest itself through returns to capital (aggregate consumption would flow through to returns to capital), but to begin, consumption is first viewed as an expense on a household's bottom line. Further, consumption is intimately tied to the savings of households, this aspect is also explored here. The role of savings being particularly important in Piketty's inequality, $r > g$ (Solow, 2014). In Piketty's model, if savings were independent of income, then in the long run the wealth inequality distribution would converge to the wage inequality distribution, and the $r - g$ differential would have little relevance. However, given that wealth inequality is greater than income inequality, greater savings can exacerbate inequalities particularly in terms of Piketty's (2014a) inequality.

Consumerism has long been noted as a major transformative force in capitalist society by Marxists and social scientists alike. Typically, it has assumed various definitions depending on the ideological strain of the writer. Marxists, for example, view consumerist society as the means to the valorisation of capital, with the proliferation of consumer goods a necessary means to this end. Further, consumerism is as an important social force through which entrepreneurs and, more generally, corporations can expand the scale of their markets. In general, consumerism is a set of values and techniques whose role is to develop the scale of consumer markets beyond what would ordinarily be necessary. For our purposes, the definitions of Ewen (1976) and Galbraith (1958) are adopted. Ewen (1976) defined consumerism as 'mass participation in the values of the mass-industrialised market' (p. 54). Perhaps more importantly, the rise of advertising and sales and the recognition of the desire for consumers to emulate their 'neighbours' enabled the transformation of society into mass consumer participation, which had a substantial impact in terms of market scale. Galbraith (1958) recognised the importance of both in his book, *The Affluent Society*. On the first, he wrote:

> As a society becomes increasingly affluent, wants are increasingly created by the process by which they are satisfied. This may operate passively. Increases in consumption, the counterpart of increases in production, act by suggestion or may proceed actively to create wants through advertising and salesmanship. Wants thus come to depend on output.... [I]t can no longer be assumed that welfare is greater at an all-round higher level of production than at a lower one. It may be the same. (Galbraith, 1958, p.158)

It is important to emphasise that consumerism was not necessarily created via the tool of advertising, but can emerge naturally without direction in a capitalist system.

For Marxists, the development of consumerism is viewed strictly within the context of labour and capitalist relations. Marxists conceptualise consumerism as a process directed by corporations seeking to move labour discontent and resentment in the work environment and channel it into the desire for goods to escape the dissatisfaction and drudgery associated with mass production. Lane (1962) for example, argues:

> The more emphasis society places upon consumption – through advertising, development of new products, and easy instalment buying – the more will social dissatisfaction be channelled into intra-class consumption rivalry instead of interclass resentment and conflict. (p. 80)

The element of social dissatisfaction is developed by Bauman (2007), stating that the 'subjective sense of insufficiency' compared to the wealthier is then aggravated by an 'increasing relative (comparative) deprivation, both reinforced rather than mitigated by economic growth in its present, deregulated, *laissez-faire* form' (p. 41).

Whether consumerism is due to the growth of advertising or whether output creates a concomitant increase in wants diverts attention away from the most relevant aspect of consumerism, the notion of relative consumption. Relative consumption can be defined as the extent to which individuals or households observe their neighbour (however broadly neighbour is defined) and strive to emulate or surpass them in their display of material well-being.[1]

To establish the role of consumerism in depressing wealth accumulation amongst the lower and middle classes, a range of statistics are considered. Since a measure of consumerism does not exist, alternative measures of consumption and associated ratios are considered. This is done through three avenues. Firstly, has the average propensity to consume (APC) increased since the 1960s or 1970s across the industrialised world? Secondly, have the incomes of the lower and middle classes grown enough to sustain rising consumption levels? Thirdly, what has occurred with the saving rates of the lower- or middle-class households relative to the rich?

On the first question, the APC, defined as national consumption divided by national income, demonstrates substantial variance since the 1960s across all seven countries. The range of observations resides between 0.51 and 0.75, depending on the year and country, as observed in Fig. 4.1. Of the seven countries included in the sample, four have shown increasing propensities to consume out of current income. The largest economy, the US, also shows a

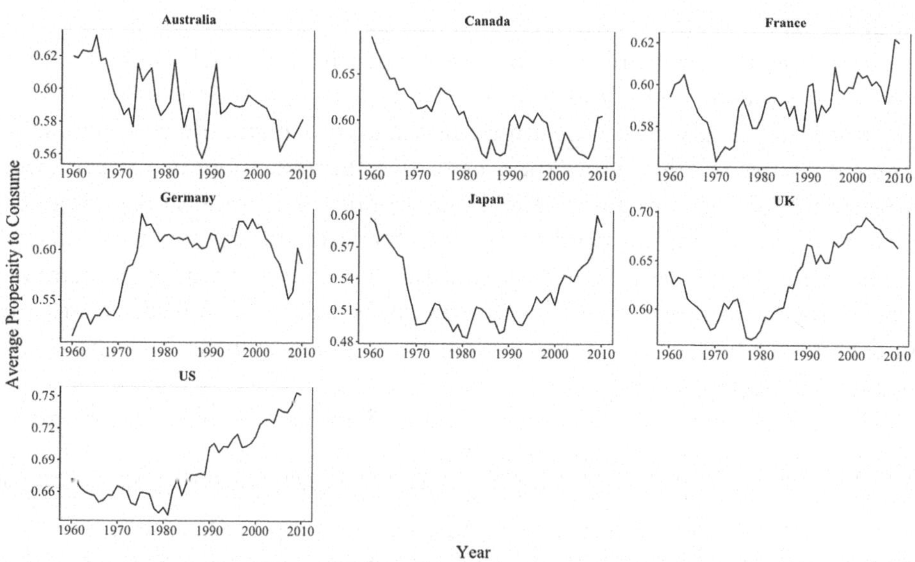

Fig. 4.1 Average propensity to consume, 1960–2010. (*Source*: Calculation based on data from respective countries national accounts)

[1] At this point, it needs to be emphasised that this section is mainly concerned with the role of consumption in *depressing* wealth accumulation amongst working and middle-class households. The issue of whether consumption in itself has driven up both the top wealth and income shares is partly considered in terms of entrepreneurial risk further below.

steep increase in the APC measure from the lowest observation in 1979 at 0.64 to approximately 0.75 over the last two years of the sample. Both Japan and the UK have also shown similar increases, but neither attains the absolute level exhibited by the US. Japan demonstrates a marked increase of 24% from 0.48 in 1981 to 0.60 in 2009. The APC in the UK increased 22.1% from 0.57 in 1978 to a peak of 0.69 in 2003. France also shows a marked increase in APC during the 1980s and 1990s compared to the lows observed in the 1970s. In contrast, both Australia and Canada have exhibited downward sloping trends since the 1960s. Germany has had a relatively stable APC since the mid-1970s, with a mean of 0.6079, despite a precipitous increase in the 1960s and 1970s.

At what level of the distribution (wealth or income) has the increased propensity for consumption arisen? For Australia and the UK, there is enough statistical information at a disaggregated level to suggest that the less fortunate do consume much more than the wealthy (asset or income rich) relative to their wealth or income. Table 4.1 presents the aggregate distributional patterns of consumption in Australia and the UK as a proportion of wealth, savings and income from 2003 to 2011 for Australia, and for the UK from 2008 to 2013.

Regarding the consumption to wealth ratio in Table 4.1 Panel 1A, the poorest Australian households consume, on average, 4.4 times their annual net worth in contrast to the wealthiest households, which only consume 0.04 times their net worth. Across the wealth distribution, there is a continuing downward shift in this ratio. The consumption to income and savings to income ratios in Panels 1B and 1C are less dramatic, but the relative disparity between the fourth wealth quintile and the highest wealth quintile demonstrates the extent to which the less fortunate, as well as the middle classes are under greater budgetary pressures than the highest quintile households to sustain a lifestyle standard.

The savings rates of the wealthiest tend to dominate the observations associated with lower income groups in Australia. In Panel 1C of Table 4.1, the Australian household savings rate of the highest wealth quintile ranges between 31.5% and 20.6% throughout the sample period, with a mean of 25.9%, in contrast to the average rate for the poorest wealth quintile at 2.8%. The second wealth percentile shows a substantial increase in the saving rate over the course of the sample, but also a considerable degree of variance relative to the mean (cv = 0.37). Both the third and fourth quintiles reveal a substantially lower savings rate compared to the wealthiest households, averaging 10.5% and 10.1%, respectively. The most affluent households on average appear to exhibit greater savings rates while maintaining extremely low

Table 4.1 Consumption and savings ratios by quintiles, Australia and the UK

Australia					
Panel 1A: Consumption to wealth					
	Lowest	Second	Third	Fourth	Highest
2003–2004	5.136×	0.498×	0.201×	0.113×	0.049×
2005–2006	3.340×	0.444×	0.186×	0.112×	0.046×
2007–2008	5.682×	0.600×	0.242×	0.139×	0.052×
2009–2010	4.045×	0.449×	0.185×	0.107×	0.045×
2011–2012	3.885×	0.531×	0.207×	0.113×	0.049×
Panel 1B: Consumption to income					
	Lowest	Second	Third	Fourth	Highest
2003–2004	1.018×	0.908×	0.904×	0.899×	0.794×
2005–2006	0.989×	0.876×	0.929×	0.941×	0.766×
2007–2008	1.445×	1.044×	1.135×	1.142×	0.851×
2009–2010	0.942×	0.772×	0.873×	0.884×	0.712×
2011–2012	0.905×	0.759×	0.866×	0.848×	0.685×
Panel 1C: Savings to income					
	Lowest	Second	Third	Fourth	Highest
2003–2004	−1.80%	9.20%	9.60%	10.10%	20.6
2005–2006	1.10%	12.40%	7.10%	5.90%	23.4
2007–2008	−0.50%	18.30%	9.70%	7.60%	25.3
2009–2010	5.80%	22.80%	12.70%	11.60%	28.8
2011–2012	9.50%	24.10%	13.40%	15.20%	31.5
Source: Australian Bureau of Statistics (2014)					
UK					
Panel 2A: Consumption to income					
	Lowest	Second	Third	Fourth	Highest
2008	1.298	1.156	1.099	1.02	0.773
2012	1.159	0.988	0.968	0.911	0.732
2013	1.164	0.978	0.985	0.938	0.743
Panel 2B: Savings to income					
	Lowest	Second	Third	Fourth	Highest
2008	−23.00%	−9.60%	−4.20%	3.40%	26.80%
2012	−11.20%	5.90%	7.90%	13.60%	31.50%
2013	−12.50%	6.20%	5.40%	10.20%	29.70%

Notes: Panels 1A and 1B represent simple ratios of average consumption/average wealth and average consumption/average income, utilising current prices. Panel 1C provides the average savings rates of households across the wealth distribution, estimated as average household savings/average household income. Panels 2A represents a simple ratio of average consumption to average income, utilising current prices. Panel 2B provides the average savings rates of households across the wealth distribution, estimated as average household savings/average household income
Source: Office for National Statistics (2015)

consumption levels relative to their wealth. According to the Australian Bureau of Statistics (ABS) data upon which Table 4.1 is constructed, the average annual consumption level for the poorest quintile is AUD93,938 compared to AUD167,441 for the highest quintile. For the third and fourth quintiles, consumption is AUD133,799 and AUD133,600, respectively.

Turning to the UK consumption to income ratio, presented in Panel 2A, a similar pattern is observed.[2] The highest income quintile exhibits the lowest ratio. Over the years 2008 to 2013, it has averaged 0.749× compared to 1.207× and 1.017× for the lowest and third quintiles, respectively. As in Australia, there is a noticeable disparity between the fourth income and the highest income quintiles demonstrating once again the substantial advantages of the wealthier households, even between the two highest quintiles. The savings to income ratio better uncovers the extent to which savings diverge between the various quintiles. On average the lowest quintile savings rate is *negative* at 15.57% over the period for which data is available. Moving to the next quintile it only rises to 0.38%. The middle class (Fourth quintile) averages 9.07%. For the highest quintile an average of 29.33% is observed and closely mirrors the magnitude observed in Australia for the same quintile.

International data on the distribution of savings rates on a time series basis is lacking, but the Organisation for Economic Co-operation and Development (OECD) has been driving an initiative to harmonise and produce such statistics.[3] According to Fesseau and Mattonetti (2013), for the highest quintile, the variation between countries' savings rates is large, ranging between approximately 20% (New Zealand) and 41% (US). Progressing further down the income quintiles greater variation is revealed. At the lowest quintile, the majority countries exhibit a negative savings rate, with the US demonstrating the greatest negative saving rate at 80%. Conversely, France is the only country to show a positive savings rate, albeit close to zero.

What is driving the substantial savings rates of the wealthiest households in contrast to the poorest? Consumerism can partly explain the savings behaviour of the poor, but not of the wealthiest households. Given the finding of Carroll, Slacalek, & Tokuoka (2014) that those with low wealth to income ratios (but high incomes from entrepreneurial activity) consume less, a natural issue to consider is how much more those receiving substantial income flows from entrepreneurial activities are saving and why. Dynan, Skinner, and Zeldes (2004) explore whether there is any relationship between higher

[2] No data on the basis of wealth was available to make a direct comparison with Australia.

[3] Again, as with the UK, no OECD data based on wealth was available to make a direct comparison with Australia.

lifetime income individuals and the fraction that they save. Interestingly, they find that wealthier individuals faced with greater entrepreneurial risk will also exhibit a propensity to save in amounts higher than non-entrepreneurs. For example, 'the estimated median savings rates that range from zero for the first quintile to 22 percent for the fifth quintile to 49 percent for the top 5 percent of the sample' (Dynan et al., 2004, p. 426). Dynan et al. (2004) conclude that ultimately, the wealthy save more because of the entrepreneurial risk they face. Savings rates are not necessarily due to consumer preferences being different compared to lower wealth classes.

The role of entrepreneurial income in wealth distribution has been examined by Quadrini (1999, 2000), Gentry and Hubbard (2004) and Hurst and Lusardi (2004). Quadrini (1999) finds that the key to upward mobility in the US is whether one is from a business family or an entrepreneur. More specifically:

> While worker families (both new and old), tend to stay in or move to lower positions of wealth, both new and old business families tend to stay in or move to higher positions. Therefore, the undertaking of an entrepreneurial activity is an important way through which families switch to higher wealth classes. (Quadrini, 1999, p. 8)

These findings are reinforced by Gentry and Hubbard (2004), who, using the US Survey of Consumer Finances, find that both new and continuing entrepreneurs tend to exhibit greater savings and that business income is an important part of this saving and wealth accumulation process. Significantly, the act of exiting entrepreneurship appears to result in 'dissaving'. Again, this finding suggests that savings by entrepreneurs are not necessarily tied to preferences but are due to chance associated with business or market processes instead. Dynan et al. (2004) argue that the observation that savings increase across the wealth distribution due to entrepreneurial activity signifies that savings (and as a corollary, wealth) are a matter of chance:

> Our finding that differences in saving behaviour across income groups are also an important source of the overall variation in wealth of the US population suggests a diminished role for choice. For example, wealth accumulation because of government or private policies that differentially affect saving (such as asset-based means testing or the availability of 401(k) plans) cannot be readily attributed to tastes or preferences. (p. 438)

Such a finding contradicts the view that the ultra-wealthy are solely a product of prudent decision making in savings. Rather, it is the risks of business and the associated stochastic process of free enterprise that have the most impact upon their consumption and savings behaviour.

Returning to the original issue of a potential link between the lack of upward mobility among the middle and lower classes and the greater propensity for the poorer to consume rather than save, two questions can be posed. Firstly, if diminishing savings rates (and increased consumption) are observed amongst poorer households, is this driven by disincentives to save? Secondly, are high consumption rates among the poor simply fuelling increased income growth among the rich, entrepreneurial classes? Bertrand and Morse (2013) allude to the possibility of 'reverse causality, where higher consumption by middle- and low-income households in a [US] state raise top income levels in that state' (p. 27). The existence of such a reverse causality could potentially be determined through an indirect channel via statistics on credit growth and the financialisation of household balance sheets.

Household Financialisation: Fuelling the Poor Consumer

The phenomenon of financialisation has often been used to describe a variety of observed economic outcomes in recent times. For example, financialisation is often observed at the corporate level where remuneration of upper management is tied to financial contracts. Alternatively, financialisation has been viewed as a process through which commodities typically outside the realm of financial markets have been packaged into investment vehicles that are actively traded on secondary markets across the globe.

Krippner (2005) provides one of the first formal definitions. Financialisation is defined as the 'pattern of accumulation in which profits accrue primarily through financial channels rather than through trade and commodity production' (Krippner, 2005, p. 174). This definition is formed from a broad body of studies on the changing nature of corporate activity, through any number of mechanisms. For example, Fligstein (1990) presents evidence on the increasing influence of finance in the organisation of corporate governance control structures for large enterprises in the US. The broadest definition, however, is provided by Epstein (2002) and encapsulates the multi-faceted nature of the phenomenon:

> Financialization refers to the increasing importance of financial markets, financial motives, financial institutions, and financial elites in the operation of the economy and its governing institutions, both at the national and international level. (p. 1)

Given the scope of financialisation, attempts to recast it as an element behind one of the variables in Eq. (4.1) may appear an intractable exercise, but there are aspects to which one can infer the impact of these developments on the dynamics of the wealth equation on households over recent history.

Here, it is posited that the increasing financialisation of household balance sheets (either the wealthy or poor) is having an impact in both reducing the potential for upward mobility and fuelling the substantial growth of wealth by the globe's richest citizens, including those in the finance industry. The ability of financialisation to impact household finances through wealth is not only tied to the capacity to generate greater returns through financial advice but also to enhance consumption beyond one's means. In Eq. 4.1, the two channels via which financialisation can impact is consumption (credit growth) and capital income (r_t^i).

The growth of credit demonstrates a remarkable association with the degree of wealth accumulation across the advanced economies. Figure 4.2 depicts the relationship between the average debt-to-income ratio in an economy and its wealth to income ratio since the 1960s. The strongest association between borrowing rates and wealth to income ratios is to be found in Canada (0.95) and the UK (0.94), followed by Australia (0.93). The US exhibits the lowest

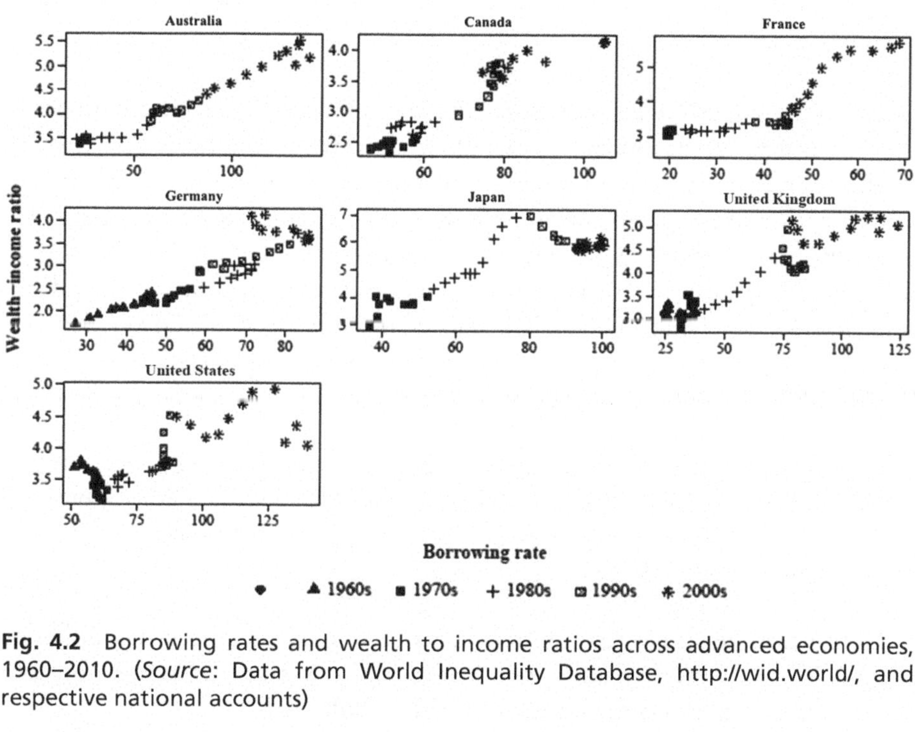

Fig. 4.2 Borrowing rates and wealth to income ratios across advanced economies, 1960–2010. (*Source*: Data from World Inequality Database, http://wid.world/, and respective national accounts)

degree of association between the variables (0.79), followed by France (0.87), Japan (0.86) and Germany (0.870). The link between credit growth and macroeconomic activity has been explored in a recent study. The findings of Stockhammer and Wildauer (2015) establish that economic growth across the OECD has largely been a debt-fuelled process—rather than being driven by productivity growth by itself. The question is at which level of the wealth distribution this is being driven.

The impact of debt on households can be viewed from both the consumption side of the equation or from the investment returns perspective. The first view posits that the rise of financial products aimed at households is largely emblematic of the rise of the type of consumerism briefly explored in the section above on consumerism. Cynamon and Fazzari (2013) examined this possibility in their study of the US Survey of Consumer Finances. Particularly, they considered whether the growth in US aggregate demand through household consumption is due to the rise of household credit. Adopting a Minsky perspective, Cynamon and Fazzari (2013) find that:

> With financial innovation and greater access to debt, the year-by-year budget constraint has become soft.... [H]ouseholds mimic the behaviours they observe around them, from both real people and media models, assuaging their uncertainty in the perceived comfort of acting like others in their social reference group. (p. 25)

Given the growth of an economic elite who made their fortunes in finance, the 'softening' of the budget constraint may provide an inkling as to why wealth to income ratios have increased to such an extent in the US. There are, however, alternative perspectives. Trumbull (2012) argues that the liberal use of credit by poorer or low-income households was largely a cultural development in which easy access to credit was construed as a form of welfare substitution. Indeed, Trumbull (2012) rejects the notion of consumerism or materialism per se as a catalyst for increasing borrowing rates, arguing that, for the US, at least:

> the link that came to be made in the United States between credit access and social welfare was not a product of wage stagnation and welfare exhaustion in the 1970s, but instead traces its roots to the early years of the twentieth century in the United States. (p. 14)

In contrast, he argues that in France, access to credit was seen in a different light, with both the left and right historically rejecting the notion of easy access to credit markets for households (Trumbull, 2012).

The existence of different attitudes towards household borrowing rates across the seven countries would seem to imply differing patterns of household behaviour. Figure 4.3 shows the historical trends of private household debt to income ratios across the five countries. In every instance, the household debt-to-income ratios have demonstrated substantial growth rates. The four Anglo-Saxon economies have in the past decade exhibited the highest debt to income ratios in excess of 1×, with both Australian and US households exhibiting the greatest propensity to assume debt. France exhibits the lowest propensity to assume debt below those of the Anglo-Saxon economies, but has exhibited a dramatic increase since the mid-1990s.

The aggregate increases in debt to income ratios may be fuelled across the whole wealth distribution, but the evidence suggests different dynamics across different percentiles, particularly amongst poorer and lower-income households. Fligstein and Goldstein (2015) find that poorer households in the US avail themselves of credit products more readily than wealth accumulation assisting products:

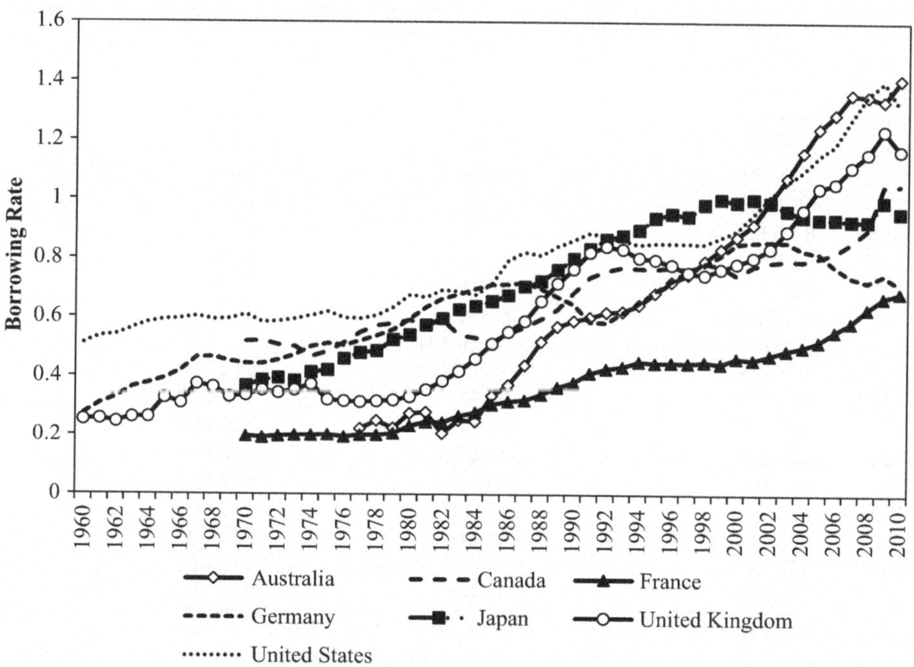

Fig. 4.3 Debt to income ratio of advanced economies, 1960–2010. (*Source*: Data from World Inequality Database, http://wid.world/, Piketty and Zucman (2014) and respective national accounts)

> For the 40% of households living at the bottom … life chances have declined dramatically in the past 20 years. Their income growth is negative, they are vulnerable to not having enough money to survive.... When they borrow, they tend to use their borrowing for routine household expenses such as paying bills, medical expenses or financing education. The rapid expansion of credit availability to those in the bottom 40% has not produced a finance culture. (p. 23)

The recent publication of household debt distribution data by the US Congress Budget Office (CBO) reveals the extent of debt levels among the lower wealth percentiles. Debt here is defined as nonmortgage debt. Table 4.2 Panel A provides some details on the evolution of average debt levels to average wealth across the three broad wealth percentiles as defined by the CBO. Beginning with the bottom 25th percentile, the debt to asset ratio averaged 92.13% (σ = 17.4%) over the 1989–2007 period. By 2010 and 2013, however, the debt to asset ratio had exponentially increased to 300× times total assets. The process driving this has not only been an accumulation of

Table 4.2 Debt to total assets, US households

Year	Bottom 25th percentile	25th–50th percentile	50th–90th percentile
Panel A, debt to total assets:			
1989	110.0%	18.3%	5.5%
1992	65.0%	15.5%	4.4%
1995	83.3%	17.2%	5.1%
1998	117.6%	19.4%	5.4%
2001	89.5%	17.5%	4.6%
2004	87.5%	18.3%	5.0%
2007	92.0%	20.2%	4.9%
2010	1600.0%	26.7%	5.5%
2013	3300.0%	28.3%	6.1%
Panel B: Average debt levels of US households			
1989	$11,000	$11,000	$14,000
1992	$13,000	$9000	$10,000
1995	$15,000	$11,000	$12,000
1998	$20,000	$14,000	$16,000
2001	$17,000	$14,000	$17,000
2004	$21,000	$15,000	$20,000
2007	$23,000	$19,000	$21,000
2010	$32,000	$16,000	$19,000
2013	$33,000	$17,000	$21,000

Source and Notes: Congressional Budget Office (2016). *Trends in Family Wealth, 1989 to 2013.* Assets consist of financial assets, home equity and other assets. Other assets are defined as including real estate (non-residence) and business equity net of loans. For home equity, mortgage debt is subtracted from the primary residency. Debt in the table refers to nonmortgage debt, and includes a household's consumer debt, and other debt (primarily student loans).

debt, but enormous falls in the value of home equity and a corresponding rise in credit card and student loan debt. In contrast, the 50th–90th percentile exhibit very little variation over the entirety of the sample provided. Overall, the 50th–90th percentile's average proportion of debt to assets was 4.99% with little variation (σ = 0.40%).

The ratio approach may obscure some of the dynamics in relation to debt. Panel B Table 4.2 shows the average amount of household debt in dollar terms. Across the three percentile ranges for which data are provided, debt levels have systematically increased since 1989. However, the largest debt burden is on average upon the poorest households. For example, in 2013 the average debt burden was USD33,000 for the bottom 25th percentile, compared to USD21,000 of the 50th–90th percentile. The mean growth rate of debt for the poorest 25th percentile is 15.9% since 1989, compared to 6.8% for the 50th–90th percentile.

The phenomenon of poorer households being unable to increase their income and accumulate wealth, and consuming out of credit, is not restricted to the US. As mentioned above, Australia exhibits the world's highest household debt to income ratio. Have the record levels of household borrowing led to a greater concentration of household debt by the lower classes as in the US? Table 4.3 presents the distribution of household debt (mortgage and

Table 4.3 Distribution of Australian household debt

	Share of household debt from		
	Home loan	Credit card	Other
Percentile of net worth			
	2002		
Less than 20	6	28	37
20–39.9	37	49	41
40–59.9	47	32	26
60–79.9	42	29	27
80–100	33	22	25
	2006		
Less than 20	5	28	51
20–39.9	40	37	46
40–59.9	48	30	31
60–79.9	45	28	31
80–100	36	18	30
	2010		
Less than 20	6	50	67
20–39.9	42	46	78
40–59.9	50	34	69
60–79.9	46	28	67
80–100	38	27	63

Source: Reserve Bank of Australia (2012)

nonmortgage debt) in Australia across wealth percentiles. Home loans are mainly held by households in the 40%–59% and 60%–79% wealth percentiles, with the proportion increasing from 47% and 42% in 2002 to 50% and 46% by 2010, respectively.

Significantly, the two lowest wealth percentiles have credit card debt as the largest proportion of debt, which rose over the years for which the Reserve Bank of Australia provides data. In 2002, 28% of the poorest households had credit card debt, which increased by 2010 to 50%. In contrast, only 22% of the wealthiest households held credit card debt in 2002, increasing marginally to 27% in 2010. Other personal debt increased across all wealth percentile ranges from 2002 to 2010, and especially among the lowest two percentiles.

The UK also acutely demonstrates the impact of financialisation upon the poorest of households. Figure 4.4 plots the ratio of debt to income against average income for UK households. Between GBP4,500 and GBP15,000 the level of debt held ranges between 1.2× for the poorest households to approximately 0.2× for those on GBP15,000. Beyond this point, the average level of debt to income ratio gradually decreases.

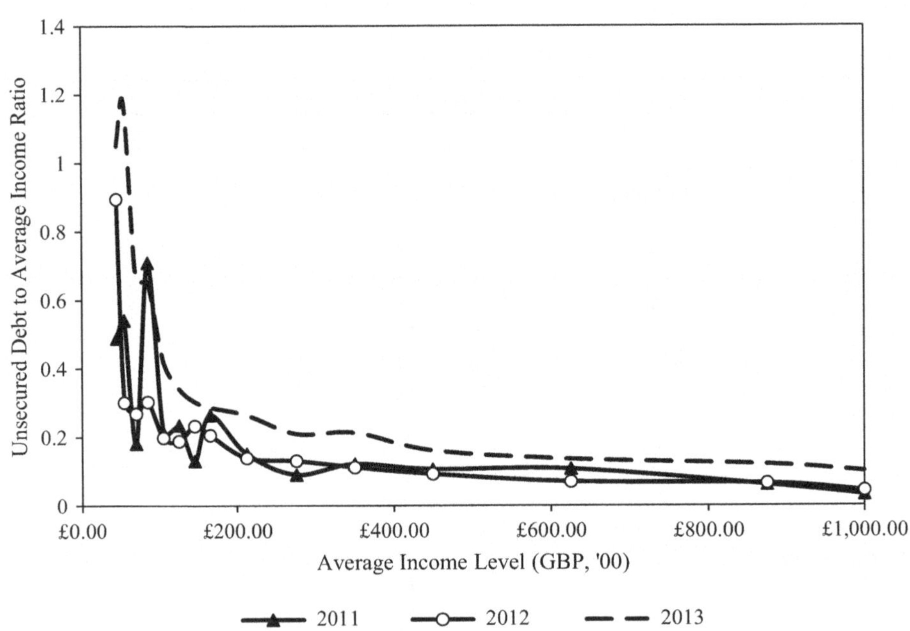

Fig. 4.4 Distribution of household unsecured debt to income, UK 2011–2013. (*Source*: Bank of England, NMG Consulting Survey 2011, 2012 and 2013)

Income Inequality: The Rise of the Top 1%

Under Eq. 4.1, a key element in the wealth accumulation process is the size of income. Obviously, ceteris paribus, higher incomes result in greater wealth accumulation. Here, the degree of wealth inequality is thus highly contingent upon the degree to which the highest income percentiles can increase their income shares. Further, the structure of income at the top is of major relevance. Piketty's (2014a) inequality relationship, $r > g$, suggests that the returns to capital (capital income) are of paramount import to any analysis of wealth distribution. As a first step, it is necessary to first establish the level of income inequality, then how that income is generated. Fortunately, there is substantial evidence available to this end.

The evolution of income inequality has received considerable attention in the literature since the 1960s. Quantifying income inequality can take two approaches in general. One approach that is often employed to determine the level of income inequality in the economy is the Gini coefficient. An alternative approach is to examine the distribution of income via various percentiles or fractals of the income distribution. A significant advantage of this method is that it effectively accounts for the extremities in a distribution. In contrast, Gini coefficients place weight on the median observations, potentially underemphasising the amount of inequality present in the tails of a distribution (Piketty, 2014a).

The data used here is the share of national income accruing to the top income 1% percentiles. The WWID provides various country-by-country data across different income share percentiles as discussed in Chap. 3. For some countries, the database provides a structural division between the share of income from either labour or capital. This aspect of the database is particularly important considering the growth of income generating financial products. If, in Western economies, credit growth has been a defining characteristic of the impact of financialisation on household balance sheets for the poor, the increase of income generation from wealth holdings is the defining characteristic on the right-hand side of the wealth distribution. Saez and Zucman (2014) document that income derived from capital has consistently and increasingly accrued into the hands of the wealthy. This structure of top incomes is explored later on in the chapter.

To begin, income shares for the top 1% are depicted for the six advanced economies in Fig. 4.5. Income here is defined as *pre*-tax income, combining income derived from both labour and capital. In all instances, the top 1%

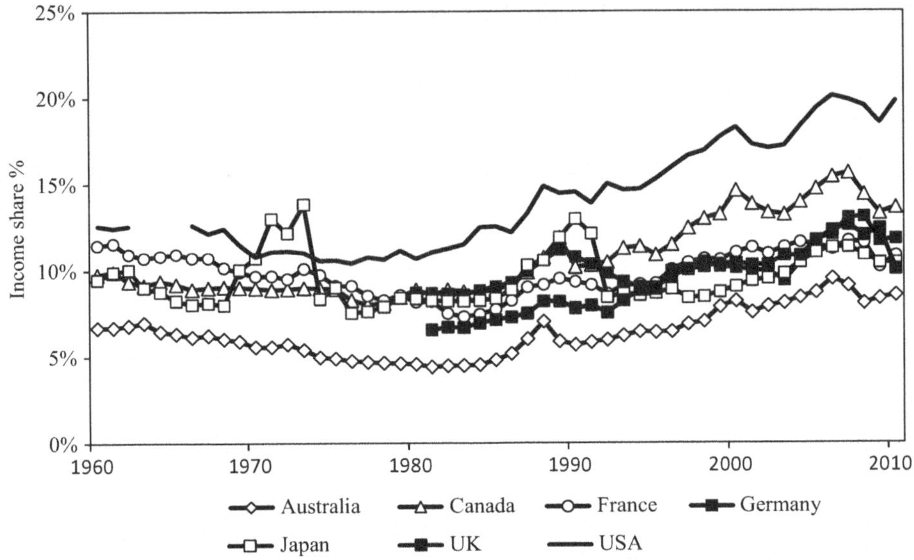

Fig. 4.5 Top 1% income share, 1960–2010. (*Source*: Income shares were obtained from the World Wealth and Income Database. The data is accessible from https://wid.world/)

income share is observed as increasing across all countries since the late 1970s. For the US, the 1960s and 1970s show approximately 8.07% of income being captured by the top 1% income group. This period in part corresponds to the 'great compression' mentioned at the start of Chap. 4. The lowest share over these two decades is observed for Australia at 6.08% followed by the UK at 7.2%, while the highest is observed in Germany at 11.2%.

From the 1980s, there is a precipitous increase in the income shares of the top 1% across the sample. Both the US and the UK exhibit significant increases. Over the two-decade period, 1990–2010 the mean income share going to the top 1% share in the US increased to 15.35% from 8.07% (1960 to 1979). No less steep is the observed increase in the UK, where the income share rose from 7.2% (1960 to 1979) to 12.52% over the 1990 to 2010 period. On average, most other countries reveal increased income shares for the top 1% albeit less than those observed in the US and the UK. In Australia, the mean income shares over 1990 to 2010 increased to 8.20% compared to 6.08% over the 1960 to 1979 period. Canada demonstrated an increase of similar magnitude, increasing from 8.84% to 10.69% across the same two periods. France and Germany exhibit little variation across the span of the two periods. Germany's top 1% share increased only marginally to 11.21% from 11.20%. France's top income share decreased from 8.83% to 8.20%.

Increasing levels of income concentration at the top income percentiles across the globe have varied explanations. Neoclassical economists emphasise the increasing returns to skill and education. Keynesians or institutionalists point to a shift in the bargaining power of high-income earners or managers over those further down the income (or wealth) distribution.

The most recent econometric study on the determinants of income inequality is by Dabla-Norris et al. (2015). Their study utilised a cross-country longitudinal approach and examined the drivers of income inequality along various dimensions with a focus on the top 10%. These drivers encompass a variety of elements, including:

- Trade openness
- Financial openness and deepening
- Technological growth
- Skill and education premiums
- Labour market institutions
- Government spending

Their regression estimates found that of the above, three features appear to have had the most dramatic impact upon income inequality over the past 30 years. These include labour market institutions, technological growth and financial deepening.

The role of labour market institutions is measured as degree of regulatory control over firing and hiring, collective bargaining and the setting of minimum wages. Dabla-Norris et al. (2015, p. 15) find that labour market flexibility has been particularly beneficial to the top 10% income decile and conclude that 'labor market flexibility benefits the rich and reduces the bargaining power of the lower-income workers'. Similarly, Jaumotte and Buitron (2015) view the decline in unionisation across the globe as giving rise to higher shares in the top 10%—once again achieved largely through the bargaining power of workers and top income shares. The weakening of unions and the commensurate decrease in the bargaining power of workers has largely increased the proportion of capital income received by capitalists (Jaumotte & Buitron, 2015, p. 31). This shift, however, has been brought about by governments shifting support to capital over labour. This process is particularly evident in the radical labour market policy shifts with the elections of Margaret Thatcher in the UK in 1979, Ronald Reagan in the US in 1980 and the Howard government in Australia from the mid-1990s. In the UK, 'the Thatcher government's union reforms of the 1980's included limits on closed union shops, secret ballots, … weakened labor unions and led to a decline in union membership' (Bronars, 2013, para. 5). Similarly, in the US, the Reagan administration terminated the PATCO strikers, that began a trend to turn the US 'back to a 'union-free environment' not seen since the 1920s' (Evans, 2016, p. 118).

The causal link between flexible labour markets and, or, de-unionisation and the growth of top income shares, although recognised as important, is not the only policy force in increasing *wealth* inequality. Piketty (2014a) stresses this point by arguing that it is wealth inequality to begin with that drives income inequality—through the returns to capital. Here taxation can have a substantial impact on reducing capital returns. In Eq. 4.1, capital income is reduced by the rate of capital income tax: $r_t^i \mathrm{n}\left(1-\tau_k\right)$. As will be shown in the discussion on taxation further on, tax shifting between wage and capital represents a real issue via which the wealthy can minimise tax paid given that capital is taxed lower than wage income.

Further, enhanced bargaining power of top executives or management enhances remuneration of this class. In this context, Piketty, Saez, and Stantcheva (2014) emphasise the impact of tax policy on *pre*-tax incomes in which unions have little if any role. The correlation between decreasing top marginal income tax rates and top wage incomes is not merely a statistical association but demonstrates a causal link. This causality story essentially argues that senior executives (and presumably, the owners of capital), with lower top tax rates, demanded greater compensation. Emphasising the role of incentives, Piketty (2014a), and Piketty et al. (2014) argue that top income earners were prepared to fight now for greater income, since they got to keep more of the money they received. Labour unions, however, have little role in these empirical specifications whereas other institutional forces come to the fore.

These 'institutional' factors primarily appear to be associated with the economic power found in the highest echelons of the corporate hierarchy. For example, corporate governance practices, in reality, tie remuneration packages of top executives to prevailing social norms rather than performance. The argument goes that with a shift in taxation policy, it is now permissible for executives to gain higher salaries as society permits this implicitly through government taxation policy. Performance does not provide an adequate explanation itself as the marginal productivity story would maintain. For example, empirical evidence suggests that executives receive large bonuses for increased sales or profit during periods of high economic growth (Bertrand & Mullainathan, 2001).

The second major force according to the Dabla-Norris et al. (2015) is the impact of technological growth. The advancement in technology can affect income inequality through two mechanisms. Jan Tinbergen's (1975) provided the main impetus for this viewpoint proposing that to a significant extent income inequality was the outcome of the race between education and technology. There are two channels through which technology can impact upon income inequality. Firstly, a required tertiary qualification to utilise the technology may demand a premium for the worker's skill set, thereby increasing incomes for those possessing the requisite skills. In the second channel, technological progress replaces unskilled workers or reduces their incomes. The first of these channels is the standard neoclassical marginal productivity story. Piketty (2014a) argues that although technological change or growth certainly has an impact, the strength of this effect is not as pronounced as ordinarily expected. Advanced economies which have demonstrated significant technological progress or growth, such as Sweden, have not shown a concomitant increase in income inequality. Empirically, the evidence shows that income inequality is not as pronounced in other societies or economies (such as Sweden) compared to, for example, the US or the UK despite sharing similar levels of technological growth. Pressman (2015) summarises Piketty's argument as follows: 'The fact that there are large national differences [in income inequality] shows that marginal productivity is not driving the sharp rise in top incomes in Anglo-Saxon nations. The problem appears to be institutional rather than economic' (p. 301).

The Structure of Income at the Top: Inequality of Capital Income

Here, findings on the distribution between capital and labour income at the highest income percentiles are examined. According to Krugman (2014), research into income inequality has largely neglected or missed the emergence of an economic elite whose income is derived not from labour but capital. As Krugman (2014) points out, the general thrust of inequality research focused upon the rise of large managerial and chief executive officer (CEO) compensation packages since the mid-1980s. Capital income though was largely neglected. *Capital* income here is defined as comprising capital gains, dividends, interest receipts, rents and business profits. The significance of capital income in the compensation structure of the wealthy is particularly important for the distribution of wealth, in so far as the Piketty (2014a) framework contends. Capital income, through the return to capital, r, is the main driver of inequality by amplifying initial disparities in accumulation models such as that presented in Eq. 4.1. In societies where high wealth concentration prevails it represents a particularly important mechanism through which inequality is maintained.

There are some a priori reasons to expect that capital income may represent a substantially greater element of total income for the wealthiest income groups. In previous sections, the increasing financialisation of household balance sheets was viewed as depressing wealth accumulation for the poorest households through the accumulation of credit. Financialisation might be playing a similar role on from the asset side for the wealthy households. For example, Fligstein and Goldstein (2015) find evidence that the upper and upper middle classes in the US from 1989 through to 2007 'adopted a more aggressive attitude towards risk and engaged in more financial activities to support their lifestyles' (p. 23). The greater risk tolerance among wealthier households for riskier investments has been tested (see e.g. Tsigos and Daly, 2016). It is sufficient to note here that such risk-taking enables rapid wealth accumulation by the upper classes compared to the lower classes in the long run through capital gains, dividend or interest receipts so long as the return to capital is greater than national income growth.

By way of a brief introduction, the extent to which the wealthy dominate capital income shares is presented in Fig. 4.6. The data is sourced from the Luxembourg Income Study (n.d.), which provides a distributional breakdown of income up to the 95th percentile. At the highest income tier, mean capital

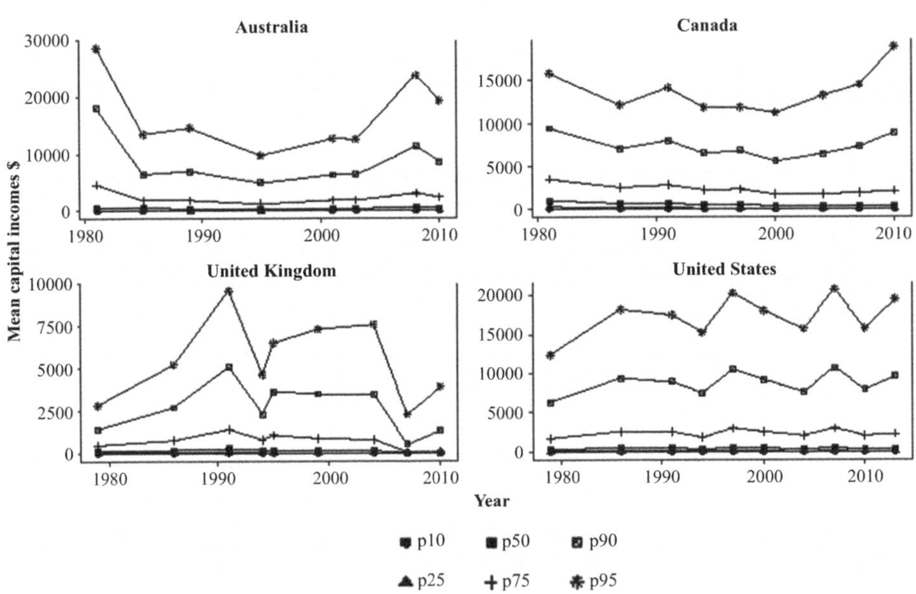

Fig. 4.6 Distribution of capital income across the Anglo-Saxon economies by wealth percentiles. *Note*: All amounts are in US dollar terms, real base 1990. (*Source*: Data retrieved from Luxembourg Income Study (n.d.))

incomes have remained relatively stable, ranging between USD13,750 (Canada) and USD17,372 (US), but from 2000 there is a noticeable increase in Canada and Australia. Among the middle classes, the range is considerably lower, with the highest mean being USD545 (Canada) and the lowest USD389 (US). At the 75th percentile, it increases to approximately USD2,330 for all countries. For the 95th percentile it increases dramatically to USD20,000 for Australia, Canada and the US.

Although useful as a guide, the Luxembourg Income Study data stops at the 95th percentile and does not provide further information on the structure of incomes at the very highest echelons of the income distribution. Examining the structural breakdown between labour and capital income-by-income group percentiles at the very top provides a better examination of the shifting changes utilising data sourced from the World Income and Wealth database. Below, the structure of top incomes, the proportion of income derived from capital or income, is presented at three different percentiles: top 1%, top 0.1% and the top 0.01%. By examining the data across the three percentiles, the shifting predominance or composition between income classes over time can be observed, and the reasons for the shifts can be explored.

The income structure decomposition for the top 1% is presented in Fig. 4.7. Since the late 1970s to early 1980s, the top 1% earners have increasingly

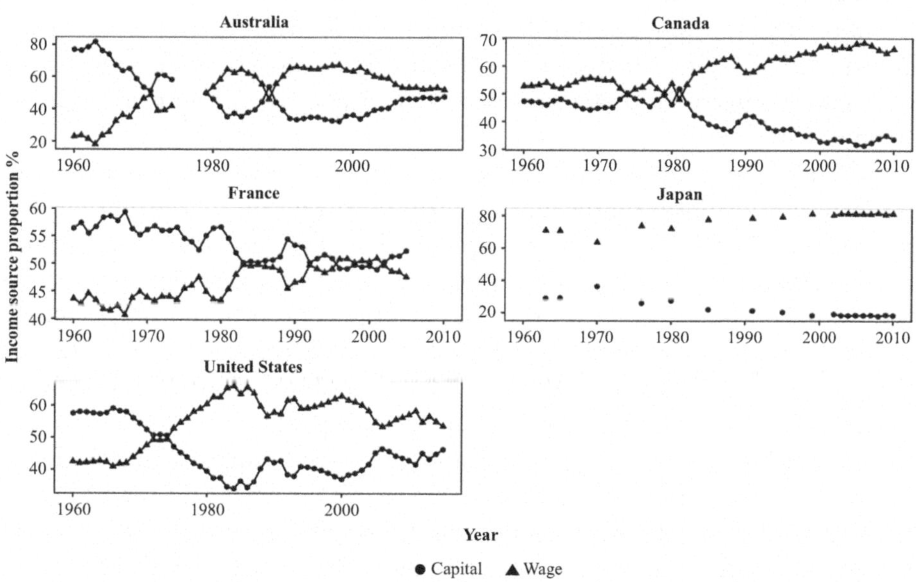

Fig. 4.7 Capital and labour income shares, top 1%. (*Source*: Income proportions were obtained from the World Wealth and Income Database. The data is accessible from https://wid.world/)

earned their income from 'non-capital' income sources. The shift is most acutely observed in Australia, Canada and the US. In the US, the proportion of earned income has averaged 59.10% since 1975 to 2010. Australia has a similar average at 59.62%. Canada has similarly exhibited a relatively high portion of earned income, averaging 61.03%. Japan is well ahead with the 79.67% of the top 1% sourcing their income from non-capital labour. Only France deviates from the patterns observed in the other sample countries. There, although capital income demonstrates a decreasing trend since the 1960s, it has on average represented the majority source of income to the contemporary period for the top 1%. Taking a similar time frame from 1975 to 2005, 51.77% of the top 1% income earners in France received income from capital sources. Although labour income did at one stage constitute the majority of income for a brief period between 1996 and 2001, it subsequently reversed.

Who, precisely, are the top 1% of earners? It is ultimately dependent upon national context. Typically, the bulk of the top 1% of income earners are characterised as being part of the professional and managerial classes. Saez (2006), for example, contends that the increasing income share of the top 1% observed in the Anglo countries is being driven not by increasing or higher capital incomes, but 'highly paid executives [who] seem to have replaced the capitalists and rentiers of the early part of the century at the top of the income distribution' (Saez, 2006, p. 238). In contrast, the French experience shows the dominance of capital income. This may, in part, be driven by the high rate of inheritance observed in France relative to the Anglo-Saxon countries, as identified in Chap. 3.

Advancing to a smaller more prosperous income percentile group, the top 0.1% reveals *significant* differences compared to the top 1% in the income dynamics of the wealthy. The relative proportion of income sources for the top 0.1% is presented in Fig. 4.8. Two important observations can be made regarding the data. Firstly, except for Canada, income derived from capital income sources now dominates. In the US and Australia, there were brief periods throughout the 1980s and 1990s where this observation does not hold. However, by 2002 the relative pre-eminence of capital income holds. Further, the observed proportion of capital income appears to be approaching the levels in the early observation period, from 1960 to the late 1970s. In the US, there is a degree of overlap between capital and non-capital income. For non-capital income, the highest spike occurs in the year 2000, which coincidently corresponds with the largest influx of new entrepreneurs from the fields of information technology and finance as presented in Chap. 3. However, since then capital income has once again become the dominant source of income.

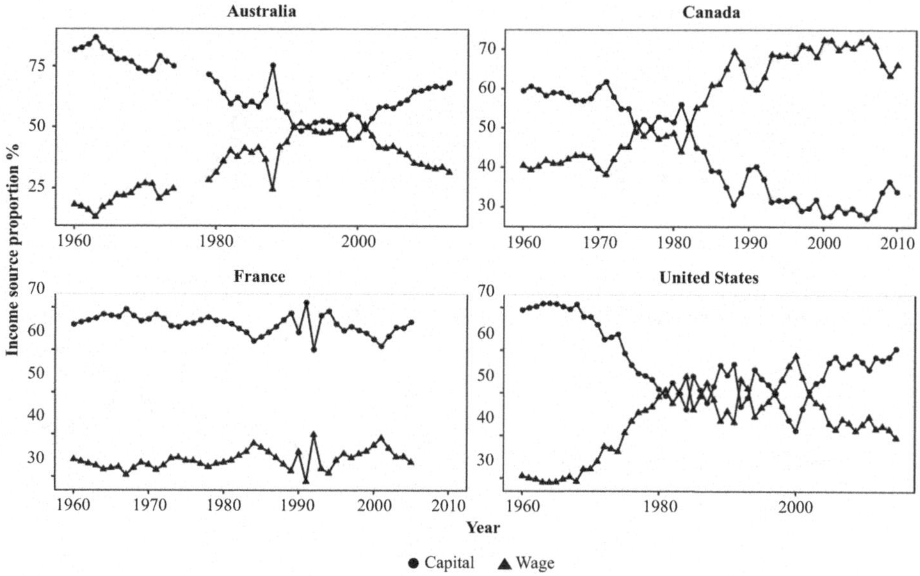

Fig. 4.8 Capital and labour income shares, top 0.1%. (*Source*: Income proportions were obtained from the World Wealth and Income Database. The data is accessible from https://wid.world/)

In France, capital income continues to dominate the income structure. Between 1960 and 2005, the average proportion of income from capital was 66.01% (σ = 2.2%), with no discernible trend up or down. Inheritance potentially explains the large role of capital incomes in France at both the 1% and 0.1% level. Daumard (1980) demonstrates that inheritance has always played a significant role in French economic life. Prior to the First World War, the annual inheritance flow as a fraction of national income in France averaged 24%. The destruction wrought by the two World Wars had pushed this portion down to 4% by 1945. However, by 2010 the inheritance flow had increased to approximately 14% (Piketty, 2014a, p. 378). Australia's experience largely follows that of the US, where the relative proportion of the two income sources converge between 1985 and the early 2000s before the ascendency of capital income becomes established again.

Further advancing along the income distribution, to the top 0.01%, reveals trends like those presented in Fig. 4.9 for the top 0.1%. Figure 4.9 shows the evolution of the top 0.01% income structure across the four countries for which data are available. The trends and relative contributions of capital and non-capital income to overall income for the top 0.01% mostly follow those observed for the top 0.1%, though capital income dominates for a greater

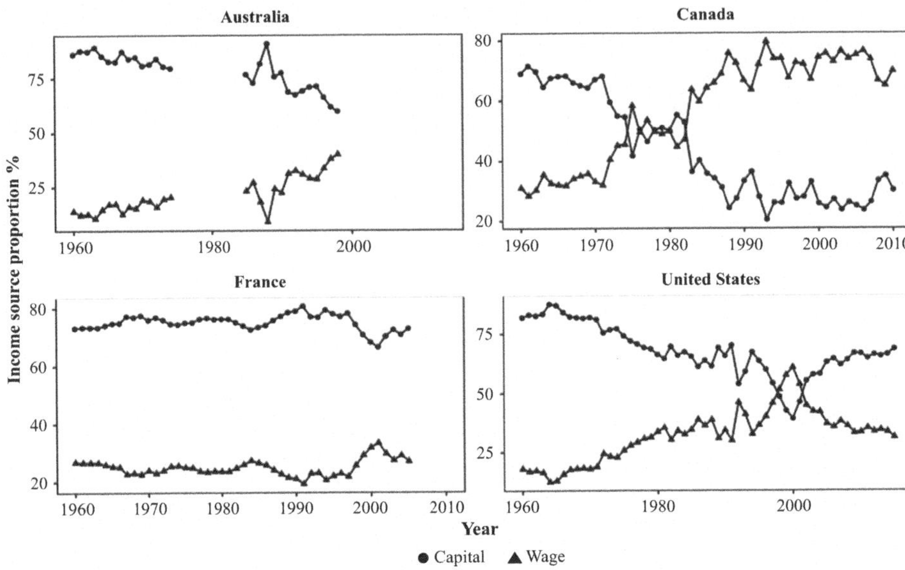

Fig. 4.9 Capital and labour income shares, top 0.01%. (*Source*: Income proportions were obtained from the World Wealth and Income Database. The data is accessible from http://www.wid.com/)

length of the period. In the US, only between 1998 and 2001 is there a sharp but momentary increase in labour income, such that it dominates income derived by capital income. Beyond 2001, capital income once again dominates rising towards the proportions observed in the 1980s. For Australia, data on the top 0.01% is only available up to 1998. At least up until this point, a downward trend in the proportion of capital income emerges but is still well above non-capital income. Assuming Australia's proportional income shares follow those of the US, it is reasonable to expect these levels to be maintained throughout the 2000s. Both France and Canada largely show patterns that are like those observed in Fig. 4.8.

In Chap. 3, the relationship between return to capital and national income growth was discussed. The greater returns to wealth relative to income growth invariably result in greater wealth concentration. At least in the Piketty (2014a) framework, capital income represents one of the major forces driving wealth accumulation and concentration at the top of the wealth pyramid. At the very highest income levels, this appears to be an accurate representation of economic reality. Capital income, at least for those countries that data exists, dominates at the top.

Tax and Inequality

The role of taxation policy in suppressing the amassment of great fortunes is now considered. The relationship between taxation policy and wealth accumulation arises through three channels, as presented in Eq. 4.1. There is, of course, the direct impact on labour incomes which becomes more pronounced with progressive taxes. Secondly, there are taxes on capital income flows (corporate taxes, dividend taxes or capital gains taxation). Thirdly, there is the potential for direct taxes on the stock of wealth via estate or inter vivos gift taxation. This section explores the evolution of all three channels since 1960s. Further, the role of tax evasion via off-shore financial centres (OFC) is, briefly, considered.

Top Marginal Income Tax Rates

To begin, a comparison of the changes in the top marginal income tax rates for labour is examined since 1960. The impact of income taxation can be either direct in the sense of *after*-tax incomes or indirect on *pre*-tax incomes (see e.g. Leigh, 2009; Piketty et al., 2014). Both aspects are explored here.

Overall, all countries demonstrate a fall in the top marginal income tax rates as presented in Fig. 4.10. The overall trends across all seven countries

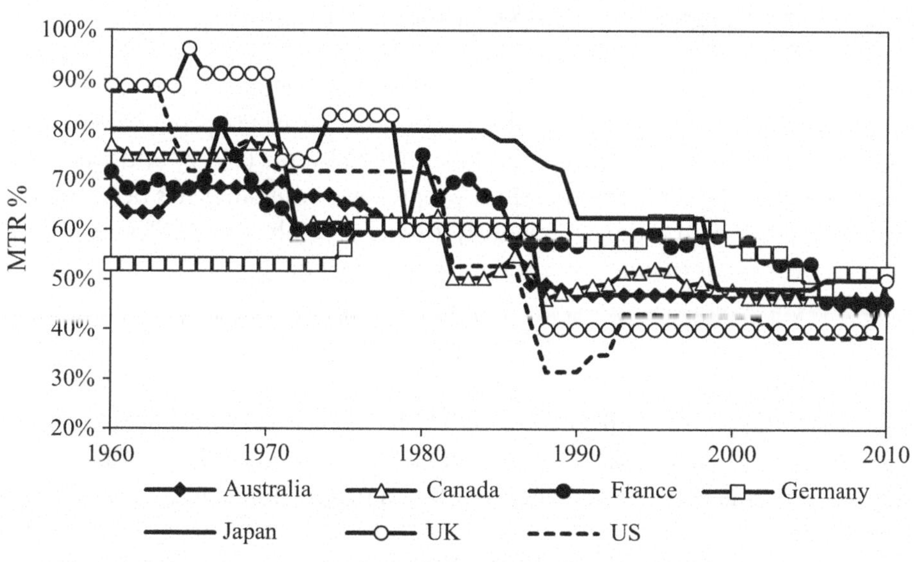

Fig. 4.10 Top marginal income tax rates, 1960–2010. (*Source*: Top marginal income tax rates data from Piketty, Saez, and Stantcheva (2012))

seem to follow a path that can be divided into three different epochs. In the first epoch, roughly corresponding to 1960 to the early 1970s, top income tax marginal rates were high. Except for Germany (in relative terms), all countries exhibited significantly higher top income tax rates during the 1960s. The maximum income tax rate was in the UK at 90.0%, followed by the US (78.7%) and Japan (74%). The second epoch begins in the mid-1970s. By the mid-1970s, the average top income tax rates had fallen substantially, with some decreasing by more than 10%. France and the UK registered the largest decreases, dropping by 11.2% and 11.6%, respectively. The third epoch in tax policy changes across most countries manifests in the late 1980s through to 2010. On average, all countries exhibited significant falls in the top income tax rates over the 1990 to 2010 period. The lowest average top marginal income tax rates were to be found in the US (39.89%) and the UK (40.45%). Australia also imposed significantly lower marginal tax rates on the highest incomes, now averaging 46.63%. Continental Europe also enforced lower tax rates on top incomes during this period but maintained these at levels higher than the Anglo countries in the sample. France decreased its top tax rate to an average of 54.44%. Germany somewhat goes against the behaviour of other states in maintaining a stable top income tax rate over the sample period. From 1960 to 2010, the average top income tax rate was 56.45%. Over the 1990–2010 period, it had barely changed at 56.08%.

Income Tax Progressivity, Kakwani Index Estimates

Measuring the impact of income tax policy changes upon after-tax income distribution can involve the use of various measures of tax progressivity. Two well-known measures are those developed by Kakwani (1977) and Reynolds and Smolensky (1977). The use of tax progressivity measures has been used in income distribution studies previously (see e.g. Leigh, 2005). The Kakwani (1977) measure of income tax progressivity is estimated as:

$$P = \frac{\left(G - G^*\right)}{\left[\tau / \left(1 - \tau\right)\right]} \tag{4.4}$$

where G is the pre-tax Gini coefficient, G^* is the post-tax Gini coefficient and τ is the average income tax rate. According to Kakwani (1977), when $P > 0$ the tax system is progressive, when $P = 0$ it is proportional and when $P < 0$ it is regressive.

Figure 4.11 presents the Kakwani index across the advanced economies. Some facts emerge from the trends across the economies. Firstly, most countries appear to follow a U-shaped pattern in income tax progressivity. For example, in Australia, tax progressivity peaked in 1974 under the Whitlam

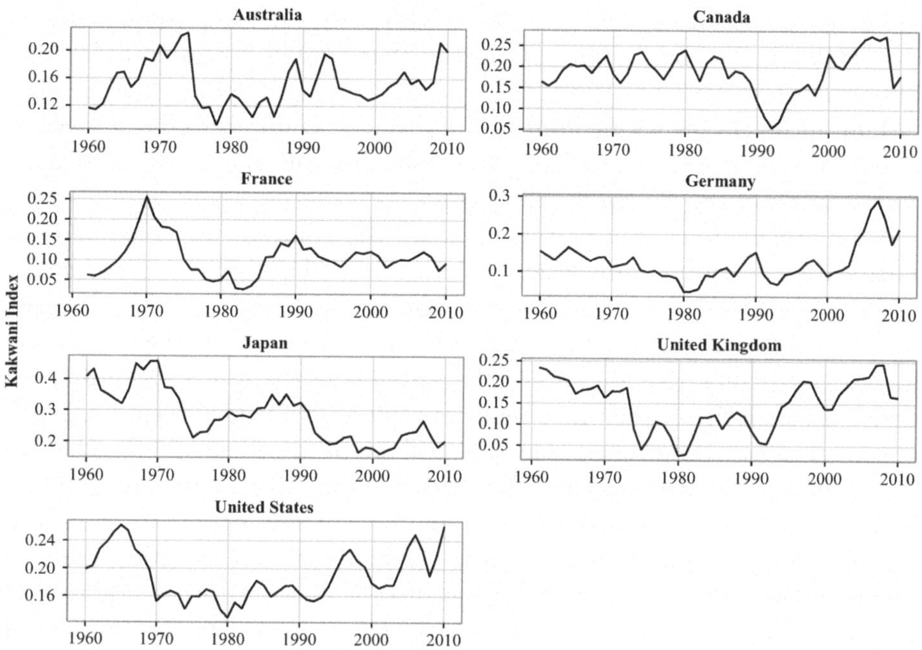

Fig. 4.11 Kakwani income tax progressivity, 1960–2010

Government, before undergoing a precipitous decline until the late 1980s and before slight increases in the index throughout the 2000s, peaking in 2009. The shape of the Australian Kakwani Index calculated here follows that of Leigh's (2005) own calculations with a different index. Leigh (2005) applied the Suits Index measure of tax progressivity, who also noted an increase in tax progressivity from the 1990s to 2000s. The US tends to follow a similar pattern, although the U-shape is more clearly delineated compared to Australia. Enhancements in tax progressivity per the Kakwani Index are also observed in the UK, Canada and Germany. The only country that deviates from the observation of increased tax progressivity is Japan; wherein the index decreased from a high of 0.55 in 1969 to approximately 0.20 in 2010 converging to the average observed for other countries. It should be noted that Japan demonstrated enormous entrepreneurial activity during the 1960s and 1970s.

The observation that tax progressivity has increased since the 1980s and 1990s across the advanced industrialised economies ostensibly conflicts with the observed decrease in top tax rates depicted in Fig. 4.10 and the increase in top income shares as discussed previously. Numerous studies have shown a causal link between taxation rates and income shares. Alvaredo et al. (2013) demonstrate that for the countries discussed here, the reductions in top marginal tax rates were highly correlated with a surge in top income shares (at the 1% level). DeLong (1998) points out that the US generated hardly any billionaires from 1930 to 1980. The existence of a highly progressive taxation system in the US constituted one of the strongest counters to the emergence of billionaires. The reversal in tax policy coincides with the almost immediate reappearance of the American billionaire.

Four explanations may partly conciliate the contradictory observations. Firstly, the estimation of the Kakwani Index utilised the after-tax *and* transfer income Gini coefficient. Transfers can, potentially, have a significant impact on inequality beyond taxation. Secondly, it was noted on the section on income inequality, that the ultra-rich, particularly the top 0.1% and above derive the majority of their income from capital (dividends, interest receipts, or capital gains). These forms of income will not be impacted upon by changes in top marginal income taxes rates. Thirdly, the Gini coefficient tends to be less effective in capturing the extreme tails of the income distribution, placing greater emphasis on the median (Piketty, 2014a). Fourthly, the data on top income shares examine before-tax income shares. Very few studies have considered after-tax income shares which may permit a better estimate of progressivity of income tax rates.

Implicit Tax Rates Derived from Top Pre- and Post-tax Income Shares

An alternative to the tax progressivity indexes is to estimate the direct impact of income tax on top incomes. The arithmetic impact of income tax on the top income shares is hard to assess across the all seven countries given a lack of data in this area. Previous studies by Atkinson and Salverda (2005) on the UK, Veall (2012) on Canada and the US (Piketty & Saez, 2006) permit some assessment of the arithmetic impact of taxation on the top shares. Figure 4.12 presents the 'implicit tax rate' of the 1%. It is calculated as:

$$\tau_{IR} = 1 - \left[\frac{\text{before tax share of the top } 1\%}{\text{post tax share of the top } 1\%} \right] \tag{4.5}$$

where τ_{IR} is the implicit tax rate.

For the UK and the US, the implicit tax rate on the top 1% shows a dramatic fall between 1960 through to 1980. The implicit tax rate for the two countries went from a mean of 28.9% (UK) and 27.6% (US) in the 1970s to

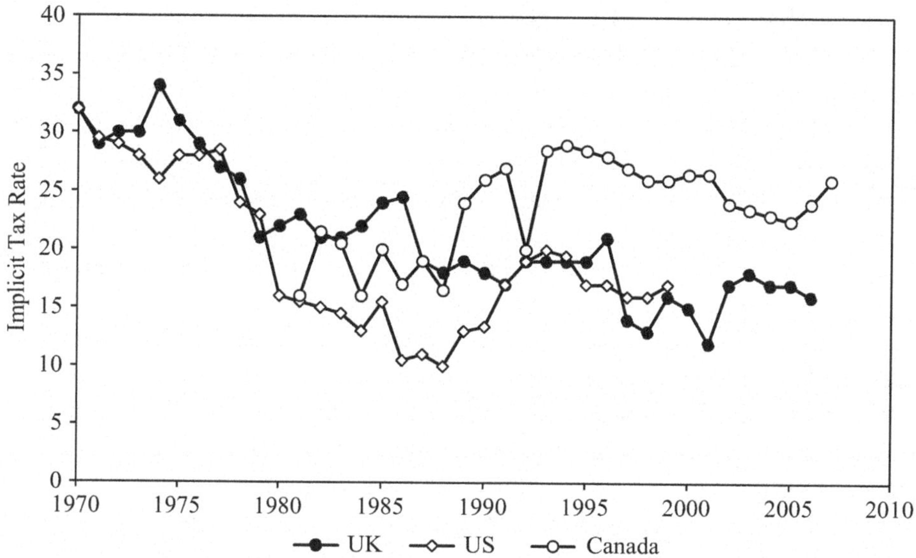

Fig. 4.12 Implicit income tax rates, 1970–2006. (*Source:* UK estimates from Atkinson and Salverda (2005), Canadian estimates from Veall (2012) and US estimates from Piketty and Saez (2006))

21.4% and 13.4% in the 1980s, respectively. The subsequent two decades experienced slight reversals to this trend. By the 1990s, both the UK and the US had converged to implicit tax rates of 20%. In contrast, the Canadian experience somewhat reverses the observations in the UK and US. In the 1980s the mean implicit tax rate was 19% increasing to 26.4% in the 1990s and 24.7% in the 2000s. In contrast to the Kakwani Index, these estimates do suggest that the tax burden has systematically decreased across the UK and US, but data limitations limit the inferences that can be made.

Response of Pre-tax Top Income Shares to Income Tax Rate Changes

Numerous studies have econometrically examined the relationship between marginal tax rates and top *pre*-tax income shares. Cross-country studies have typically found a correlation between the two, but the strength of the relationship is highly varied. Roine, Vlachos and Waldenström (2008) found that countries that experienced substantial reductions in the top marginal income tax rates only experience modest increases in top income shares. Numerically, a 10% decrease in the top marginal tax rate was found to be associated with a 0.4 percentage point increase in the share of the top 1%. However, Roine et al. (2008) also conclude that high marginal tax rates have an equalising effect beyond the direct impact of taxation such as societal norms briefly discussed previously on executive pay. Another cross-country study finds a stronger effect. Atkinson and Leigh (2013) analyse the impact of a reduction in top marginal tax rates on top income shares across five Anglo-Saxon countries. They determine that a reduction in the top marginal rate can explain between one-third and one-half of the rise in the income share of the top percentile.

Country-specific studies of the impact of changes in the top marginal tax rate upon top income shares largely corroborate the findings of cross-country studies, though some results establish no clear relationship. Dilnot, Kell and Webb (1988) analysed the US 1979 top income tax reduction. They found that the level of tax receipts remained mostly constant from 1978 to 1985. The stability in tax receipts implying that incomes increased following the tax cut. The Canadian experience ostensibly reflects that exhibited by both UK and US. Saez and Veall (2005) find top income shares largely track income tax reductions, but this may represent a spurious correlation between the two variables. Instead, they argue that Canadian income shares more closely track US income shares. The authors suggest this is due to the competitiveness of the US after-tax regime relative to that of Canada. Workers with highly marketable skills move(d) to the US if after-tax compensation was more attractive there compared to Canada.

Studies on Europe reveal that the relationship between pre-tax income shares and tax rates may be somewhat ambiguous. Piketty (1998) and Landais (2007) both consider the relationship between income taxes and top income shares in France over time. Both find that personal income tax rates have had an insignificant impact on income shares. Piketty (1998) finds that the elasticity of taxable income with respect to taxation is far lower than what is observed in the US. Evidence from Germany shows evidence more in line with that of the US. For Germany, Gottfried and Schellhorn (2004) find that the elasticity of taxable income to changes in the tax regime is quite substantial for Germany, estimating an elasticity of approximately 1—far higher than 0.4 for France.

A significant outlier is Japan. Moriguchi and Saez (2008) do not find any surge in top income shares in recent decades. As Fig. 4.11 depicts, Japan has demonstrated a significant reduction in top income tax rates. In their conclusion, Moriguchi and Saez (2008) contend that neither changes in technology nor tax policies alone can explain the relative stability of top Japanese incomes shares, despite significant variations in both. Instead, economic policies beyond tax to those such as institutional arrangements surrounding corporate governance, and the lasting influence of occupation reforms of the US in the post-war era constitute greater influences on top income shares. Tax evasion and avoidance are, for the case of Japan, also largely dismissed as an explanation for its low-income inequality trends (in recent decades). For countries beyond the focus of this study, empirical results demonstrate a clear relationship between falls in the top marginal income tax rates and increase in top income shares. For Sweden, Roine and Walenström (2008) find a significant inverse relationship between the two variables over the twentieth century. Similarly, in Finland the same causality is established.

The differing impact of reductions of the top marginal tax rate on pre-tax income shares could be explained by any number of alternatives as advanced in the literature. Leigh (2009) argues that there are two channels: (1) an immediate work disincentive effect and (2) a lagged effect via capital accumulation. Alvaredo et al. (2013) argue that the impact of a reduced tax rate on pre-tax top income shares can be affected via three potential channels. These include:

1. An increase in hours of work supplied due to a fall in the income tax rate.
2. Increased rent-seeking activity by executives or owners of enterprises. The increased rent seeking manifests through bargaining power.
3. Decreased tax avoidance.

On decreased tax avoidance Morelli, Smeeding and Thompson (2014) state that the:

> reduction in top marginal tax rate could indeed reduce the propensity to evade taxation, increasing the tax collection and therefore income reported at the top. Hence, the increase in inequality may be due to a reduction in tax avoidance due to lower tax rates for richer groups. (p. 86)

Similarly, Reynolds (2007), for example, argues that the large growth in the top 1% income share, particularly during the 1980s, is owed to a shift in the tax base from corporate to personal income tax. Alvaredo et al. (2013) empirically examine all three hypotheses. They argue that impact of changes in the top marginal tax rate upon pre-tax income shares are largely emblematic of greater institutional changes that favour the bargaining positions of executives. Decreased tax avoidance and increases in hours of work supplied (the marginal productivity story) are found to have little explanatory power.

Capital Income Tax and Base Shifting Between Income Sources

It has been shown that capital income is the dominant form of income amongst the highest earners. Therefore, it may be taxes related to capital income that might bear the clearest impact on capital income shares. Stilwell and Jordan (2007, p. 155) articulate the ultimate impact of this when stating that '[t]he unequalising effects of government policy have been further compounded by cuts in company taxes, dividend imputation and reduction of the effective rate of capital gains tax' (p. 155). The evolution of statutory corporate tax rates and tax rates on dividends since the early 1980s are presented in Fig. 4.13. Across all countries, there is a marked downward trend in both rates. In the 1980s, Australia's average corporate tax rate was approximately 45%. By 1999, this had decreased to 37%, before falling again in the 2000s. Throughout the 2000s, the average tax rate remained at 30%. The other sample countries largely mirror the Australian experience. In the 1980s, Japan's, the UK's and the US's average corporate tax rate was 42%. Germany exhibited the highest average through the 1980s at 56%. By the 2000s, all countries maintained corporate tax rates at or below 35%. The largest decrease is observed for Germany down to an average of 23% throughout the 2000s compared to 56% in 1980s.

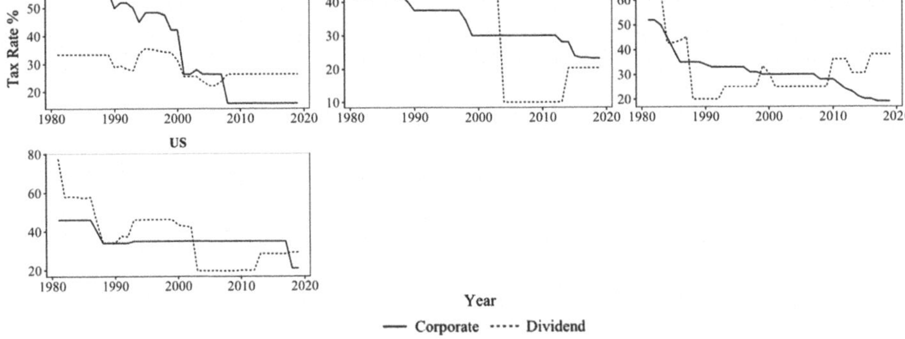

Fig. 4.13 Dividend and corporate tax rates, 1980–2010. (*Source*: OECD Tax Database. Retrieved from http://www.oecd.org/tax/tax-policy/tax-database.htm)

The dividend tax rates also underwent significant falls across the sample. Since the early 1980s, taxes levied on dividends ranged 45%–80%. In line with reductions in the corporate tax rate and top marginal income tax rates, the dividend tax rate was systematically decreased across all the countries in the sample. By 2010, most of the advanced economies taxed dividends between 10% and approximately 30%. The lowest tax rates in 2010 are observed in Japan (10.00%) and the US (19.99%). Australia, Canada, France and Germany all exhibited taxation rates ranging between 26.38% (Germany) to 30% (Australia).

Focusing solely on income taxes negates the various means via which the wealthy can circumvent or hide their large incomes from tax authorities by alternating between different income sources as required to exploit tax rate differentials (whilst also benefitting from decreases in the actual rate of taxation). Being wealthy permits routing earnings through other channels that are taxed effectively lower. The most obvious example of shifting between tax bases is that of executive compensation alternating between the use of wage compensation to stock options.

Directly measuring the impact of taxation on capital income is vastly more challenging due to the ways the wealthy can shift earnings between wages, dividends or capital gains. Piketty, Saez and Zucman (2013) recognise the potential for shifting income between different sources when stating: 'Sometime [sic] it is not all obvious to decompose these flows into a pure labor component (payment for labor services) and a pure capital component (compensation for capital ownership)' (p. 2). The point which Piketty et al. (2013) are conveying being that there is tremendous scope for the wealthy to shift income bases depending upon which provides the most favourable tax treatment.

The impact of changes in capital income taxes relative to wage income taxes can be observed through even casual empiricism. In Australia, dividend tax policy till 1986 implemented a classical tax approach to dividend payouts. In 1987, Australia abandoned the classical approach to dividend taxation and adopted a dividend imputation system. The change in policy also implemented a concomitant and drastic decrease in the tax payable on dividends. Dividend tax rates fell from 58.23% in 1986 to 18.4% in 1987. Commensurately, the top 0.01% share of capital income went from 59.94% in 1986 to 68.6% in 1986 and 82.64% in 1988. Throughout the 2000s, the dividend tax rate hovered at approximately 25%, while the capital income share of the top 0.1% averaged at 73%. Similar falls are observed across other countries in response to changes in the dividend tax system. The US registers one of the largest decreases on dividend tax. Throughout the 1980s the average tax rate on dividends was 52%, in the 1990s it fell to 43% before another precipitous fall to 26%. The large fall was met with a commensurate shift in the structure of top incomes in the US to that of capital income. Empirical studies on tax base shifting are sparse, though Gordon and Slemrod (2000) provide one of the best examples. Utilising time series data, they found that a one-point increase in the differential between the corporate tax rate and labour income tax rate 'raises reported personal labor income by 3.2%, and results in a fall in the reported corporate rate of return of 0.147 percent' (Gordon and Slemrod, 2000, p. 46).).

Wealth and Estate Taxation

Wealth and estate taxes have long been considered as a means of addressing perceived inequalities (Kopczuk, 2013). Taxation on stocks of wealth can take two forms, taxes on intergenerational transfers (after death or inter vivos) and taxes on an individual's net worth. For Piketty (2014a) a tax on the stock of wealth represents a key proposal to emerge from his treatise on wealth. In this subsection, the historical trends in both are considered as well as a brief review of the predictions of theoretical models and empirical studies that consider the impact of taxes in either form.

Intergenerational and Estate Taxes

To begin, intergenerational transfer and estate transfers are considered. For brevity, both are referred to as inheritance taxes from this point. Figure 4.14 depicts the top tax rates on inheritances across the seven economies. Across all countries, with the exception of France, there has been a systematic decrease in the rate of taxation applicable to estates. Both Canada and Australia abolished their respective estate taxes in the 1970s. The abolition of the Canadian federal estate tax in 1971 was viewed in the era as being 'important in terms not of revenue but of what it symbolized: a retreat from decades of attempts to alter wealth distribution through taxation' (Bird, 1978, p. 134). In Australia, the *Estate Duty Amendment Act 1978* abolished estate duties that had been in place since 1915. Just as in Canada, the abolition of inheritance taxes had little impact on state revenues but represented a signal that Australia, as a nation, now appeared unconcerned by the concentration of wealth (Pedrick, 1982).

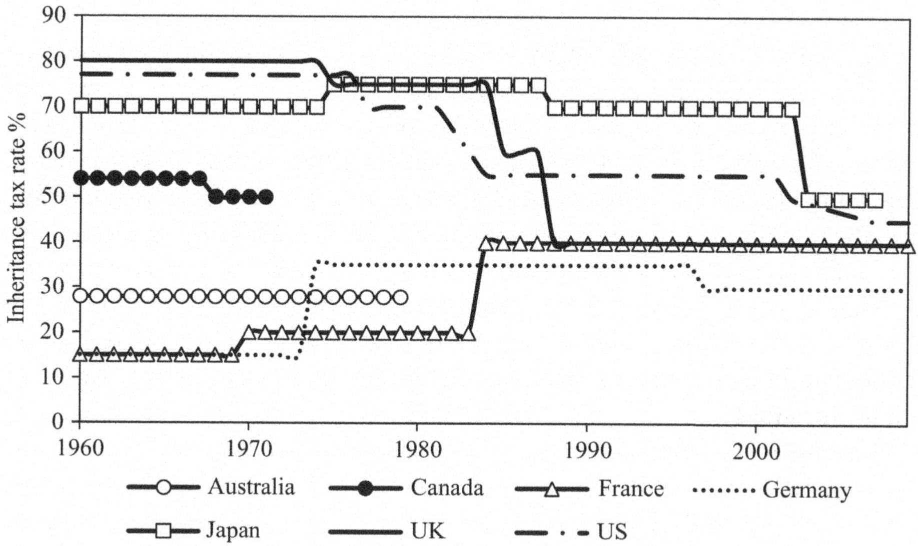

Fig. 4.14 Top inheritance tax rates %. (*Source*: Plagge, Scheve, and Stasavage (2010). Comparative Inheritance Taxation Database)

In contrast to Australia and Canada, the other Anglo countries, the US and UK have both maintained inheritance taxes to the present day. In the US, the *Revenue Act 1940* had set top tax rates on inherited estates at 77% with a threshold of USD20,000. The rate remained stable until 1976, though the threshold had increased to USD40,000. In line with the observations in relation to income tax rates, and capital incomes, the inheritance tax rate underwent a substantial transformation. The *Economic Recovery Act of 1981* decreased the top tax rate to 65% and was further reduced in subsequent years to 55% and the threshold exemption to USD325,000 in 1984 and further increasing to USD675,000 in 2001. The largest shake up in US inheritance taxes occurred in 2001 with the passing of *The Economic Growth and Tax Relief Reconciliation Act of 2001*. The new act provided for a ten-year schedule in decreases to the top tax rate to 45% in 2009 with the goal to repeal estate taxes, but was overturned by Congress. At the time of writing the top tax rate had been further reduced to 40%. The UK has also demonstrated similar falls to the US, with the top inheritance tax rate of 80% in 1960 decreasing to 40% with the passing of the *Finance Act 1987*. Roach (2003) finds that despite the falls in estate and gift tax rate, it remains the most progressive tax component in the US federal system.

Since the mid-1980s, the highest inheritance tax rates have been enforced by Japan. In 2003, tax rates fell to 50%, but remained above the rates observed in other countries. Data from the Japanese Ministry of Finance shows that both inheritance tax revenues and the proportion of estates taxed have decreased significantly. In 1993, the amount of inheritance tax revenue raised was approximately 3 trillion Yen. By 2012, this had decreased to approximately 1.5 trillion Yen. In 1997, approximately 7% of estates were taxed. By 2012, this was reduced to approximately 4%. This outcome appears primarily to be driven by an increase in the exemption threshold from 70 million Yen in 1988 to 275 million Yen. Further, the dramatic falls in Japanese real estate values would have had an impact in the number of estates meeting the minimum threshold.

Turning to continental Europe, both France and Germany have maintained modest levels of inheritance tax, but the progressivity of it has increased since the 1970s and 1980s. In contrast to the US and UK where the progressivity of inheritance taxes has declined significantly, for the two continental economic powers, it has increased. Piketty and Saez (2006) argue that the overall impact of the increase in estate and gift taxes is to have improved the *overall* progressivity of those nations' tax systems relative to the UK and US.

The review of inheritance tax rates only considers the progressivity of inheritance taxes and not their impact upon the wealth distribution. The relationship between inheritance taxes and the wealth distribution is ambiguous. Pedrick (1982) and Bird (1978) when advocating the reintroduction of death taxes were themselves sceptical of their overall *direct* impact on moderating wealth inequality. Pedrick (1982), for example, states that:

> In both countries [the UK and the US] there are still family fortunes of huge size notwithstanding that these family fortunes have passed through several generations with death taxes featuring rates that reach to seventy per cent. Plainly death taxes in the United Kingdom and the United States have been avoidable with expert guidance. (p. 453)

As mentioned in the above quote, much of these great fortunes escaped taxation through the rise of the professional family offices and trusts. Tuckman (1973) long recognised taxes directly on wealth, at least in the US, could be readily circumvented even in periods of high tax progressivity. Large family foundations such as the Ford Foundation or similar schemes by the Du Ponts largely rendered the effectiveness of estate taxes blunt (see e.g. Tuckman, 1973, pp. 60–61).

A scarce number of theoretical papers have analysed the impact of changes in estate taxation on the distribution of wealth, with ambiguous results. Stiglitz (1978) utilising a general equilibrium framework finds that estate taxes may *increase* inequality. In the general equilibrium framework, estate taxes reduce capital accumulation and increase returns to capital.[4] Assuming that the elasticity of substitution between labour and capital is less than one, it will result in a greater amount of capital income than is ordinarily received by the wealthy in the main. Dynamic general equilibrium models which have been augmented by more assumptions in relation to certain risks largely conclude that repealing estate taxes (or implementing them) will have minor impact on overall wealth distribution (Cagetti & De Nardi, 2006; Castañeda, Diaz-Gimenez, & Rios-Rull, 2003).

Empirically, there is little contemporary work that considers the impact of estate and gift taxes on inheritance flows. Atkinson (2012) finds that the proportion of the UK population liable for estate taxation has fallen considerably today compared to the first half of the twentieth century, which may have significant implications for equity. For the US, Blinder (1976) found that even estate taxes of up to 60% had very little impact on distribution. Similarly, Verbit (1978) finds estate taxes had little impact on the distribution of wealth from 1920 to 1970 in the US.

Net Wealth Taxes

An alternative approach to tax estates is a net wealth tax. In Chap. 3, it was shown that wealth to income ratios have substantially increased across all the advanced economies since the 1960s. According to Joumard, Pisu and Bloch (2012), a wealth on tax even at a modestly low rate could generate significant revenues for the state. Despite the mounting evidence of large increases in wealth to income ratios, national governments have largely ignored this as both a potential source of redistributing wealth or raising revenue. At the time of writing, only France, Norway (up to 0.7% at the municipal and 0.4% at the national level) and Switzerland (varies at the cantonal level) continue to levy a wealth tax. Germany abolished their wealth tax in 1998 as it was ruled unconstitutional. Australia, Canada, Japan, the UK and the US have never imposed an overall net wealth taxation (Price & Dang, 2011).

The French net wealth tax was introduced in 1981 by the Socialist Party. Labelled the solidarity tax on wealth (*Impôt de solidarité sur la fortune*), the tax

[4] This relationship is largely rejected by the empirical data presented by Piketty (2014a) that has shown a high degree of capital or wealth deepening and relative high returns to capital.

was briefly repealed in 1986 but once again reinstated in 1989. The purpose of the scheme was to finance the minimum income scheme aimed at assisting those who could not find work and were not entitled to unemployment benefits. In terms of direct economic effectiveness, the tax is a significant generator of income for the French state. Piketty and Saez (2006) estimate that the solidarity tax pushes the average tax rate in France up to 60%, and approaches the progressive tax regimes observed in the Anglo-Saxon countries in the 1950s and 1960s.

The impact of the solidarity tax on France's wealth distribution is difficult to assess. Much like other taxes, the behavioural response of individuals and households typically does not always accord with the intended purpose of the tax. Amoils and Read (2015) tracked the movements 323,400 French high net worth individuals from 2000 to 2014. During this period, they found that 42,000 high net worth individuals emigrated from France, blunting the overall effectiveness of the state's policy. Further, it was found that the majority of these individuals moved to countries that offered favourable tax treatment, including Luxembourg, Switzerland and the UK.

The ability of the wealthy to either move to more favourable locations due to tax advantages or just shift wealth into jurisdictions with favourable tax treatment is considered in the next section.

Tax Avoidance and Evasion: Emergence of Off-Shore Financial Centres

Amongst the wealthy, a preferred method of minimising the effects of tax is via tax minimisation schemes through off-shore financial centres (OFC). What precisely are off-shore financial centres? The definition of an OFC has undergone substantial revision, particularly over the past two decades. At one end, the term off-shore financial centre is largely just a synonym, or a contemporary spin, for tax haven. Desai, Foley and Hines (2004) define: 'Tax havens are low-tax jurisdictions that provide investors opportunities for tax avoidance' (p. 1). International governmental bodies have typically expanded the boundaries of OFC's roles beyond the strict tax evasion definition. For example, the 1998 OECD report, Harmful Tax Competition, is significantly more expansive than that of Desai et al. (2004). For the OECD (1998, pg. 23), a tax haven is defined as a jurisdiction that imposes or possesses:

1. No or only nominal taxes
2. Lack of effective exchange of information

3. Lack of transparency
4. The absence of a requirement that the activity be substantial

Point (4) was an important inclusion as it recognised that these jurisdictions are typically synonymous with the 'booking device' term, wherein transactions are not related to any real-world activity such as the creation of a shell company.

The term 'tax haven' has subsequently become much more inclusive. Working towards an operational definition of off-shore centres, Zoromé (2007) argued that the surveyed literature typically compromises three core definitional elements if aggregated. According to Zoromé (2007, p. 4):

> Three distinctive recurrent characteristics of OFCs have emerged from these definitions: (i) the primary orientation of business toward nonresidents; (ii) the favourable regulatory environment (low supervisory requirements and minimal information disclosure) and; (iii) the low-or zero-taxation schemes.

Another definition provided by Di Nicola (2006, p. 3), provides a similar meaning:

> An offshore centre is a country which provides to the residents of other countries the opportunity to establish companies and to use its financial services for activities outside this centre, offering in most of the cases some advantages such as low taxation rates. In other words, the aim of the users of the offshore centres is to take advantage of the lower tax rates offered by the offshore centre which is not synonymous to tax evasion as is the general perception.

The importance of an operational definition is essential from three aspects. Firstly, there is, of course, the taxation dimension, and the associated lost taxation revenue due to tax avoidance related to off-shore centres. Secondly, there are substantial anomalies in international payments data of which offshore centres play a significant role. Thirdly, establishing a more inclusive definition of an offshore centre necessarily permits a wider context on how ultra-high net worth individuals can hide their wealth, often in plain sight, in *jurisdictions not necessarily associated with tax havens* in the popular mind.

Exploring the full impact of OFCs wealth accumulation is beyond the scope of this study. Zucman's (2014) study presents numerous estimates as to the wealth hidden in these centres and the tax revenue lost. For the wealthy of the US, at least $1.2bn is estimated to be held in OFCs, or 4% of financial wealth. Although small in relative terms, Zucman estimates that this equates to a $36 bn tax revenue loss. Notable in Zucman's estimates, is the dominance of Europe, with an estimated $2.6 trillion held in OFCs, representing a tax revenue loss of $75 billion. Although the advanced economies hold the most wealth in *absolute* terms, developing regions maintain the highest proportions of their respective wealth in these centres. Both Russia ($200 bn) and the Gulf countries ($800 bn) maintain up to and over 50% of their financial wealth in OFCs. Wealthy individuals in Latin America and Africa also hold a large proportion of their wealth in these centres.

Estimates of the amount of wealth held in off-shore financial centres or tax havens vary substantially depending upon the methodology employed. Zucman (2014) derives the $7.5 trillion estimate via the presence of anomalies in the national accounts of countries. Henry (2012) furnishes vastly higher estimates, valuing the total wealth held in tax havens between $21 trillion and $32 trillion in financial wealth. More recent estimates by Henry (2016) further present divergent estimates particularly for the developing world. Henry (2016) estimates that flows into OFCs from the developing world total approximately $12.1 trillion compared to Zucman's (2014) estimate of $3.5 trillion. The major variations occur concerning Russia (Zucman estimate of USD200 billion, Henry estimate of USD1.3 trillion) and Asia (Zucman estimate of USD1.3 trillion, Henry estimate of USD4.5 trillion).

Previous estimates have tended to align with Zucman (2014). In the same year, the NGO Oxfam (2000) estimated that OFCs held in custody between $6 and $7 trillion in financial wealth. In 2007, the Boston Consulting Group estimated the wealth hidden in tax havens at approximately $7.3 trillion.

Notwithstanding the divergent estimates of wealth in OFCs, the cost to societies and their national governments in the form of lost tax revenue are substantial, even when assuming the conservative estimates of Zucman (2014). Zucman (2014) estimates that being able to tax the top 0.1% of the population's wealth would impact significantly not only on government revenue but reduce global wealth inequality to a material degree. Zucman (2014, p. 53) argues that assuming 'all unrecorded offshore wealth belongs to the top 0.1%, eradicating offshore evasion would thus raise as much revenue as increasing the top 0.1%'s federal income tax bill by close to 18%'.

The revenue loss estimates of Zucman (2014) do make some simplifying assumptions that potentially overestimate the losses from OFCs. The US estimated revenue loss assumes that income tax is paid at the dividend rate of 30% and an estate tax of 40%. Clarke (2016) points out that the effective tax rates paid by the top 1% are below both these estimates, and that, further, the return on capital that Zucman (2014) assumes at 7% is historically high.

International Effectiveness: A Note on the Political Economy of Tax Treaties and Havens

- Thwarting the returns to wealth by reducing the level of tax avoidance and evasion in tax havens has received policy attention on a global and regional scale. At an international level, the core mechanism through which personal capital incomes can be taxed is via the implementation of an information exchange between two countries. The two primary forms of information exchange entail automatic exchanges or direct information requests by a government to another national government. Although the former is viewed as the more effective means of detecting tax evasion or avoidance, it is often the latter that is enshrined in bi- and multi-lateral treaties (Keen & Ligthart, 2006).

The primary international institutional framework for dealing with tax evasion is through the OECD (Hanlon, Maydew, & Thornock, 2015). Beginning with a working group on tax havens in 1998 (OECD, 1998), the OECD issued a report listing 35 jurisdictions as tax havens. According to Hanlon et al. (2015, p. 8):

> By 2002, 31 of the countries had agreed to cooperate with the OECD, though implementation in some cases took much longer. By 2009, there were no countries on the OECD blacklist and only four countries on the grey list… and those were labelled as "other financial centers" rather than tax havens.

The decision by tax havens to cooperate with OECD seemingly has had a positive impact if considered from the viewpoint of the number of treaties signed. Table 4.4 lists the number of double tax treaties (DTCs) and tax

Table 4.4 TIEAs/DTCs signed between G20 summits

Summit	Signed treaties
G20 Washington DC Summit (15 Nov, 2008)	44
G20 London Summit (2 Apr, 2009)	65
G20 Pittsburgh Summit (25 Sep, 2009)	229
31 Dec, 2009	364
G20 Toronto Summit (26 Jun, 2010)	524
G20 Seoul Summit (12 Nov, 2010)	606
13 Oct, 2011	725

Source: *OECD*, http://www.oecd.org

information exchange agreements (TIEA) since 2008. The turning point was the G20 London Summit where states proposed a four-tier system of blacklisted havens. Since then the number of treaties has increased from 65 to 725 by October 2011. Although the growth is on the surface impressive, it potentially masks two problems. Firstly, a proportion of the treaties would be DTCs. Double tax treaties have been criticised as being ineffective in the instance of tax havens as they permit a requested party to remain concealed behind bank secrecy. Sheppard (2009) argues that this is particularly present in the treaties signed by Luxembourg and Switzerland. The provision to permit bank secrecy and confidentiality effectively provides a mechanism for Switzerland and Luxembourg to rebuke requests for information on the basis of the secrecy clauses. Secondly, the use of direct tax agreement between a country and a tax haven country may not be appropriate as the latter may have very low or no taxes on income or profits to begin with.

By contrast, TIEAs are meant to provide a more effective legal mechanism of reducing tax evasion. Tax information exchange agreements are far less broad in scope than DTCs as they are specifically designed to focus on information exchange. The effectiveness of TIEAs can be considered both from a legal efficacy perspective and from an economic perspective where the portfolio responses of individuals can be observed.

Legally, numerous problems have been identified with the efficacy of TIEAs in their current form. Firstly, a tax haven may not possess the information in a form to be useful to tax authorities (Sullivan, 2009). Often this may be due to the tax haven not requiring clear identification when individuals set up accounts or shell companies. For example, the British Virgin Islands do not require any identification of shareholders or directors despite being home to thousands of registered corporations. Therefore, a request for information may not give rise to any genuinely useful information. Secondly, tax information exchanges only take place on a request basis (Sullivan, 2009). For tax authorities, this presents two significant impediments to prosecuting cases of tax evasion. First, requests for information require significant effort on the part of tax authorities involving the use of detailed evidence and case arguments. Assuming such an application is made, the matter would likely be tied up in courts for years—beyond that provided by the statute of limitations in each jurisdiction (Sheppard, 2009). The onus upon tax authorities is such that use of TIEAs is low. In the US, only 894 information requests were made between 2006 and 2010. Contrast this with the estimated 19,000 US residents who maintained bank accounts at a *single* Swiss bank.

The empirical evidence on the economic efficacy of tax treaties is small, and that which does exist is mixed as to their efficacy. A recent study by Hanlon et al. (2015) investigate a form of tax evasion termed 'round-tripping' where individuals conceal funds in offshore tax havens and plough those funds back into the US securities markets. Specifically, they test whether foreign portfolio investment into the US from tax havens decreases with information exchange initiatives covering the period 1984–2008. Hanlon et al. (2015) report that their regression model estimates show reduced inbound foreign portfolio investment from tax haven countries after the OECDs initiatives to combat tax evasion since 1998. However, a potential issue of the Hanlon et al. (2015) analysis is that it does not model for the possibility that the decrease in inbound foreign investment via tax havens is compensated by an increase in investment flows from other havens that have not signed a treaty with the US.

The analysis of geographical portfolio shifting between tax havens largely reveals that the effectiveness of tax treaties is mostly rendered ineffective due to the bilateral nature of said treaties. Gorea (2015) specifically explores this possibility for US investors for the period 2002 to 2013, a period that saw greater tax treaty formulation activity than the period covered by Hanlon et al. (2015). Two findings of significance emerge from Gorea's (2015) study. Firstly, no statistically significant evidence is found that the amount of debt and equity held by a tax haven is reduced by the signing or implementation of a tax treaty between the US and a tax haven. Secondly, and most importantly, the signing and/or implementation of a treaty is found to have a statistically significant impact on the flow of equity and debt funds into havens that have not signed a bilateral treaty with the US.

Alternative investments in the form of bank deposits also represent an important aspect of offshore tax haven services. The evidence on the response of bank deposit flows to tax treaties is limited but mainly signals the problems inherent in bilateral tax treaty arrangements. A recent investigation by Johannesen and Zucman (2014) analysed the response of bank deposit flows in a panel setting, covering 52 tax havens and 220 potential country partners for the period 2004–2011. In line with the findings of Gorea (2015), Johannesen and Zucman (2014) find that in response to the establishment of a tax treaty, deposits invariably flow to the least compliant tax havens. Hence, although there have been shifts in the allocation of deposits, global levels of deposits held in off-shore accounts have largely remained stable.

While the TIEAs represent a multilateral approach (in so far as it is designed by the OECD), unilateral attempts have been made at increasing tax compliance. These have largely emanated from the EU in the form of the EU Savings Directive and from the US in the shape of the *Foreign Account Tax Compliance Act* (FATCA). The EU Savings Directive was introduced in 2005 and provided that Swiss banks withhold tax on interest income on the accounts of EU residents. As an incentive to EU resident savers, '[s]avers can escape the withholding tax if they voluntarily declare their income to their home country tax authority' (Johannesen & Zucman, 2014, p. 87). Although the EU directive has not provided a major increase in revenues, Johannesen and Zucman (2014) do attribute it improving tax compliance modestly. A major factor of differentiation between the EU Saving Directive and TIEAs was that the former incorporate elements of automatic information exchange.

Summary

The purpose of this chapter was to place the accumulation and distribution of wealth in the context of broader socioeconomic mechanisms.

The chapter adopts the overall framework of Saez and Zucman (2014) who decompose wealth accumulation per an accounting identity. The disparity in wealth accumulation was explored in the context of the great consumerist and financialisation forces that have had an impact on households. The degree of consumption has increased since the 1960s across most countries. However, the propensity to consume *decreases* with household wealth in both the US and Europe. In Australia, too, the extent of consumption as a proportion of wealth diminishes with wealth percentiles, and the highest wealth percentile exhibits the lowest relative consumption to wealth.

It was found that capital income is increasingly becoming an important source of wealth accumulation relative to labour income for the wealthiest households. Conversely, the poorest households are increasingly assuming greater debt levels, as demonstrated by the Australian, UK and US data, to sustain consumption levels.

In addition, for countries that data is available, capital income was found to constitute an increasing share of income for the wealthiest households. The exception to this observation is Canada where labour income dominates even at the highest income percentile.

The reduction in the level of taxation was also advanced as a contributory factor to the process of wealth accumulation. Since the 1980s, the level of top marginal tax rates has systematically declined across most advanced countries. Pre-tax income shares have also increased, in line with less rigorous oversight from tax authorities. Further, tax base shifting potentially has had an impact on wealth accumulation with the wealthy shifting their main sources of income between capital and labour whenever it is advantageous to do so. Calls to mitigate the impact of tax evasion were considered. The considerable amounts of wealth held in off-shore financial centres make it an important aspect of taxation policy. However, the political will to deal with these issues may mitigate the effectiveness given the adoption of bilateral framework.

References

Alvaredo, F., Atkinson, A. B., Piketty, T., & Saez, E. (2013). The top 1 percent in international and historical perspective. *Journal of Economic Perspectives, 27*(3), 3–20.

Amoils, A., & Read, N. (2015). *Second citizenship & the migration of HNWIs 2000–2014*. New World Wealth. Retrieved from http://nebula.wsimg.com/

Atkinson, A. B. (2012). *Wealth and inheritance in Britain from 1896 to the present*. Retrieved from http://piketty.pse.ens.fr/files/Atkinson2012.pdf

Atkinson, A. B., & Leigh, A. (2013). The distribution of top incomes in five Anglo-Saxon countries over the long run. *Economic Record, 89*, 31–47.

Atkinson, A. B., & Salverda, W. (2005). Top incomes in the Netherlands and the United Kingdom over the 20th century. *Journal of the European Economic Association, 3*(4), 883–913.

Australian Bureau of Statistics. (2014). *Australian National Accounts: Distribution of Household Income, Consumption and Wealth, 2003–04 to 2011–12*. Retrieved 20 February, 2015, from http://www.abs.gov.au/

Bauman, Z. (2007). *Work, consumerism and the new poor*. Maidenhead, UK: Open University Press.

Bertrand, M., & Morse, A. (2013). Trickle-down consumption (NBER Working Paper No. 18883). Retrieved from National Bureau of Economic Research website https://www.nber.org/papers/w18883.pdf

Bertrand, M., & Mullainathan, S. (2001). Are CEOs reward for luck? The ones without principals are. *The Quarterly Journal of Economics, 116*, 901–932.

Bird, R. M. (1978). Canada's vanishing death taxes. *Osgoode Hall Law Journal, 16*(1), 133–145.

Blinder, A. S. (1976). Intergenerational transfers and life cycle consumption. *American Economic Association, 66*, 87–93.

Bronars, S. (2013). How Margaret Thatcher Tuned Great Britain's Labor Markets Around. *Forbes*. Retrieved from http://www.forbes.com/

Cagetti, M., & De Nardi, M. (2006). Entrepreneurship, frictions, and wealth. *Journal of Political Economy, 114*, 835–870.

Carroll, C. D., Slacalek, J., & Tokuoka, K. (2014). *The distribution of wealth and the marginal propensity to consume* (No. 1655). European Central Bank Working Paper Series. Retrieved from https://www.ecb.europa.eu/

Castañeda, A., Diaz-Gimenez, J., & Rios-Rull, J. (2003). Accounting for the U.S. earnings and wealth inequality. *Journal of Political Economy, 111*, 818–857.

Clarke, C. (2016). What are tax havens and why are they bad? *Texas Law Review, 95*(1), 59–79.

Cynamon, B. Z., & Fazzari, M. (2013). *Inequality and household finance during the consumer age* (No. 752). Levy Economics Institute Economics Working Paper Archive. Retrieved from http://www.levyinstitute.org/

Dabla-Norris, E., Kochhar, K., Suphaphiphat, N., Ricka, F., & Tsounta, E. (2015). *Causes and consequences of income inequality: A global perspective* (No. 15/13). IMF Staff Discussion Notes. Retrieved from https://www.imf.org/

Daumard, A. (1980). Wealth and affluence in France since the beginning of the nineteenth century. In W. D. Rubinstein (Ed.), *Wealth and the wealthy in the modern world* (pp. 90–121). London: Croom Helm.

DeLong, J. B. (1998). *Robber barons*. Retrieved from http://www.uni-muenster.de/PeaCon/dgs-mills/mills-texte/RobberBarons.htm

Desai, M. A., Foley, F. C., & Hines, J. R. (2004). Economic effects of regional tax havens (NBER Working Paper No. 10806). Retrieved from National Bureau of Economic Research website https://www.nber.org/papers/w10806.pdf

Di Nicola, A. (2006). Offshore financial centres and corruption: A toolkit for KNAB investigators. *Transcrime*. Retrieved from http://www.knab.gov.lv/

Dilnot, A., Kell, M., & Webb, S. (1988). The 1988 Budget and the structure of personal taxation. *Fiscal Studies, 9*, 38–47.

Dynan, K. E., Skinner, J., & Zeldes, S. P. (2004). Do the rich save more? *Journal of Political Economy, 112*, 397–444.

Epstein, G. (2002). *Financialization, rentier interests, and central bank policy*. Paper presented at the PERI conference on Financialization of the World Economy, University of Massachusetts, Amherst. Retrieved from http://www.peri.umass.edu/fileadmin/pdf/financial/fin_Epstein.pdf

Evans, L. (2016). *And justice for all … even teamsters*. Morrisville, NC: Lulu Publishing.

Ewen, S. (1976). *Captains of consciousness: Advertising and the social roots of the consumer culture*. New York: McGraw Hill.

Fesseau, M., & Mattonetti, M. L. (2013). *Distributional measures across household groups in a national accounts framework* (No. 2013/04). OECD Statistics Working Papers..

Fligstein, N. (1990). *The transformation of corporate control*. Cambridge, MA: Harvard University Press.

Fligstein, N., & Goldstein, A. (2015). The emergence of a finance culture in American households. *Socio-Economic Review, 3*, 575–601.

Galbraith, J. K. (1958). *The affluent society*. New York: Houghton Mifflin Company.

Gentry, W. M., & Hubbard, R. G. (2004). Entrepreneurship and household saving. *Advances in Economic Analysis & Policy, 4*(1), 1–55.

Goldin, C., & Margo, R. A. (1992). The great compression: The wage structure in the United States at mid-century. *The Quarterly Journal of Economics, 107*, 1–34.

Gordon, R., & Slemrod, J. (2000). Are 'Real' Responses to Taxes Simply Income Shifting between Corporate and Personal Tax Bases?. In J. Slemrod (Ed.), *Does Atlas Shrug: The Economic Consequences of Taxing the Rich* (pp. 240–279). New York: Russell Sage Foundation.

Gorea, D. (2015). *Catch me if you can: U.S. Tax Treaties and Shifts in Offshore Investments.* Working Paper, European University Institute.

Gottfried, P., & Schellhorn, H. (2004). *Empirical evidence on the effects of marginal tax rates on income – The German case* (No. 15). IAW Discussion Papers Institut für Angewandte Wirschaftsforschung.

Hanlon, M., Maydew, E. L., & Thornock, J. R. (2015). Taking the long way home: U.S. tax evasion and offshore investments in U.S. equity and debt markets. *Journal of Finance, 70*, 257–287.

Henry, J. S. (2012). The price of offshore revisited. *Tax Justice Network.* Retrieved from http://www.taxjustice.net/

Henry, J. S. (2016). More than $12 trillion stuffed offshore, from developing countries alone. *Tax Justice Network.* Retrieved from http://www.taxjustice.net/

Hurst, E., & Lusardi, A. (2004). Liquidity constraints, household wealth, and entrepreneurship. *Journal of Political Economy, 112*, 319–347.

Jaumotte, F., & Buitron, C. O. (2015). Inequality and Labor Market Institutions. *IMF Staff Discussion Note*, SDN/15/14.

Johannesen, N., & Zucman, G. (2014). The end of bank secrecy? An evaluation of the G20 tax haven crackdown. *American Economic Journal, 6*, 65–91.

Joumard, I., Pisu, M., & Bloch, D. (2012). Tackling income inequality: The role of taxes and transfers. *OECD Journal: Economic Studies.* Published online first. https://doi.org/10.1787/eco_studies-2012-5k95xd6l65lt

Kakwani, N. C. (1977). Measurement of tax progressivity: An international comparison. *The Economic Journal, 87*, 71–80.

Kaldor, N. (1960). *Essays on value and distribution.* Glencoe, UK: Free Press.

Keen, M., & Ligthart, J. E. (2006). Information sharing and international taxation: A primer. *International Tax and Public Finance, 13*(1), 81–110.

Kopczuk, W. (2013). Taxation of intergenerational transfer and wealth. In A. J. Auerbach, R. Cherry, M. Feldstein, & E. Saez (Eds.), *Handbook of public economics, volume 5*. Amsterdam: Elsevier.

Krippner, G. R. (2005). The financialization of the American economy. *Socio-Economic Review, 3*, 173–208.

Krugman, P. (2014. May 8). Why we're in a new Gilded Age. *The New Review of Books.* Retrieved from http://www.nybooks.com/articles/2014/05/08/thomas-piketty-new-gilded-age/

Landais, C. (2007). *Les hauts revenus en France (1998–2006): Une explosion de inégalités?.* Working Paper, Paris School of Economics.

Lane, R. E. (1962). *Political ideology: Why the American common man believes what he does.* New York: The Free Press.

Leigh, A. (2005). Deriving long-run inequality series from tax data. *The Economic Record, 81*, S58–S70.

Leigh, A. (2009). Top incomes. In W. Salverda, B. Nolvan, & T. M. Smeeding (Eds.), *The Oxford handbook of economic inequality*. Oxford, UK: Oxford University Press.

Luxembourg Income Study. (n.d.). *LIS Web Tabulator*. Retrieved on 10 June, 2015, from http://www.lisdatacenter.org/

Meade, J. E. (1964). *Efficiency, equality, and the ownership of property*. London: George Allen & Unwin.

Meade, J. E. (1975). *The just economy*. London: George Allen & Unwin.

Morelli, S., Smeeding, T., & Thompson, J. (2014). *Post-1970 trends within-country and poverty: Rich and middle income countries* (No. 356). CSED Working Papers, Centre for Studies in Economics and Finance, University of Naples, Italy.

Moriguchi, C., & Saez, E. (2008). The evolution of income concentration in Japan, 1886–2005: Evidence from income statistics. *The Review of Economics and Statistics, 90*, 713–734.

OECD. (1998). *Harmful tax competition: An emerging global issue*. Retrieved from http://www.oecd.org/tax/transparency/44430243.pdf

Office for National Statistics. (2015). *Results from the OECD exercise on the Distribution of Household Income, Consumption and Savings*. Retrieved on 1 December, 2015, from https://www.ons.gov.uk/economy/nationalaccounts/uksectoraccounts/datasets/resultsfromtheoecdexerciseonthedistributionofhouseholdincome consumptionandsavings

Pasinetti, L. (1962). Rate of profit and income distribution in relation to the rate of economic growth. *Review of Economic Studies, 29*, 267–279.

Pedrick, W. H. (1982). Oh, to die down under!: Abolition of death and gift duties in Australia. *Western Australian Law Review, 14*, 438–468.

Piketty, T. (1998). Les hauts revenus face aux modifications des taux marginaux supérieurs de l'impôt sur le revenu en france, 1970–1996. *Economie et prévision, 138–139*, 25–60.

Piketty, T. (2014a). *Capital in the twenty-first century*. Cambridge, MA: The Belknap Press of Harvard University Press.

Piketty, T. (2014b). Capital in the twenty-first century: A multidimensional approach to the history of capital and social classes. *The British Journal of Sociology, 65*, 736–747.

Piketty, T., & Saez, E. (2006). The evolution of top incomes: A historical and international perspective. *American Economic Review, 96*, 200–205.

Piketty, T., & Saez, E. (2014). Inequality in the long run. *Science, 344*, 838–843.

Piketty, T., Saez, E., & Stantcheva, S. (2014). Optimal taxation of top labor incomes: A tale of three elasticities. *American Economic Journal: Economic Policy, 6*, 230–271.

Piketty, T., Saez, E., & Zucman, G. (2013). *Rethinking capital and wealth taxation*. Working Paper. Retrieved from http://piketty.pse.ens.fr/files/PikettySaez Zucman2013RKT.pdf

Piketty, T., & Zucman, G. (2014). *Appendix of Capital is back: Wealth-income ratios in rich countries 1700–2010*. Retrieved on 10 June, 2015, from http://gabriel-zucman.eu/files/PikettyZucman2013Data.zip

Plagge, A., Scheve, K., & Stasavage, D. (2010). *Comparative inheritance taxation database*. ISPS Data Archive, http://hdl.handle.net/10079/dz08kx8

Pressman, S. (2015). *Understanding Piketty's capital in the twenty-first century*. London: Routledge.

Price, R. W., & Dang, T. (2011). *Adjusting fiscal balances for asset price cycles* (No. 868). OECD Economics Department Working Papers, OECD Publishing. https://doi.org/10.1787/5kgc42t3zqkl-en

Quadrini, V. (1999). The importance of entrepreneurship for wealth concentration and mobility. *Review of Income and Wealth, 45*, 1–19.

Quadrini, V. (2000). Entrepreneurship, saving and social mobility. *Review of Economic Dynamics, 3*, 1–40.

Reserve Bank of Australia. (2012). *Household Debt – Distribution – E7*. Retrieved on 20 February, 2015, from http://www.rba.gov.au/

Reynolds, A. (2007). *Has U.S. income inequality really increased?* (No. 586). Cato Institute Policy Analysis Series.

Reynolds, M., & Smolensky, E. (1977). *Public expenditures, taxes, and the distribution of income: The United States, 1950, 1961, 1970*. New York: Academic Press.

Roach, B. (2003). *Progressive and regressive taxation in the United States: Who's really paying (and not paying) their fair share?* (No. 03-10). Global Development and Environment Institute Working Paper.

Roine, J., Vlachos, J., & Waldenström, D. (2008). *The long-run determinants of inequality: What can we learn from top income data?*. Working Paper, Stockholm University.

Roine, J., & Walenström, D. (2008). The evolution of top incomes in an egalitarian society: Sweden, 1903–2004. *Journal of Public Economics, 92*, 366–387.

Saez, E. (2006). Income and wealth concentration in a historical and international perspective. In A. J. Auerbach, D. Card, & J. M. Quigley (Eds.), *Public policy and the income distribution*. New York: Russell Sage Foundation.

Saez, E., & Veall, M. R. (2005). The evolution of high incomes in Northern America: Lessons from Canadian evidence. *American Economic Review, 95*, 831–849.

Saez, E., & Zucman, G. (2014). *Wealth inequality in the United States Since 1913: Evidence from capitalized income tax data* (NBER Working Paper No. 20625). Retrieved from National Bureau of Economic Research website http://www.nber.org/papers/w20625

Sheppard, L. (2009). Don't ask, don't tell, part 4: Ineffectual information sharing. *Tax Notes*, 1411–1418.

Slemrod, J. (2000). The economics of taxing the rich. In J. Slemrod (Ed.), *Does atlas shrug? The economic consequences of taxing the rich* (pp. 2–28). Cambridge, MA: Harvard University Press.

Solow, R. M. (2014, April 22). Piketty is right. *New Republic*. Retrieved from http://www.newrepublic.com/

Stiglitz, J. E. (1978). Notes on estate taxes, redistribution, and the concept of balanced growth path incidence. *Journal of Political Economy, 86*, S137–S150.

Stilwell, F., & Jordan, K. (2007). *Who gets what?: Analysing economic inequality in Australia*. Cambridge, UK: Cambridge University Press.

Stockhammer, E., & Wildauer, R. (2015). *Debt-driven growth? Wealth, distribution and demand in OECD countries* (No. 1503). Post Keynesian Economics Study Group.

Sullivan, M. A. (2009). Proposals to fight offshore tax evasion. *Tax Notes*, 264–268.

Thurow, L. (1975). *Generating inequality*. New York: Basic Books, Inc..

Tinbergen, J. (1975). Substitution of academically trained by other manpower. *Review of World Economics, 111*, 466–479.

Trumbull, G. (2012). Credit access and social welfare: The rise of consumer lending in the United States and France. *Politics and Society, 40*, 9–34.

Tsigos, S., & Daly, K. (2016). "Fair go" for all? Wealth and risk aversion of Australian households. *Australian Economic Papers, 55*, 274–300.

Tuckman, E. (1973). *The economics of the rich*. New York: Random House.

Veall, M. R. (2012). Top income shares in Canada: Recent trends and policy implications. *Canadian Journal of Economics, 45*, 1247–1272.

Verbit, G. P. (1978). Do estate and gift taxes affect wealth distribution? *Trusts & Estates, 117*, 598–616.

Zoromé, A. (2007). *Concept of offshore financial centers: In search of an operational definition* (WP/07/87). IMF Working Paper.

Zucman, G. (2014). *The hidden wealth of nations: The scourge of tax havens*. Chicago: The University of Chicago Press.

5

Sources of Great Fortunes in the World

The objective of this chapter is to focus upon high net-wealth individuals and their associated sources of wealth. To this end, the chapter:

- Assumes a cross-regional comparison—to better analyse and identify the sources of great fortunes today.
- Explore the historical economic, political and social conditions when many of the fortunes were first made on a region-by-region basis.
- Investigate the role of self-made and inherited wealth and how representative they are across sections of the globe.
- How inherited wealth is transferred and managed by subsequent generations.
- Where appropriate, the links between great fortunes and government policy, particularly in sustaining inherited fortunes.

Introduction

This chapter analyses two aspects of wealth accumulation via a cross-regional comparison. Firstly, it explores the industrial activities that have enabled individuals and family dynasties to amass great fortunes and places this process firmly in its social, economic and/or political context. Secondly, it examines the extent to which individuals made their fortunes through their own entrepreneurial effort as opposed to inheritance, focusing on why inheritance levels among the ultra-rich should differ between advanced economies and, where relevant, how that wealth is sustained across generations.

S. Tsigos, K. Daly, *The Wealth of the Elite*, https://doi.org/10.1007/978-981-15-2148-5_5

Much like the Gilded Age, entrepreneurship appears to have played the dominant role in the process of massive wealth accumulation observed today. Although the US continues to lead the world in producing large fortunes, the phenomenon appears to have been replicated across the globe, as first observed in Chap. 3. However, given the disparate paths in historical and institutional developments across the globe, there may be substantial differentiation in not only the patterns of entrepreneurial development, but also how societies accept the emergence of a patrimonial capitalism.

The term 'patrimonial capitalism' or patrimonialism is a concept characterised by notions of inheritance, state paternalism and a concentration of wealth. The degree to which one of these characteristics dominates is contingent upon whether the approach is based on an economic or sociological analysis. Piketty's (2014a) use of the term appears to be largely centred on the notion that the economic elite's fortunes are mainly derived through inheritance rather than entrepreneurship. Piketty (2014a) argues that the concentration of wealth savings behaviour alone cannot explain the concentration of wealth, but must be combined with evidence on the importance of inherited wealth.

This chapter in scope is most closely aligned to Kaplan and Rauh (2013) who use a similar database (US Forbes 400). Their explanation for the rise of great fortunes in modern society is ensconced in theories of human capital and the return to skills as exemplified by the information technology entrepreneur. However, this book strives to firmly place the sources of great fortunes, and to quote Watkins (1907), '[to] changes in external conditions' (p. 5). It argues that the sources of great fortunes are just as much due to the existence of fortuitous historical and political circumstances from which traditional notions of randomness can then come to the fore. As the countries examined have high levels of human capital, if Kaplan and Rauh's (2013) thesis were correct, a wealthy elite in highly technical industries would be expected to emerge in other countries where these skills exist to a similar degree. By restricting their analysis to skills scalability and human capital for example, Kaplan and Rauh (2013) ignore the role of both family and state patrimony in the growth of great fortunes. Further, they do not consider the type of risks assumed under which initial self-made fortunes were made, and what sort of investments are subsequently made in states of inheritance.

To explore the first objective, the key trends and defining patterns of growth among the most prominently represented industries across the relevant regions are considered in order to (1) systematically identify patterns of variation in the industrial sources of wealth; (2) the era when the first big opportunities arose; and (3) the general political, social and macro conditions that ensured significant payoffs. Differentiating self-made from inherited wealth at an intra-industry level is important for a number of reasons. Firstly, the preponderance of inheritance in each industry may signal significant barriers to new entrants into an industry. As argued by Figueroa (2008) and Bodley (1999), the existence of an economic elite erects barriers to entry (see Chap. 2). In addition, Shorrocks (1988) argues that such barriers may exist because of the unique risks ensconced in certain projects are more optimally performed (from an atomistic not socially optimal perspective) at different wealth levels. Secondly, the dominance of patrimony may, ceteris paribus, result in lower economic growth (Piketty, 2014a).

Finally, it will be argued that how wealth is sustained, particularly in family dynasties, may be intimately bound up in a movement towards a more rentier-based wealth class than one derived from purely entrepreneurial effort. The following questions are also asked: why should inheritance come to dominate a given country's wealth ranks? And how is it possible that family dynasties are able to secure and often expand the scope of their influence and control across an industry or industries?

As detailed in Chap. 3, rates of return across the advanced economies have demonstrated a secular downward trend since the 1960s, while the wealth accumulated has significantly increased. Although the decrease has been far from uniform across the advanced economies of the world, it does signal that entrepreneurial effort may have been higher during the 1950s to 1970s. Piketty (2014a), it will be recalled, argues that periods of high entrepreneurial effort are usually synonymous with higher rates of return and high national income growth. A natural question then to consider is how do entrepreneurs or those who inherited wealth respond? Watkins (1907) argued that it is during periods of high returns that entrepreneurs emerge. Conversely, when confronted with low returns, the degree of entrepreneurial application will diminish to the extent that they can easily increase their fortunes through speculative ventures beyond their expertise. The means through which this is achievable is not clearly outlined but Watkins (1907) offers various possibilities, chiefly speculation brought upon by the emergence of abstract financial property. Alternatively, in contemporary times, diversification (be it through mergers or acquisitions or greater asset allocation diversity) may provide such means through which already wealthy entrepreneurs shift from entrepreneurial activity to a rentier-style existence. For family dynasties, it is posited that this tendency is just as pronounced. This theme can be further motivated in the theoretical framework of Shorrocks (1988) discussed in Chap. 2.

Lastly, the relationship between government and the ultra-rich is an area lacking in the literature (Medeiros & de Souza, 2014). The relation is multifaceted and need not necessarily be due to direct subsidisation of capitalist interests, and will manifest itself substantially different depending upon the historical trajectory of a country's political and economic landscape. This chapter makes a modest attempt at exploring the relation between state and capitalist interest in various historical guises.

This chapter offers policy implications, as it demonstrates that many of the great technological and welfare enhancing activities enacted by entrepreneurs, upon which today's great fortunes were built, were not blunted by more onerous tax regimes or high labour wages throughout the 1950s, 1960s or 1970s. Indeed, Solow (2014) argues that the 'rich-get-richer' dynamic of Piketty's (2014a) thesis does not necessarily work 'through individual incentives to innovate' (para. 22). Hence, policy that seeks to blunt wealth accumulation should not necessarily be inhibited by arguments relying on notions of stifling innovation or unfairly reducing returns to human capital.

This chapter is divided along regional and country dimensions to facilitate the organisation of a large amount of data under consideration. The first section explores the billionaire factory of North America. Despite the rise of East Asia and reassertion of Western Europe as an economically powerful bloc, North America still remains the primary driver of the extraordinary growth of billionaires in the past 30 years. The second section shifts to Western Europe, focusing on Germany, France and the UK. The third investigates the rise of great fortunes in the new economic powerhouses of India, China and Russia. East Asia, specifically Japan and South Korea, is the focus of the fourth section. These two countries, despite sharing similar cultural and historical underpinnings, have exhibited dramatic and divergent evolutionary paths in the rise of their respective billionaires. The fifth section examines Australia and New Zealand, which, despite their relatively small population bases, have exhibited a sizable growth in vast fortunes in the past decade.

North America: Billionaires' Factory

In our era, how did the US once again manage to emerge at the forefront of producing individuals who can accumulate extreme wealth? The detailed regional exploration of billionaires begins with North America, which here includes the US, Canada and Mexico. The bulk of the billionaires do come from the US, although there are notable examples from both Canada and Mexico. For example, Mexican Carlos Slim often vies for the richest individual in the world with Bill Gates and Warren Buffett. Watkins (1907) and Rubinstein (1980) both recognised that during the Gilded Age, the US led

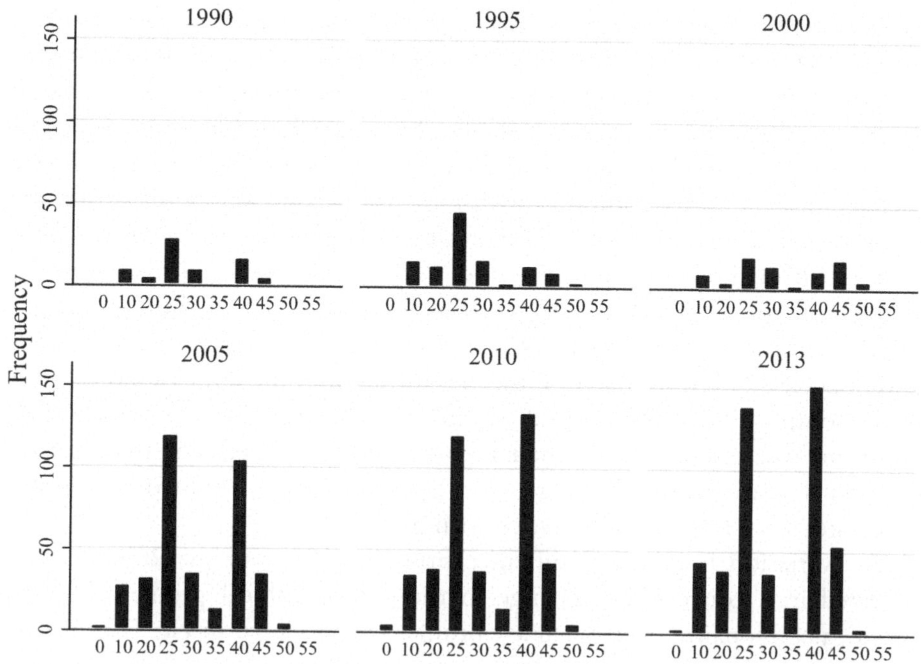

Fig. 5.1 Distribution of North American billionaires by GICS industry group. *Notes*: The chart provides a visual summary of the distribution of individuals across North American industries using the two-code GICS. The data is presented on a 5-year interval basis. The numbers for associated sectors are: **10:** Energy, **15:** Materials, **20:** Industrials, **25:** Consumer Discretionary, **30:** Consumer Staples, **35:** Health care, **40:** Financials, **45:** Information Technology, **50:** Telecommunications, **55:** Utilities. (*Source*: Forbes (1990–2013), authors' compilation from various secondary sources)

the world not only in terms of the size of fortunes, but also in the number of ultra-rich. In contemporary times, how did the average North American billionaire establish their fortune? Figure 5.1 presents the distribution of North American billionaires by industrial group.

The first salient detail that should be noted in Fig. 5.1 is that no industry has shown a general retreat overall, with at most ephemeral reversals during the outbreak of crises. Across every industry, there is a demonstrable increase in the population of billionaires. This increase is particularly evident between 2000 and 2005 with certain sectors registering a three-fold increase. Contrary to popular perception, these increases are not necessarily tied to 'new economy' industries *only*. For example, consumer discretionary increased by almost 380% from 29 billionaires in 1990 to 139 in 2013, exhibiting one of the slowest growth rates at 8.7% per annum. Finance, which includes banking, diversified financials, insurance and property, has demonstrated even greater growth, increasing from 17 in 1990 to 151 by 2013, the equivalent of a 790%

increase in their population ranks and a 13% per annum growth rate. In 2013, financial services represent the bulk (31.1%) from where North American great fortunes emanate. IT has, unsurprisingly, demonstrated exceptional growth, albeit from a smaller base. In 1990, there were four billionaires in IT, which increased to 53 in 2013, the equivalent of a 1225% increase or a 12% per annum growth rate. The second key point is that the year-on-year distribution of billionaires across industries has been far from uniform throughout the sample period. Rather, a dramatic shift between the 1990s and the 2000s is observed. According to Fig. 5.1, throughout the 1990s, consumer discretionary (25), industrials (10), consumer staples (30) and financials (40) dominated. However, throughout the 2000s a radical shift in the composition in the sector distribution is observed. Now, materials (15), consumer discretionary (25), financials (40) and IT (45) all tend to dominate the North American billionaire wealth ranks. The combined sub-group accounted for 71.1% of billionaires during 2013.

The variation in sector dominance from the 1990s to the 2000s is also reflected in a concomitant change in the demographical profile of North America's billionaires. The mean age profiles are presented in Fig. 5.2. At first

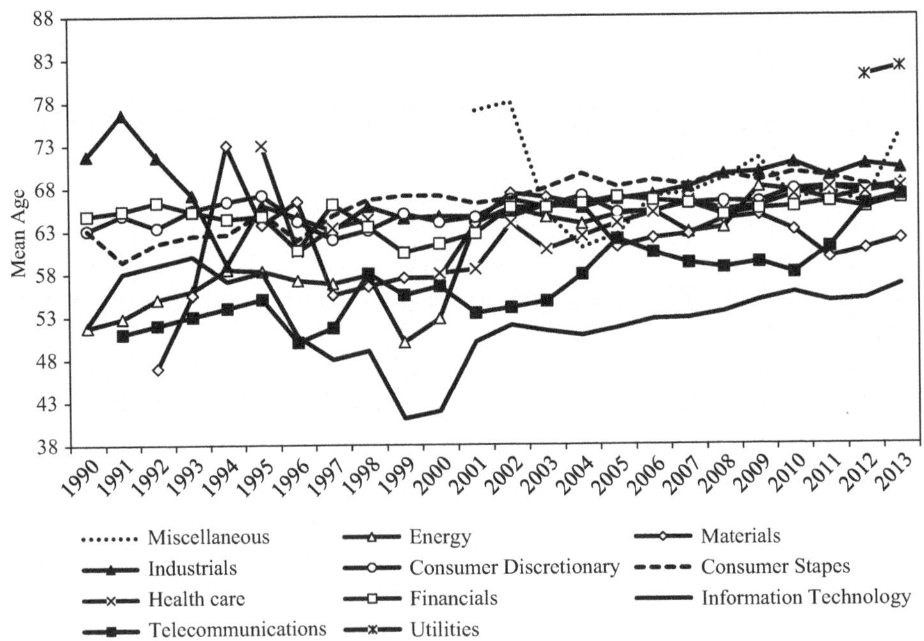

Fig. 5.2 Mean age profile by industry in North America, 1990–2013. (*Source*: Forbes (1990–2013), authors' compilation from various secondary sources)

glance, there is substantial cross-sectional variation in the mean age exhibited by the various industries. The mean age ranges from a low of 50 in IT and services to a high of 82 in utilities. Overall, the mean age is 66, in line with the US study by Canterbery and Nosari (1985), who attribute this finding to a life-cycle dynamic. Across time, all industries demonstrate a general upward trend although there appear to be bouts where much younger individuals enter the billionaire ranks.

The large oscillations to an industry's mean age appears to be clustered in the late 1990s. IT, energy, telecommunications and financials all registered drops in the mean age throughout this period. The substantial drops in IT are particularly revealing. In 1994, the peak mean age was 60, before decreasing to the mid and low 40s between 1996 and 2001. The decrease in the average of age of the IT entrepreneur coincides with an influx of youthful individuals in Internet-related enterprises. However, since 2001 there has been a long steady increase to the mid-50s. Finance, too, registered a drop during this period, although by no means as dramatic. Throughout the sample, the mean age of billionaires in financial services is 65. Between 1999 and 2003 it remained below the long-term trend, due largely to the influx of new rich from the hedge funds industry.

In general, the changes in the mean age distribution across time and industry coincide with the large jumps in the overall trend of billionaire numbers. However, there are some industries that exhibited robust growth in numbers, which is not necessarily due to recent entrepreneurial effort. Consumer discretionary is dominated by the retail and media industries—both of which have experienced a dramatic swelling in their ranks since 2000. Despite the growth in both, deep analysis reveals them to consist of mainly older individuals who have been in enterprise for many years.

The infusion of younger individuals could be driven by inheritances (intergenerational wealth transfers), new industry or growth in mature industries due to substantial technological advancement. In Chap. 3, it was shown that when compared to the rest of the globe, North America exhibited the lowest proportion of inheritances suggesting that one of the latter two is at work. The natural issue arises as to how widespread this trend has been across the North American industrial structure, or whether it is just a few key industries that have induced this trend. Figure 5.3 presents the proportion of inheritances in North America by industrial grouping since 1990. Most industries exhibit decreasing levels of inheritance, with only a few registering stability or slight increases. Of the former, industrials, financials, materials and telecommunications have demonstrated the largest falls. Consumer staples (μ =71%), energy (μ =63%) and materials (μ =62%) have generally exhibited, on average over

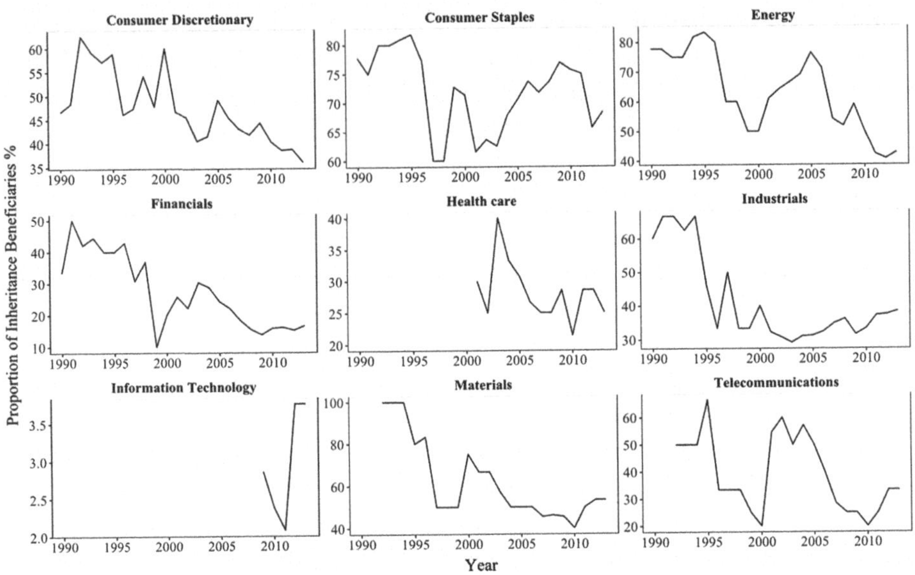

Fig. 5.3 Proportion of inheritances by industry in North America, 1990–2013. (*Source*: Forbes (1990–2013), authors' compilation from various secondary sources)

the sample period, majority patrimony. In contrast, financials (μ =28%), health care (μ =22%) and IT (μ =3%) all exhibit the lowest levels of inheritance.

Of the three largest growth industries, (financials, IT and consumer discretionary), consumer discretionary has generally demonstrated a close to even split between inheritance and self-made individuals (μ =48%). How and why these three industries should demonstrate the most growth in the past two decades and why inheritance proportions can vary between industries are explored in further detail below.

Consumer Discretionary

The realm of the consumer discretionary spending has been a consistent producer of billionaires, albeit at a slower rate relative to other North American industries. Figure 5.4 presents the sample trend since 1990 in each of the consumer discretionary industrial subgroups. Since 1990, the number of billionaires finding a fortune in consumer discretionary spending has grown annually by 12%. The largest representative is media, averaging 40% of the number of billionaires in the consumer discretionary sector throughout the sample period, followed by retail (32%), consumer services (19%), consumer durables and apparel (8%) and automobiles and components (1%).

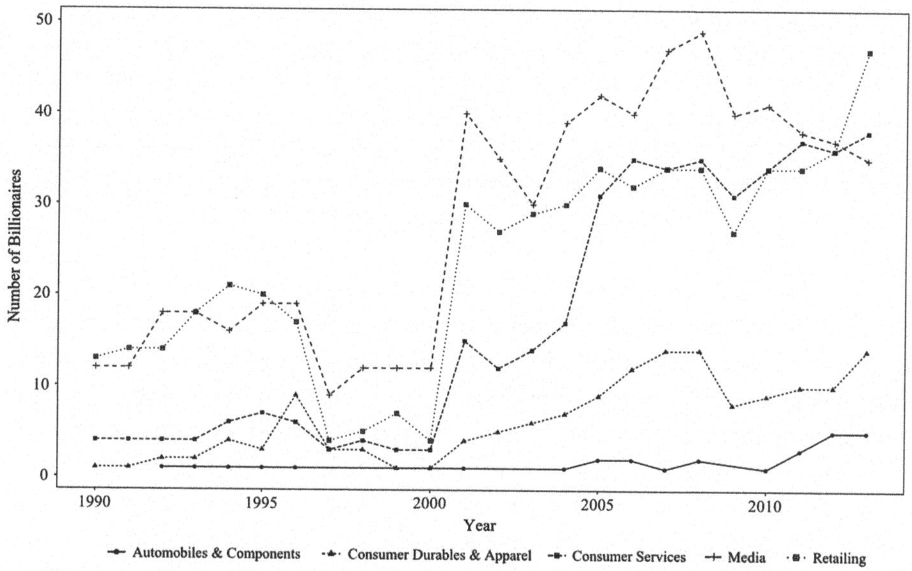

Fig. 5.4 Consumer discretionary sector trends in North America, 1990–2013. (*Source*: Forbes (1990–2013), authors' compilation from various secondary sources)

In total, 35 individuals found their fortune in media as of 2013, having fallen from a high of 49 in 2008. Some portion of the decrease can be explained by death, where the subsequent inheritance was divided up into individual portions falling below the one billion-dollar *Forbes* threshold. Examples include the co-founder of The Weather Channel and head of Landmark Communications, Frank Batten, who died in 2009 (Hevesi, 2011), and John Kluge, who was once rated the wealthiest man in the world in the late 1980s after making his fortune by buying and selling broadcast and cellular properties (Berger, 2010). After Kluge died in 2010, his wealth was shared among his three children, despite some media outlets stating that the fortune had disappeared (Martel, 2014). In 2009, Leonore Annanberg passed away with an estimated net worth of $1.7 billion, and the estate was divided up between numerous beneficiaries (McFadden, 2009).

Overall, however, except for personal risks or death, media appears to have been a robust source of wealth in North America in the recent past. A major reason for this appears to have been a large increase in mergers and acquisitions between various media companies, generating enormous returns to owners. Bagdikian (2000) shows that the process of concentration in media is greater in the past 20 years compared to any prior period:

> In 1983, fifty corporations dominated most of every mass medium and the biggest media merger in history was a $340 million deal .... [I]n 1987, the fifty companies had shrunk to twenty-nine.... [I]n 1990, the twenty-nine had shrunk to twenty three.... [I]n 1997, the biggest firms numbered ten and involved the $19 billion Disney-ABC deal, at the time the biggest media merger ever .... [In 2000] AOL Time Warner's $350 billion merged corporation [was] more than 1,000 times larger [than the biggest deal of 1983]. (pp. xx–xxi)

From 2000, the number of media moguls increased from 8 to 35, suggesting that the scope for wealth creation in media is still there, though it tends to be associated with older individuals who have long been in the media game or those via intra-generational inheritance. Of course, the rise of the Internet must constitute one of the determinants that have caused an immense increase in the number of media moguls, with their content now being able to reach a global audience rather than just the US. Rosen's (1981) argument that advanced technological communications platforms increases returns to scale becomes easily attainable. Given the association between scale and technology the Internet provides an ever-greater pool from which new individuals will make large fortunes. Moreover, the scale attainable suggests that accumulation through mergers and acquisitions is not likely to let up anytime soon with newer content providers and delivery systems vying for both the North American and global markets.

Closely mirroring the growth in media has been the growth in representation of the consumer services. Over 1996–2003, the number of billionaires averaged 15; however, over the 2005–2013 period the mean number of billionaires ballooned to 48. The increase has been dominated by the hospitality sector owing to both demand and supply factors. On the demand side, tourism in the US has undergone a growth, with tourist numbers far outstripping those of Europe and Asia throughout the 2000s (Hobbs & Toscano, 2014). Perhaps signifying still existent arbitrage opportunities, the growth in demand has not witnessed a commensurate rise in the supply of hotel rooms, leading to increased pricing and, therefore, substantially increased revenue for incumbents. Still on the supply side, an added force that may assist in creating greater wealth accumulation in the sector is a substantial increase in the casualisation of the US hospitality workforce. The process towards casual work was evident in 2013, with hoteliers and restaurateurs recruiting a greater proportion of part-timers than full-time employees (Hobbs & Toscano, 2014). Given the relative recent growth in hospitality, the majority of wealth is associated with self-made wealth.

The high incidence of inheritance in the consumer discretionary sector is largely driven by the retail sector. Examining the raw data, the number of retail moguls increased from just 4 in 2000 to 31 in 2001, an increase of 675%. Though it plateaued throughout the 2000s, it peaked at 46 in 2013. Of these, an average 46% inherited their wealth, with the Walton family the most famous and wealthiest. Christy, Jim, Alice and Samuel Walton all had an individual net worth in excess of $20 billion in 2013. Other inheritors litter the list with many demonstrating a propensity to diversifying the business interests through either vertical supply chain purchases or straight-out acquisitions. Charles Butt made billions by diversifying into Latin American neighbourhoods and Mexico after inheriting the family owned H. E. Butt Grocery chain. The Waltons also commandeered an aggressive position over the value chain by often negotiating at below cost for products to appear on the retail giant's shelves. In retail, at least, a winner-takes-all dynamic has arisen, through either mergers or acquisitions.

Of the self-made individuals, the majority built the foundations for their success in the 1950s or 1960s, reflecting the opportunities afforded to entrepreneurs during an era of high growth and commensurate high returns, as discussed in Chap. 3. Bernard Marcus, James Moran and Jean Coutu all successfully exploited the growing consumerism of North American society through the application of innovative retailing strategies. The strategies ensured the attainment of rapid scale across the North American landscape during the golden years of post-war capitalism.

Overall, the billionaire number increases in the consumer discretionary sector seem to be much more aligned with the randomness hypothesis of Thurow (1975) for the self-made entrepreneur. When it comes to inheritances, there is a marked tendency for growing one's wealth through acquisitions or diversification of business holdings.

Financials

Eclipsing the number and growth of billionaires in the consumer discretionary sector is the financial services industry, which is here taken to represent banking, diversified financials (including hedge funds) insurance and property investments. Financial services continue to provide fertile ground for extraordinary riches to be made, despite being the sector at the core of the Great Recession of 2008. A similar dynamic is observed during the Gilded Age when the depression of 1893 did little to dent the accumulation of wealth among the financial and propertied groups (Rockoff, 2012). Referring to

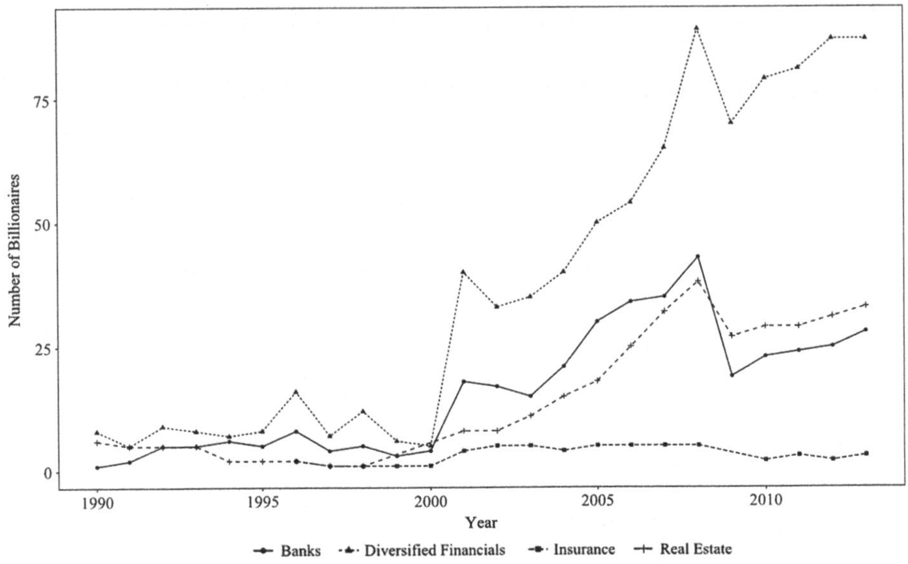

Fig. 5.5 Financials sector decomposition and trends in North America, 1990–2013. (*Source*: Forbes (1990–2013), authors' compilation from various secondary sources)

Fig. 5.5, only diversified financials and property have shown high growth over the entirety of the sample and since the Great Recession. Given that the US has a market-based financial system, it is not surprising to observe that insurance and banking have only small representation on the wealth tables. In 2013, there were 107 billionaires in diversified financials, representing a significant increase from the 84 observed in 2008. Similarly, for real estate, a high of 38 was reached in 2008, before decreasing to 27 in 2009, but then recovering to reach 41 in 2012 and 33 in 2013. The number of billionaires increased from nine in 2000 to 58 in 2001, a dramatic increase of 544%, though the majority was due to diversified financials.

A booming stock market during the late 1990s presents itself as an obvious explanation as to why the financial sector in North America is the dominant industry in producing vast fortunes. However, significant regulatory changes throughout the past 30–40 years present just as compelling an explanation in creating the necessary opportunities for such growth in the finance sector. For example, the Tax Reform Act of 1986 eliminated the attractiveness of real estate tax shelters, causing the real estate boom to go bust in the 1980s. Consequently, individuals such as Andrew Beal purchased distressed real estate loans throughout Texas, securing his meteoric rise in the wealth ranks.

A problem with dealing with the diversified financial community is that it incorporates largely disparate groupings. This study focuses on the two

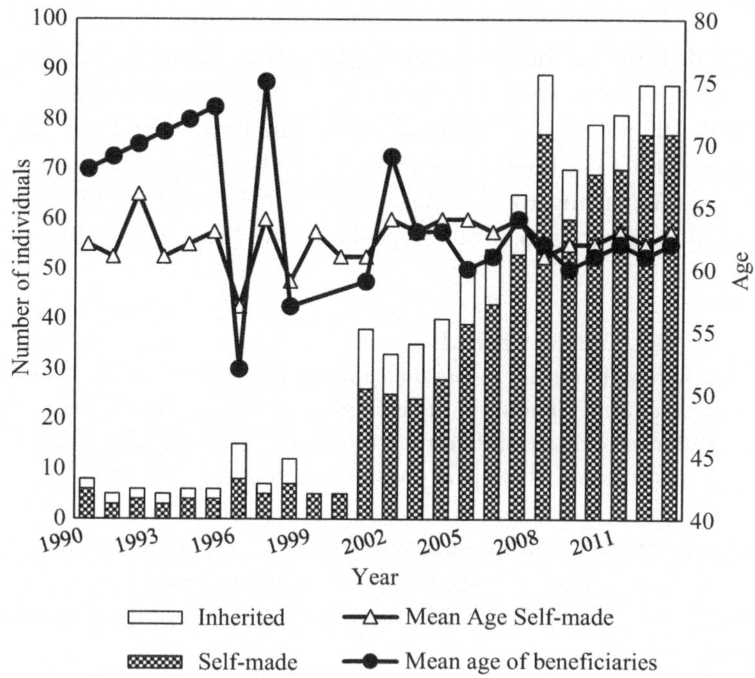

Fig. 5.6 Number and mean age of billionaires in North America: investments. (*Source*: Forbes (1990–2013), authors' compilation from various secondary sources)

sub-sectors that have brought the most growth, investments (incorporating managed fund owners) and hedge fund owners. Figure 5.6 displays both the average age and number of those engaged in the investment sector. Three items are of note. Firstly, as in other sectors of the US economy, the number of individuals who generated their wealth from investing demonstrated a dramatic increase from 2000 to 2001. In 2000, there were 5 billionaires and by 2001 there were 38, representing an increase of 660%. The US stock market downturn of 2002 only had marginal effects on the number of billionaires who remained in the rich lists. Since 2001, there has been substantial growth, with the GFC proving to be only a momentary hurdle for growth. Since 1990, the average growth rate has swollen the number of super rich by 10.9% overall (geometric mean). Taking the more extreme period, 2000–2013, the growth rate is an astonishing 24.5% per annum. By 2013, there were 87 billionaires, of which 77 were self-made and 10 inherited their wealth. Since 2002, the relative proportion of self-made individuals has increased from 68.4% to 88.5% in 2013.

Among the investment community the older cohorts mainly began their roads to wealth during the 1970s and 1980s. The timing of their entry into the industry positioned them to effectively benefit from the changing nature of the financial landscape, largely due to regulation. For example, under Regulation Q of the Banking Act of 1933, a 5.25% ceiling on savings accounts was imposed. According to Sherman (2009), this had a deleterious impact upon the ability of banks to attract capital but benefitted a new emerging class of financiers:

> In the late 1970s, inflation caused market interest rates to rise above the limits mandated by Regulation Q.... Brokerage firms and other financial institutions began to create money market mutual funds ... They quickly became popular among small investors who shifted their money out of the regulated accounts in depository institutions, which paid considerably lower interest rates. (p. 6)

The impact can be viewed clearly in Fig. 5.7, where the managed funds industry saw dramatic growth in the 1980s. More recently still, the Financial Modernization Act of 1999 allows financial services companies to achieve unprecedented scale.

Although the proportion of inherited wealth has remained relatively stable, there appear to be differences between the two groups in terms of how their

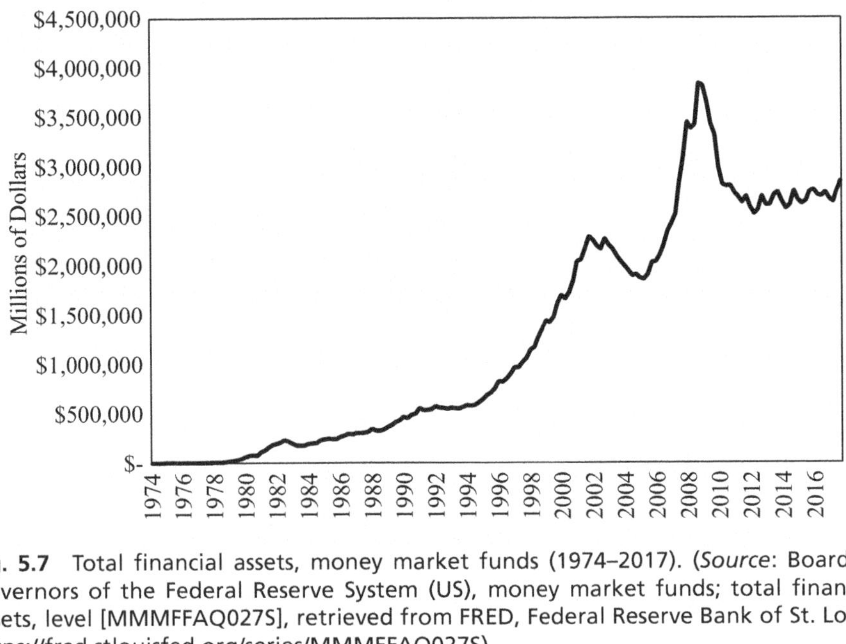

Fig. 5.7 Total financial assets, money market funds (1974–2017). (*Source*: Board of Governors of the Federal Reserve System (US), money market funds; total financial assets, level [MMMFFAQ027S], retrieved from FRED, Federal Reserve Bank of St. Louis; https://fred.stlouisfed.org/series/MMMFFAQ027S)

wealth and associated enterprise interests are handled. A sizeable proportion of self-made individuals in investments made their fortunes by targeting specific investments rather than diversifying. Previous scholarship has often identified the ability of investments to be rapidly capitalised in a Fisherian manner (Hirsch, 1911; see Thurow, 1975). Examples of such individuals abound in the US data with many making their fortunes in private equity particularly. In contrast, the inherited group generally appear to adopt much more diversified approaches to their investments.

The prevalence of diversification of inheritance can be exemplified in a number of case studies. Amongst these individuals is Lester Crown, who has appeared every year since 1990, when his father, Henry Crown passed away. The Crown family holds controlling interests in a number of corporations including a $3.8 billion equity stake in defence contractor, General Dynamics. General Dynamics, once the producer of the western world's most popular fighter aircraft, the F-16 Falcon, represents the jewel in the Crown empire, but was once in substantial jeopardy due to bribery accusations and concerns (Tamarkin, 1986). However, like all good investors, the family has substantially diversified since the 1950s and 1960s. The family now holds interests in various enterprises, including the Hilton Corporation, Chicago Bulls, New York Yankees and several property investments, including the Rockefeller Center. The importance of diversification amongst wealthy clans was emphasised by Thurow (1975) and Canterbery and Nosari (1985). The Ziff siblings inherited a large fortune when their father, William Ziff Jr., sold his publishing empire. His children, Daniel, Dirk and Robert Ziff, had no interest in maintaining management of the publishing business. Instead, the siblings diversified their inherited wealth across equities, debt and real estate, whilst providing seed funding to hedge funds (Chung, 2014). Peter Kellog, once labelled 'Peter the Predator', made his billions by being employed in his father's specialty brokerage firm, Spear, Lead, and Kellog. In 2000, the firm was sold to Goldman Sachs for $6.5 billion. Kellog cultivated a fierce reputation on Wall Street, with the brokerage firm becoming the first to control more than 10% of the stocks on the New York Stock Exchange (Sorkin, 2003; Willoughby, 1994). Even relatively minor inheritances have been grown substantially under their beneficiaries' direction. Nicolas Berggruen grew a family trust fund of $250,000 to a fortune of in excess of $1 billion by 2000 (Kahn, 2011). Echoing the flamboyant consumption patterns of the early twentieth-century wealthy, Berggruen, although nominally a US citizen, 'has had no fixed home address. He constantly roams the world on his Gulfstream IV jet, living out of five star hotels' (Kahn, 2011).

Table 5.1 Number, mean age and date of birth of hedge fund owners in North America

Year	**1994**	**1995**	**1996**	**1997**	**1998**	**1999**	**2000**	**2001**	**2002**	**2003**
Number	1	1	1	1	1	1	–	4	3	3
Average age	63	64	65	66	67	68	–	60	58	59
Average birth year	1931	1931	1931	1931	1931	1931	–	1941	1944	1944
Year	**2004**	**2005**	**2006**	**2007**	**2008**	**2009**	**2010**	**2011**	**2012**	**2013**
Number	5	7	10	13	28	24	25	26	31	31
Average age	54	56	54	56	53	55	55	56	56	57
Average birth year	1950	1949	1953	1951	1955	1954	1955	1955	1956	1956

Source: Forbes (1990–2013), authors' compilation from various secondary sources

Given the impact of hedge funds on the industry some attention is focused on the pioneers of this sector. Generally, the overwhelming majority can be described as self-made entrepreneurs from the baby boomer generation compared to the older cohorts observed in the investment community. Table 5.1 shows that since 2001, the average age of hedge fund billionaires has decreased from the mid-60s during the 1990s to approximately the mid-50s since 2002. The large, almost, generational shift is mostly attributable to a large influx over the past decade. During the 1990s, the number of hedge fund billionaires was small, just one, George Soros, born in 1931. In 2001, there were four hedge fund billionaires; by 2012 the number of billionaires had swelled to 31, an increase of 675% and representing 35.6% of the diversified financial community. With the increase, there has been a large concomitant decrease in the average age of the hedge fund billionaires, decreasing from 60 in 2001, to the mid-50s throughout the 2000s.

The growth in the hedge fund industry and the antecedent wealth it generated for its captains can be traced to two main factors. Firstly, the source and size of fund flows has dramatically changed since the 1990s. In previous decades, wealthy individuals were, typically, the main investors in hedge funds. However, the sheer scale of fund flows has now largely emanated from mutual and pension funds brimming with large pools of funds (Stulz, 2007). An important issue is why hedge funds should be attracting such significant investment flows from institutional investors and wealthy individuals. As noted in Chap. 3, real returns have been significantly decreasing since the Second World War across both North America and Western Europe. Could the search for higher returns be driving a flight to hedge funds? According to Preqin (2014), more than 80% of fund flows into hedge funds come from Europe and North America. The Preqin (2014) industry survey lists three major reasons why institutional investors favour hedge funds, including: the ability to reduce volatility; diversifying risk *premia*; and producing absolute returns.[1]

Secondly, hedge fund fee structures ensure a robust channel for wealth accumulation. Compensation contracts that are extremely favourable to the hedge fund managers ensure significant pecuniary advantages:

> [A]lmost all hedge fund managers have an asymmetric compensation contract that specifies that they receive a substantial fraction of the profits they generate .... Typically, hedge fund managers receive a fixed compensation corresponding to 1-2 percent of the net asset value of the fund ... and 15-25 percent of the return of the fund above a hurdle rate (which can be the risk-free rate). (Stulz, 2007, p. 184)

Given (*a*) the massive influx of cash flow into hedge funds, and (*b*) the generous compensation packages of hedge fund managers, it is not surprising to observe the swelling of wealth being generated in this sector.

The other great producer of wealth for North America's financial sector has been property—although close inspection of the data suggests that the scope for new wealth is limited. Figure 5.8 presents the overall number and average ages of realty billionaires in North America between 1990 and 2013. The number of billionaires languished in single digits during the 1990s, with the maximum numbering a meagre six in 1990. Throughout the 1990s, there was, in fact, a secular downward trend and by 1999 not one real estate billionaire appeared in the *Forbes* list. However, by 2001, there were 8 billionaires and by 2008 there were 38, an increase of 375%. Significantly, the majority of growth is due largely to self-made individuals and not inheritance. However, this should not be tied to recent entrepreneurial effort. The average number of inheritances over the entire sample has remained low at three with the highest recorded in 2012 and 2013 at six. Turning to the billionaires' ages, more variation and a higher mean age overall are observed compared to the other investment related sectors.

Both the stalwarts and relatively new entrants into the billionaire ranks have a long history in the property game and represent the fortuitous timing in the grand socio-demographic changes experienced by North America after the Second World War. The original propertied billionaires, individuals such as DeBartolo Sr., Taubman and Bren, all appear to have recognised the significant demographic changes of the 1960s towards suburban living. One of the wealthiest today to have recognised and exploited this large social

[1] Absolute returns taken to mean the search for investment strategies generating only positive returns.

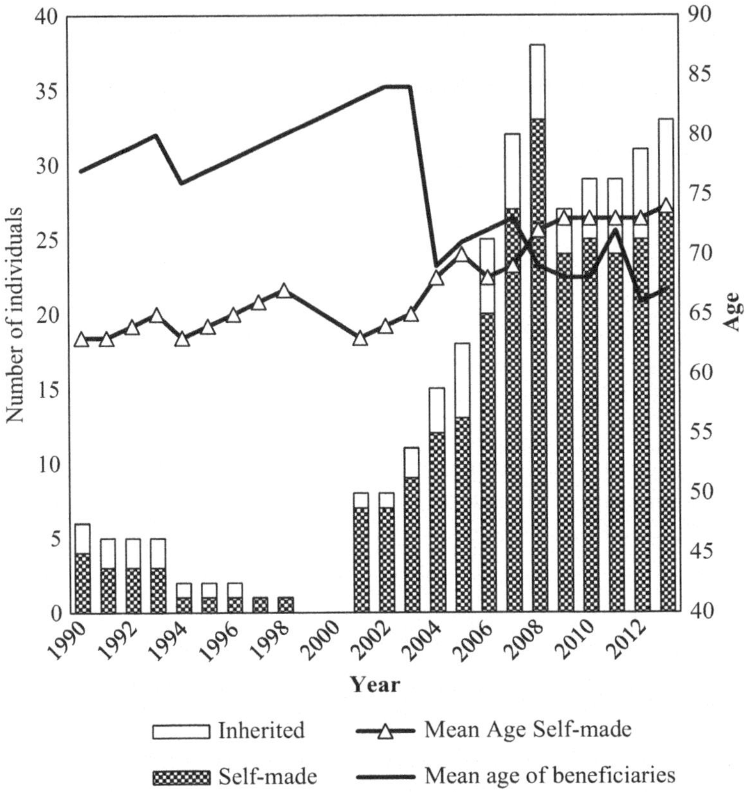

Fig. 5.8 Number and mean age of billionaires in North America: Real estate. (*Source*: Forbes (1990–2013), authors' compilation from various secondary sources)

transformation is Donald Bren who is the principal shareholder of the Irvine Company. Geographically, Bren's investments are concentrated in California, however the scale and scope of the investments is astoundingly large and diverse, spanning the roles of master planner, master builder and long-term investment across the western US state with only a few holdings beyond. According to his personal website, '[t]he Irvine Company's property portfolio exceeds 105 million square feet and includes 500 office buildings, 41 retail, 130 apartment communities, five marinas, three hotels and three golf courses, primarily in Orange County, Calif., with one-third of the investment properties in Los Angeles, San Diego, Silicon Valley and Chicago' (Irvine Company, n.d.). Self-made, Bren started on the road to commercial success when he first incorporated Bren Company in 1958. The company constructed homes in Orange County, California rapidly gained scale through the acquisition of property development rights across the county. The influence of the early investments still resonates in the present, with one newspaper stating: '[s]imply put, Orange County looks like Orange County...because of the influence of [Donald Bren]' ('The West 100', 2006). In 1963, Bren led a consortium that master planned Mission Viejo, a city in Orange County. The city is considered one of the largest ever-planned communities in the US. This investment provided the foundation for future expansion across the region.

Edward John DeBartolo, Sr. (born 1909), largely got his start via his stepfather's construction business, Michael DeBartolo Construction. In 1944, DeBartolo Sr. founded his own company, Edward J. DeBartolo Corporation. Demonstrating the entrepreneurial characteristics of alertness, DeBartolo identified a clear need for denizens of the new urban areas for central and convenient shopping centres or malls (Bryant, 1994). Indeed, DeBartolo constructed the first shopping malls in the US. Although DeBartolo identified the need, there was substantial risk in his approach. His investment style was often predicated on a risky strategy of 'Stay out in the country. That's the new downtown' (Bryant, 1994; Frieden & Sagalyn, 1991, p. 5), a philosophy that worked in his favour well into the 1960s. In later life, investment interests diversified into sporting teams—however, real estate remained the primary wealth generation activity. DeBartolo Sr.'s son, Edward John DeBartolo Jr., has maintained an active role in the real estate business. The family group holds management interests in not just shopping malls but hotels and restaurants, and for a brief time in sport with control of the gridiron team the San Francisco 49ers.

The changing demographics of the US and the opportunities it provided was also recognised by Alfred Taubman. A self-made man (his parents lost everything during the Great Depression), Taubman, like DeBartolo, recognised the importance of the shopping mall concept in the 1950s. Recognising consumer requirements to shop in locales near the new suburban areas, Taubman reasoned, 'Demographically, I looked at the numbers, and as far as I was concerned we couldn't miss. And we didn't' (Melvin & Sutton, 2015). Further, 'Suburban growth after the war … allowed us to build large developments based on new road patterns and new freeways that came in. We were able to duplicate to a great degree what occurs in a downtown, all under one ownership and one control' (McFadden, 2015 p. D8(L)). Taubman differed from DeBartolo in his mainly targeting of upmarket centres rather than investing in future suburban centres. Although they may have had different strategies, they undoubtedly had significant impact on the future evolution of American cities. In the instance of Taubman, for example, the massive wealth he generated is seen by some as 'having siphoned business and jobs from downtowns, hastening the decline of old cities like Detroit, and that by turning farmland and wilderness areas into parking lots he intensified traffic and pollution' (McFadden, 2015 p. D8(L)).

The experience of the more recent rich inductees reflects the paths of the older cohorts during the 1960s and 1970s. The brothers Herb and Melvin Simon first appear in the global rich lists in 2004. The two brothers formed a real estate investment company, Melvin Simon & Associates, in 1959. Throughout the 1950s, the brothers had acted in the capacity of lease managers before deciding to embark on the role of owners. Despite coming relatively late into the shopping mall development craze, the brothers had developed a real estate empire, and by the 1980s, it spanned across the US:

> By 1967, the company owned and operated more than 3 million square feet of retail property. It continued to expand throughout the country, adding more than 1 million square feet of property every year. By the 1980s the company opened three enclosed malls every year. (RetroIndy, 2014) Just like the DeBartolo family, the Simons diversified into sport team ownership, purchasing the Indiana Pacers in 1983.

Even in Canada, the pattern has typically followed that of the US, albeit on a smaller scale. David Azrieli started his journey to extreme wealth by developing small duplexes in Montreal before embarking on shopping malls. The pattern of development that Azrieli embarked upon largely exploited the changing social geography of Canada which underwent a process of considerable suburbanisation of residential, industry and commerce in the 1950s (Bourne, 2014). Marcel Adams, who first appeared in the *Forbes* list in 2013 at the age of 92, started his real estate investments in 1950s in Quebec. Like Azrieli, Adams focused on residential properties first before embarking on office and shopping mall complexes in the 1960s and beyond (van Praet, 2014). Amongst the 'new' blood, shopping malls and variations thereof, continue to be the money generator. Mitchell Goldhar is the main developer for Wal-Mart's Super-centres in Canada (Rocha, 2015). Goldhar's property empire is enormous having 'developed a network of more than 50 million square feet of retail space over the last 20 years, including more than 170 Wal-Mart stores' (Rocha, 2015).

A confluence of economic and policy forces throughout the 1930s to 1970s ensured that the economic structure was there for any keen entrepreneur to exploit. The creation of the Federal National Mortgage Association (Fannie Mae) in 1938 provided mortgage finance to millions of prospective and aspiring homeowners in subsequent decades. The G.I. Bill of Rights provided the backbone for a massive home development market. By 1952, the government backed approximately 2.4 million homes. The *Federal-Aid Highway Act* of 1956, which provided funding for 41,000 miles of interstate highways, ensured that viable suburban communities to develop could be connected to large regional metropolitan centres. The freeway initiative having benefits for individuals involved in the mass development of master planned communities such as Donald Bren (Forsyth, 2005). Similarly, the urban sprawl providing fertile ground in which shopping malls would become part of the wealth generating businesses for individuals like DeBartolo and Taubman.

To summarise, several salient themes become apparent among the propertied elite. Much of the wealth is generated via construction of retail centres or supplying residential housing. Ultimately, both were largely spurred on by the substantial post-war wave of urbanisation across both the US and Canada. For property, at least, the means to extreme wealth appears to be very much restricted to having identified opportunities in the post-war era and accumulated significant property holdings in the 1950s to 1970s. The surprising lack of 'youthful' wealth suggests a substantial cohort effect during the post-war era. The rise itself in the number of billionaires during the 2000s is obviously associated with the boom in property prices—however, a substantial element in their success is fortuitous timing since their investments during the 1950s and 1960s placed them in a position to ride the property boom of the 1990s and beyond.

Information Technology

In popular media, whenever billionaires are brought up, reference is typically made to those who made a vast fortune in IT. Indeed, given that Bill Gates is usually considered the wealthiest man alive, this is not surprising. Even in economic debates on the merits of vast wealth, advocates of the rich will often highlight names from this industry. The name of the late Steve Jobs is often evoked (see e.g. Mankiw, 2013). Further, a cursory glance across industry news would often suggest that many of those who made their fortunes are still very young, a trend that has continued since the 1960s with the pioneers of the microchip architecture. More recently, individuals such as Jeff Bezos (Amazon) and Mark Zuckerberg of Facebook fame have continued the trend of relatively young individuals making rapid wealth gains in IT. In many respects, these individuals are often accorded a similar status to the individuals who spurred on the industrial revolution in the UK in the early nineteenth century. A significant difference, however, is that the industrialists of that era

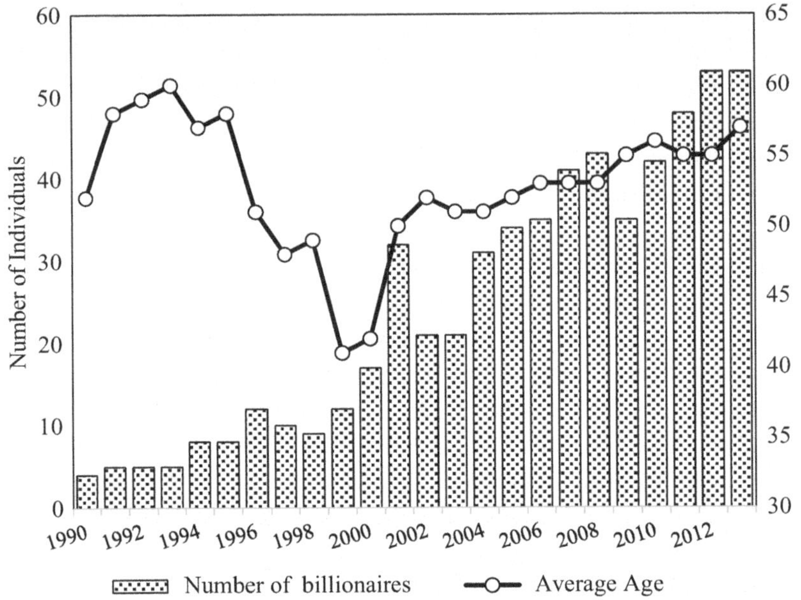

Fig. 5.9 Number and mean age of billionaires in North America: information technology. (*Source*: Forbes (1990–2013), authors' compilation from various secondary sources)

were never at the pinnacle of the wealth tree compared to what is observed with the wizards of the digital revolution.[2]

Figure 5.9 presents a breakdown of the IT sector over time along the dimensions of average age and the number of billionaires. The sample is not divided by inherited and self-made wealth as only two had inherited wealth: Henry Ross Perot Jr., the son of the former US presidential candidate, Henry Ross Perot, and Laurene Jobs, the widow of the Apple cofounder Steve Jobs. Overall, the average digital billionaire is aged 53, though the average age did demonstrate a marked downward trend throughout the 1990s to 2000. Only with the influx of new entrepreneurs from Internet-related enterprises is the average age depressed. By 2001, with the dot com crash largely sorting the winners and losers in the Internet game, the average age once again started to slowly rise and continued to do so particularly between 2004 and 2013, suggesting maturation in the industry. The increase in the average age has not, however, appeared to diminish for the computer or IT industry's capacity to generate significant wealth. By 1999, there were 12 billionaires in this industry, by 2001 it had jumped to 32, by 2010 it was 48 and by 2013 it had

[2] As Rubinstein shows, the financial and propertied classes dwarfed the wealth of the British industrialists in the 1800s.

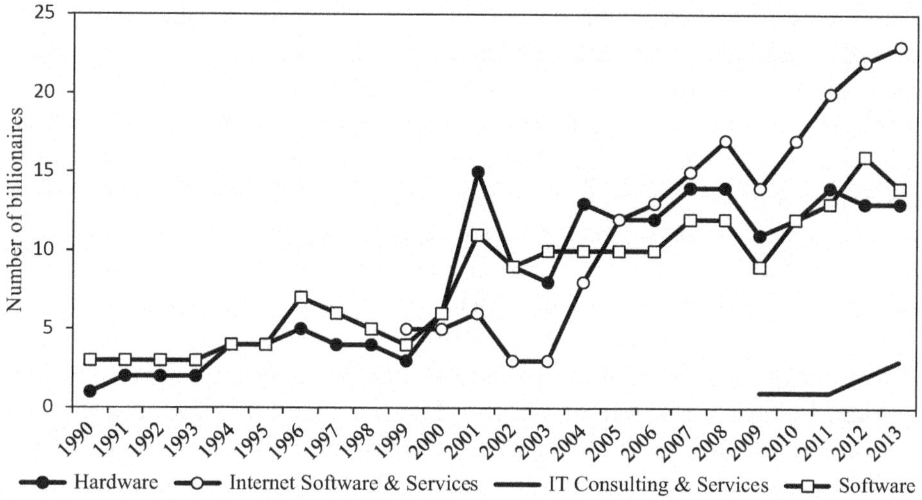

Fig. 5.10 Information technology sector decomposition and trends in North America, 1990–2013. (*Source*: Forbes (1990–2013), authors' compilation from various secondary sources)

reached 53. Annually, the number of individuals added to the ranking has averaged 15% on the previous year.

Before proceeding, it is necessary to further breakdown the sample according to sub-categories. As it stands, by applying the GICS overlay the industry detail is lost. This is an important issue since the IT industry is substantially heterogeneous with many making fortunes in software development, hardware development, computer consultancy or the Internet (with the last often incorporating elements of the other three), each possessing a degree of heterogeneity in the path to great wealth.

Figure 5.10 disaggregates the sector by the four subcomponents. The chart suggests that software and hardware only experienced rapid growth in the late 1990s. The number of hardware vendor entrepreneurs averaged 3.1 in the 1990s, increasing to 8.7 between 2001 and 2013. Software demonstrates similar numbers, with an average of 4.4 individuals amassing great fortunes in the 1990s, increasing to 11.4 between 2001 and 2013. Overall, particularly when compared to the IT industry as a whole, the slow growth rates can either be explained by appeals to notions of maturing markets, as well as substantially more competition from East Asia, particularly in the hardware sector through such manufacturers as Acer, Asus, Sony and Samsung, and software development from India. Growth rates have been much more robust among Internet-connected entrepreneurs, with an average growth rate of 20% since the first billionaires made their fortunes in 1990s. From 2001, the number of Internet-related billionaires was five, increasing to 23 by 2013. This compares favourably against hardware (11.6%) and software developers (10.4%).

Among the hardware and software entrepreneurs, numerous household names abound. For example, William Hewlett and David Packard have become synonymous with the personal computer and IT hardware in general. In what appears to be a regular pattern amongst the hardware individuals, the two close student colleagues started Hewlett-Packard in David Packard's garage. Their first product, a sound oscillator required initial capital of $538 in 1939 (Packard, 1995). From these relatively humble beginnings in the electronic testing market, Hewlett-Packard would eventually enter the computer market. Indeed, it is often argued that Hewlett-Packard introduced the first personal computer, in 1968 (Clark, 2000). By the 1980s, Hewlett-Packard had expanded into all areas of computing including, PCs, portables and servers. The company once even dabbled in CPU design and fabrication taking on the likes of SUN and IBM with their own RISC based CPU, the HP-PA RISC CPU. The early move into computing was largely made possible through large government contracts in contrast to Apple a decade on who focused much more on the home computer market. Other individuals leveraged the early computer revolution and the concomitant government contracts to gain a position in the burgeoning market.

In software, Henry Ross Perot, born in 1931, now best remembered as a US independent presidential candidate in the 1990 and 1996 elections, also saw opportunity in major sales to the US government. The one-time International Business Machines (IBM) salesperson, Perot created Electronic Data Systems (EDS) in 1962. EDS's principal revenue came from the computerisation of the government's Medicare and Medicaid records in relation to the Great Society programs (Swedin & Ferro, 2005). The rise of computer equipment as a channel of wealth accumulation during these formative years can be readily observed in aggregate sales for the US. Table 5.2 shows the

Table 5.2 US computer equipment sales, 1990–1995

Year	GDP (billions)	Sales of computing equipment (billions)	Computer equipment as % of GDP
1960	513	1.5	0.3
1970	1010	10.5	1
1980	2708	55.1	2
1990	5546	154.8	2.8
1995	7117	204.8	2.9

Source: Committee on Innovations in Computing and Communications: Lessons from History (1999)

continued growth of computer equipment sales as a significant contributor to overall US gross domestic product (GDP) from the 1960s, demonstrating the significant possibilities for wealth accumulation.

As in many of the other industries, much of the innovation of these early innovators and entrepreneurs arose during an era of high-income growth and taxation. One of the main reasons for this is that much of the evolution in computing appears to have followed a process of knowledge diffusion across numerous parties rather than being tied to individual genius. The relevance of knowledge diffusion in the creation of new industries is recognised in the literature. Knowledge diffusion, for example, being identified by Rockoff (2012) as of paramount importance to the success of the early pioneers of assembly manufacturing. Perhaps the prime example of this is Gordon Moore and the subsequent technological spinoffs. Moore co-founded Intel in 1968 with Robert Noyce and was part of the infamous Silicon Valley story of the 'Traitorous Eight'. The eight, a who's who of individuals that would one day go forth and create many of the household computers components companies of today, was a cluster of brilliant engineers and scientists who were originally part of Shockley Semiconductor (who designed the first silicon diodes). The 'Eight' left Shockley in 1957 and formed Fairchild Semiconductor after which a number, including Moore, would leave to found Intel. Once Intel was formed in 1968, a key engineer at Intel, Ted Hoff developed a brilliant notion that would allow Intel to rapidly expand by bringing one microprocessor design to a variety of customers. Previous to Intel, a bespoke approach to integrated circuitry was required that swelled the costs of the technology limiting market scale. Intel developed a paradigm that still exists today—develop a single integrated circuit with general capabilities and then use software to tailor the tasks to be undertaken by the computer (Ceruzzi, 2003). Not only did Moore's brainchild ensure future success for himself personally, but it also provided the platform upon which others in the 1970s and 1980s, such as Bill Gates or Steve Jobs, would be able to grow their own business and fortunes—a process in line with the pattern of knowledge evolution in industries first observed by Jones (1831).

It must be emphasised that much of the early innovation was attributable to substantial funding of the US government. For example, 'federal contracts supported more than half of the R&D and about 35 per cent of R&D as late as 1963' (Committee on Innovations, 1999, p. 88). Direct funding was not always a necessary precursor, indeed often the research slowly disseminated through several years before a commercial application could be found. Indeed, as has often been pointed out, entrepreneurs such as Steve Jobs at Apple and Bill Gates at Microsoft 'built upon ideas developed previously, many of them with government funding' (Committee on Innovations, 1999, p. 108). Rather, the dissemination of knowledge and collaboration ensured technological progress wherein viable commercial applications were found.

Among the more recent billionaires, there is a preponderance of those making their fortunes with Internet-related businesses. What is, however, perhaps most compelling is the extent to which these individuals have amassed vast fortunes in a short span of time and the rapidity with which they have tended to diversify their business interests, as exemplified by Google's Larry Page and Sergey Brin. Google started as a student project in 1996, and in 1997 the google.com domain was registered. In 1998, Google was incorporated as a privately held company—by 2002 the two were well on their way to billionaire status. The key to Google's success and other Internet firms has been how their founders were able to monetise their technology. For Google, revenue does not come from the search engine rather it is derived from its advertising platform that uses its search engine as its base. Given that Google controls approximately 71.02% of the global search engine market share (Net Applications, n.d.), the associated advertising revenue streams would be more than enough to cement their wealth. Google's wealth generation has not been restricted to Page and Brin, with Eric Schmidt and Kavitark Shriram also gaining vast fortunes due to the two former individuals' ideas. Google has heavily diversified since its search engine beginnings. With the release of the Android and ChromeOS operating systems Google is entering the hardware and software territory of Microsoft and Apple. Closely mirroring, and slightly beating Page and Brin to the billionaire's club, were the co-founders of Yahoo, David Filo and Jerry Yang (and just a few years older too). Yahoo's original technology was developed by David Filo, who created the server-side software used to power Yahoo's web search engines. Again, although the search engine constituted the key ingredient in Yahoo's early success, its revenue stream, just like Google's, is predominately via marketing services revenue.

Mark Zuckerberg of Facebook fame is by far the most famous, debuting on the billionaire rich list in 2008 with an estimated net worth of $1.5 billion in 2008. His net worth rose substantially prior to the initial public offering (IPO) for Facebook in 2012, reaching $13.5 billion in 2011. By 2012 when the IPO was made, Zuckerberg's wealth rose by $6 billion to $17.5 billion. The ability to displace an old industry and quickly scale to a vast market is seen in the case of Jeffrey Bezos and his Amazon empire. Although Bezos's wealth could be tied with the retail sector, there are sufficient business interests that firmly centre his company into the IT sphere. Amazon gained substantial market share firstly in online book and movie sales but has since moved into product categories usually sold by bricks and mortar department stores. Further, Amazon has diversified into cloud infrastructure and tablet and phone devices. PayPal is an example of an enterprise that has radically transformed the payments system and elevated one of its founders, Peter Thiel, to billionaire status.

Western Europe: Old and New Money

In shifting focus from North America to Western Europe one is immediately struck by the central role played by old or inherited wealth compared to North America. In Chap. 3, Table 3.3 was used to compare the relative numbers of inherited and self-made fortunes between regions. Throughout the 1990s, the proportion of individuals that had inherited their wealth was approximately 73.4% for Western Europe compared to 51.4% for North America. As one shifts into the latter years of the sample, the trend in Western Europe reverses, with the self-made individual increasingly dominating the enumerated rich lists. Since 2010, there have been consecutive points in time where the self-made rich represent the majority of billionaires in Western Europe, although there is a small reversal towards inherited wealth. For example, in 2012, 43.9% of Western European billionaires had inherited their wealth; by 2013 this had increased to 46.8%. Contrasted to this are the North American observations, where only 29.4% and 29.9% had inherited their wealth in 2012 and 2013, respectively. What is influencing the dramatic and contrasting wealth structure between Western Europe and North America? To explore this question, the Western European data is discussed with reference to both the country breakdown and the main sectors of wealth generation in each.

To acquire a better understanding, the inherited and self-made groups are further disaggregated by country. The results are presented in Fig. 5.11. A cursory glance immediately reveals that there is an intra-European gulf in the proportion of old and new wealth that is masked by the aggregate data in Chap. 3. The gulf is particularly between continental Europe on the one hand and the UK on the other. For France and Germany, 71.1% and 70.8% on average inherited their wealth, respectively over the sample period. In contrast, the British billionaire composition shows a dramatic shift from 2002 to 2004, where there was a precipitous increase in the number of self-made billionaires. Here, there is a major reversal in the composition of wealth. Throughout the first half of the sample, 1990 to 2001, the mean proportion of inheritances was 73.62%. For the second half of the sample, 2002 to 2013, dramatically reverses, with the mean drastically decreasing to 25.87%.

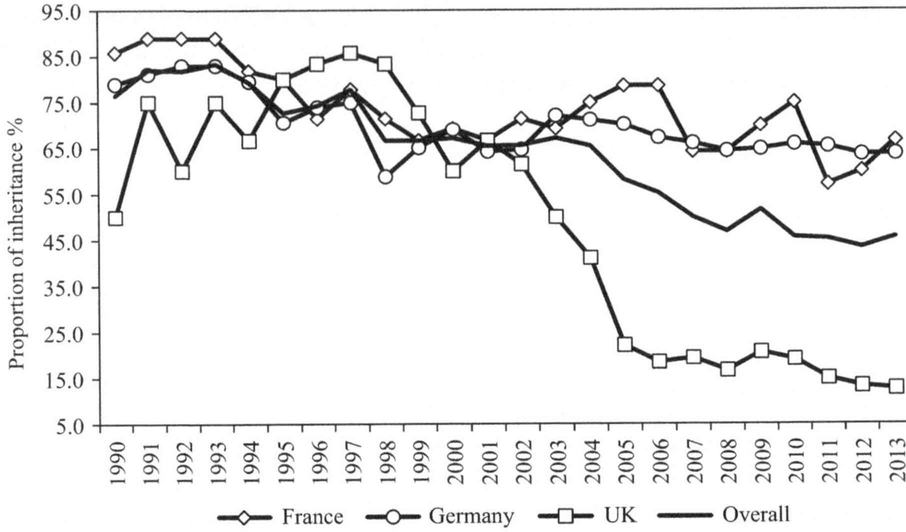

Fig. 5.11 Proportion of inheritances across Western Europe, 1990–2013. (*Source*: Forbes (1990–2013), authors' compilation from various secondary sources)

Germany: Dominance of Patronage

The gulf in inherited and self-made fortunes is particularly acute between Germany on one hand and the UK and the US on the other. Given the importance of inherited wealth for the composition and structure of Germany's largest wealth holdings, the discussion first focuses on those industries in which a few key families dominate. This includes families who made their wealth either from the pre- or post-war eras. As Fig. 5.11 establishes, the majority of Germany's elite inherited their wealth. Throughout the 1990s, this averaged in the high 70s, by the latter half of the sample the proportion of wealthy has stabilised between 63% and 65%. The industrial distribution is presented in Fig. 5.12. Of immediate interest is that inherited wealth is certainly not uniformly distributed across German industries, rather it is clustered in a few key industries. These industries are consumer discretionary (25) and food, beverages and tobacco (30). For the remaining industries where inherited wealth is present, the number of individuals is considerably low at one or two. Although this should not necessarily be taken as signifying a lack of commercial significance. Compared to the US, the UK, France and Australia it is noticeable that there is a distinct lack of property billionaires.

The low numbers are, however, associated with some of Germany's oldest family dynasties including Merck, for example. The Merck family continually

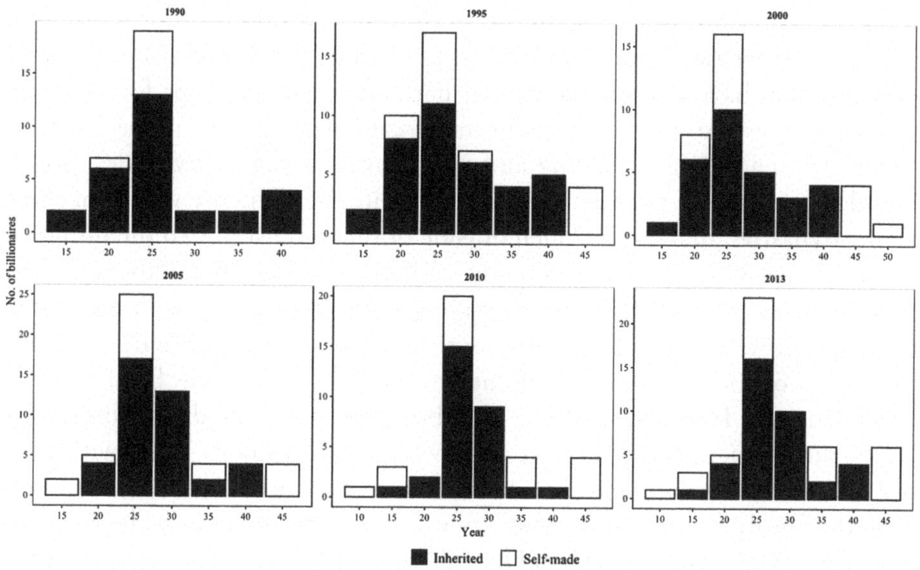

Fig. 5.12 Distribution of industries in Germany: inheritances. *Note*: The chart provides a visual summary of the distribution of billionaires across German industries using the two-code GICS. The data is presented on a five-year interval basis. The number and associated sectors are: 10: Energy, 15: Materials, 20: Industrials, 25: Consumer Discretionary, 30: Consumer Staples, 35: Health care, 40: Financials, 45: Information Technology, 50: Telecommunications, 55: Utilities. (*Source*: Forbes (1990–2013), authors' compilation from various secondary sources)

appeared throughout the early history of the *Forbes* sample, but has since been excluded. The exclusion of the Merck family from the *Forbes* lists has more to do with the diffusion of wealth across multiple family members rather than a sudden collapse in wealth, however. According to *Forbes*, by 2002, the Merck family fortune was spread across approximately 100 family members (Dolan & Kroll, 2001). Part of the dynasty's fortune is in a holding company, E. Merck KG, which the family maintains a controlling interest (approximately 70%) ownership in Merck KGaA. To place this into monetary terms, the total capital value of Merck KGaA is €565,211,241.95, of which €397,196,314 worth is owned by the family interest through E. Merck KG (Merck, 2014). The breadth of the family numbers is not surprising considering that Merck is considered one of the oldest businesses in the world, with its roots traced back to the found of the Engel Apotheke in 1668. Stretching back from the firm's founding in 1668 to the present, approximately 12 generations of Mercks have maintained a controlling interest in the pharmaceutical giant (Merck, 2013).

Industrials have traditionally been viewed as a mainstay of Germanic economic expertise. A cursory glance at the wealth ranks reveals a plethora of dynasties that have dominated the German industrial landscape for well over a century now. Among the producers of capital goods are names such as Bosch, Haniel, Diehl, Rochling and von Siemens—family dynasties mostly founded prior to the twentieth century. Despite the immense wealth of these family dynasties, many have fallen outside of the rich list due to the diffusion of wealth across successive generations. Those who have maintained a presence, such as the Loh or Happel families, have carried on the family name through diversification into construction or engineering. Friedhelm Loh, the owner of the industrial conglomerate the Loh Group, was born in 1947 (Backhaus & Hanßler, 2014). The business was initially founded by Friedhelm's father, Rudolf Loh in 1947 who passed away in 1971, with control and ownership falling to Friedhelm Loh in the same year. Friedhelm Loh grew the family fortune by diversifying into a variety of engineering and consultancy services. Similarly, Otto Happel, born in 1948, took over his parents' dust removal business in 1974 (Hillman, 2001). Happel subsequently embarked on transforming the family business in an engineering firm and sold the remaining stakes he had in the company in 2006. Similarly, the mother and son business team of Maria-Elisabeth and Georg Schaeffler developed the male head's roller bearing business into a global manufacturer.

The consumer discretionary sector possesses both the bulk of billionaires and the great number of inheritance beneficiaries. There is not much variation in the degree to which inheritance dominates across German industry. Among the inherited media wealthy, the means of maintaining wealth is through acquisitions and geographical diversification. Some of the more recent listed names are Reinhard Mohn (born in 1922) and Anneliese Brost (born in 1921). Brost inherited her stake from her deceased husband, Erich Brost, who was one of the cofounders of *Westdeutsche Allgemeine Zeitung*, one of Germany's largest newspapers. Yvonne Bauer's plan for the family business falls in line with the established pattern observed among other inherited wealth holders, of growth through acquisitions globally. For example:

> [a] flurry of recent activity suggests that Yvonne Bauer has ambitions to expand this global empire, which already extends to 15 countries.... Last month, she splashed out A$500m (£320m) to buy the Australian magazine group ACP [Australian Consolidated Press], including top-sellers such as *Woman's Day* and *Harper's Bazaar*. (Spanier, 2012, para. 9–10)

Although Germany's financial system is bank dominated, finance only has a miniscule representation. Despite the size of Germany's financial system, only four billionaires in 2013 have been found from the ranks of financiers. The number has largely remained stable since 1990. The lowest points being reached in 2010 (one) and 1998 (one). The list of finance self-made men is short, at just one. Here Karl Ehlerding, born in 1945, made his fortunes in corporate raiding, though suffered a substantial setback in 2002 when his equity investments fell by up to 80% and subsequently disappeared from Germany's wealth ranks. Of the 13 names to amass a fortune of $1 billion since 1990, only 2 have managed to appear for much of the sample period, August von Finck , Jr., and Rolf Gerling. Both individuals coming from inherited wealth. August von Finck, Jr., was born in 1930 and inherited his father's ownership stakes in Allianz and the private bank Merck, Finck & Co. He sold the stakes in 1990 and invested heavily into a diversified portfolio of real estate holdings and equity ownership in industrial companies. His inherited wealth rapidly grew under the control of his father August von Finck, Sr., particularly during the rise of Aryanisation in late 1930s Germany. During the Anschluss between Germany and Austria, the Nazi party seized control of S M von Rothschild and sold it to Merck, Finck & Co. at a very low price which allowed the latter to attain a commanding position in Europe's private bank industry (Nullen, 1970). Similarly, the von Fincks profited handsomely from war profits during the Second World War through their Allianz holdings. The success of Allianz during the war years was established through the successful cultivation of ties between the NSDAP and the upper echelons of the insurance giant, including von Finck, Sr. (Feldman, 2001). August von Finck, Jr., largely divested his family interests in the family's historical commercial interests.

Rolf Gerling (born 1954) inherited from his father Hans Gerling the family's insurance business. The family insurance business, *Gerling Konzern Versicherungs Beteiligungs Aktiengesellschaft*, did not cultivate close ties with the *Nationalsozialistische Deutsche Arbeiterpartei* (NSDAP), though it did do brisk business with it. The lack of close ties with the NSDAP allowed it to escape de-nazification processes by the Allied powers. Unlike many German families where interest in the family business continues, Gerling, just like von Flick, has diversified away from the traditional family business into diversified investments and consulting work.

The key to much of the recent strength of Germany's inherited elite seems to be tied to the extent to which many of the families have been able to diversify away from the traditional family business or diversify internationally through acquisitions. Numerous elements to Germany's modern-day legal and tax frameworks may have facilitated this process too. Firstly, strong anti-trust laws ensured the longevity and protection of German firms during the post-war era, allowing older families to maintain their commercial bases intact from competition. The German Act against Restraints on Competition prevented mergers and acquisitions allowing many of the family owned corporations to survive in the midst of much larger American corporations. However, perhaps more importantly has been the role played by estate tax in permitting the flourishing of German dynasties and ultimately their longevity. In Chap. 4, Fig. 4.14 compares the progressive tax rates across the US, Germany and France. Since the 1930s, both Germany and France have shown a lower estate tax burden on their citizens compared to the US and also demonstrate substantial inheritance representation among the ultra-rich. It is particularly telling that during the mid-1950s to mid-1970s, Germany's top inheritance tax rate was 15%, far below the 80% and 78% enforced in UK and the US, respectively.[3]

An alternative argument could be mounted that cultural differences between Germanic and Anglo capitalisms are at the core of the differences between the dominance of inherited and self-made wealth. Goldsmith's (1969) seminal work on cultural and institutional differences between Anglo-American capitalism and Germanic capitalism focused on the roles played by varying financial institutions. As outlined in Chap. 2, previous scholars have typically argued that the emergence of extreme wealth has in the past, been intrinsically tied to the design of the financial system and its associated institutions. Watkins (1907), for example, argued that what differentiated the Gilded Age from the previous feudal era was the emergence of abstract ownership forms made possible by the development of a financial system. Under a financial market based financial system, 'securities markets share centre stage with banks in terms of getting society's savings to firms, exerting corporate control, and easing risk management' (Demirgruc-Kunt & Levine, 1999, p. 2). In contrast, a bank-based financial system is characterised by 'banks play[ing] a leading role in mobilising savings, allocating capital, overseeing the investment decisions of corporate managers, and in providing risk management vehicles' (Demirgruc-Kunt & Levine, 1999, p. 2).

These definitions themselves do not signal any obvious reason why inheritance should play such a dominating role in Germany's economic elite. The ability to link the creation of vast, intergenerational family fortunes to close banking relationships is a difficult endeavour, since such direct evidence is difficult to come by, particularly given the opaque nature of Germany's

[3] Chapter 4 discussed in more general terms the impact of inheritance taxes on estates and gifts in general.

banking systems. Historically, German banks have projected an influence over industrial Germany via substantial interlocking directorates. Jeidels (1905) once argued that in Germany 'the power of the Great Banks is exercised via the legal institution of the supervisory board, rather than through direct influence of financial strength' (p. 145). Gerschenkron (1998) argues that this proximity of corporate and banking relations ensured that bank control 'extended far beyond the sphere of financial control into that of entrepreneurial and managerial decisions' (p. 225).

Recent evidence suggests that the historical case for significant German bank influence is overstated. Fohlin (2005) argues that evidence from the industrial era through to contemporary times does not support the notion that banking firms have ever actually had a substantial influence upon entrepreneurial or managerial decision making among these firms. Furthermore, bank influence is being systematically scaled back by the largest firms (Fohlin, 2005). Close government corporation in the past has protected and sustained wealth and is most likely to have been a major component in developing the composition of German wealth observed today.

In part, the longevity of some of Germany's ultra-rich family dynasties is due to favourable political environments. Germany's economic elite has been able to maintain economic pre-eminence, despite their country having succumbed to the systematic destruction of physical capital throughout the Second World War by the Allied powers. There is evidence that the German industrial elite received substantial assistance and guidance during the National Socialist regime. During the war itself, much effort was expended by both the Nazi regime and the industrialists to ensure that capital was protected. A report penned by the Allied 'Economic Warfare Division' highlights a number of mechanisms through which families such as Krupp and Rochling could maintain their economic dynasties. Their capital swelled by war profits, the Nazi regime recommended that the industrialists export their capital, as '[t]he German industrialists are not only buying agricultural property in Germany but are placing their funds abroad, particularly in neutral countries' (Schwinn, 1944, p. 3). For German industrialists this policy represented a major Nazi policy reversal that had, until this time, enacted and enforced strict controls against the export of capital—now they would receive considerable government assistance towards this end. The groundwork, however, for Germany's post war miracle went beyond simply shifting capital to foreign countries for future repatriation, Germany's industrialists themselves would require significant foreign capital to ensure the success of the 'post-war commercial campaign' (Schwinn, 1944, p. 1). At one of the meetings of the Nazi Party and the industrialists it was recommended that German firms make contact and formulate alliances with foreign companies. For their part, the Krupps argued that such an approach was already in place:

> Dr. Scheid cited the fact that patents for stainless steel belonged to the Chemical Foundation, Inc., New York, and the Krupp company of Germany jointly and that the U.S. Steel Corporation, Carnegie Illinois, American Steel and Wire, and National Tube, etc. were thereby under an obligation to work with the Krupp concern. He also cited the Zeiss Company, and Leica Company and the Hamburg-American Line as firms which had been especially effective in protecting German interests abroad and gave their New York addresses to the industrialists at this meeting. (Schwinn, 1944, p. 2)

The post-war era's denazification process did not remove these elites from German industry. Many of the heirs of this elite still maintain substantial control over Germany's industrial base in the present era.

At least for Germany's 'old wealth' there appear to be parallels between the governments of the post-Soviet Union states and China and their roles in cultivating and ensuring the continued success of an economic elite during periods of transition (discussed below). In both instances, declining political elite, vested with the control and ownership of a country's resources begin to relinquish control to capitalists. There is an important difference, however. In the case of Germany, pre-existing economic elites, although under tight control under the Nazi regime, still maintained substantial control over their own wealth and commercial interests. By contrast, in the former Soviet states and China, economic power was transferred to individuals who previously held positions of political power and then managed to rapidly establish their vast wealth through commercial enterprise, often on a global scale.

France: Moving Towards an Anglo-Saxon Model of Wealth

Turning to France, the ascendency of patrimonial capitalism is once again observed. The geographical propinquity between France and Germany at the surface suggests similar economic and social forces may be at work. Daumard (1980) argues that the primacy of inheritance in French economic life is largely rooted in a social and economic condition where inheritance represented the only reasonable way towards greater fortune. At the billionaire level, the French data depicts similar propensity for inheritance to still dominate in contemporary times. From Fig. 5.11, it is observed that the proportion of inherited wealth has ranged between a high of 78.6% in 2004 to a low

Table 5.3 French industrial distribution of billionaires, 1990–2013

	Self-made							Inherited							
Year	20	25	30	35	40	45	All	10	20	25	30	35	40	All	Total
1990		2					2		2	2	1			5	7
1991		2					2		2	3	1		1	7	9
1992		2					2		2	3	1		1	7	9
1993		2					2		2	3	1		1	7	9
1994		3					3		2	4	1		1	8	11
1995		3					3		2	4	1		1	8	11
1996		3		1			4		3	4	1		2	10	14
1997		2					2		1	3	1		2	7	9
1998		2					2			3			2	5	7
1999	2	3					5		3	4	1		2	10	15
2000	2	2					4		3	3	1		2	9	13
2001	1	3		1			5	1	2	4	2		1	10	15
2002	1	3					4	1	2	4	2		1	10	14
2003	1	3					4	2	2	3	2			9	13
2004	1	2					3	2	2	3	2			9	12
2005	1	2					3	2	2	3	2	1	1	11	14
2006	1	2					3	2	2	3	2	1	1	11	14
2007	1	2			2		5	2	1	2	2	1	1	9	14
2008	1	2			2		5	1	2	2	2	1	1	9	14
2009	1	2					3		2	2	2	1		7	10
2010		2			1		3		3	2	2	1	1	9	12
2011	1	2	1		1	1	6		2	2	2	1	1	8	14
2012	1	2			2	1	6		3	3	2	1	1	10	16
2013	1	2	1		3	1	8		2	5	6	1	2	16	24

Source: Forbes (1990–2013), authors' compilation from various secondary sources
Note: The table provides a summary of the distribution of billionaires across French industries using the two-code Global Industry Classification System (GICS). The data is presented on a five-year interval basis. The number and associated sectors are: **10:** Energy, **15:** Materials, **20:** Industrials, **25:** Consumer Discretionary, **30:** Consumer Staples, **35:** Health Care, **40:** Financials, **45:** Information Technology, **50:** Telecommunications, **55:** Utilities

of 57.1% in 2010. In absolute terms, the number of inherited billionaires, as reported in Table 5.3, has ranged between 5 (1990, 1997) and 16 (2013). In contrast, the number of self-made has never attained double-digit representation.

Table 5.3 shows that the overall number of billionaires has steadily increased over the sample period. During the 1990s, the mean number of individuals was 12. Much like the observations from the US, the late 1990s saw an increase in the overall ranks of the French economic elite, increasing from 7 in 1998 to 15 in 1999. Between 1999 and 2012, the number of billionaires has remained relatively stable, hitting a low of 10 in 2009 due to the economic crisis. However, by 2013, the ranks of French wealthy had increased to 24, its highest point throughout the sample.

Perhaps reflecting the comparative advantage of the French economy, the main industry sources for wealth appear in consumer discretionary (25) and consumer staples (30). In Germany and the US, retail and media moguls tend to dominate. In contrast, for the French, the largest fortunes tend to be found amongst purveyors of fashion or luxury goods or food producers. The wealthiest of them all is Liliane Bettencourt, born in 1922, who is the majority owner of L'Oreal. Bettencourt inherited her late husband's stake in the company. The Bettencourt story, one of patrimony is endemic in the French fashion and cosmetics industries. Similarly, the siblings, Alain and Gerard Wertheimer, perfectly exemplify this predisposition. In more recent times, the Wertheimer brothers have expanded the scale and scope of their portfolio holdings by acquiring numerous fashion houses and even a prestigious British gun maker in the form of Holland & Holland. The brothers, who are owners of the privately held group, the House of Chanel, largely owe the success to their forefathers. Their forefathers demonstrated astounding business acumen in fostering future success for their descendants. Their grandfather, Pierre Wertheimer, was instrumental. In 1917, he took over from his father in the management of the privately owned theatrical cosmetics company, Bourjois. In 1924, Wertheimer came to an agreement with Coco Chanel to distribute Coco Perfume No. 5 that received astonishing commercial success (Mazzeo, 2010). The agreement proved timely. The joint agreement endowed the Wertheimers majority ownership in the joint venture with the majority benefits accruing to the Wertheimer. Although the Wertheimers still maintain the name of Chanel, Coco Chanel herself was effectively outmanoeuvred by the Wertheimer family in the 1930s. Not even an attempt by Coco Chanel to use the Nazis during the Second World War to wrest control from the Jewish Wertheimer family could loosen their grip over the House of Chanel (Mazzeo, 2010).

The pattern of inherited wealth dominating the wealthiest echelons in French society continues across less glamorous industries. Many of these names are relatively well known globally, whilst others are much more centred on France. Dassault Aviation, originally founded by Marcel Dassault, is represented today by Serge Dassault, who took over the reins of the family business in 1986. Reflecting a pattern observed across both Germany and the US, the younger Dassault diversified across various sectors and in 1995, created a new company, Dassault Group, to reflect the more diversified nature of the firm. Similarly, Martin Bouygues grew into the Chairman and CEO of his father's business, Bouygues. Francis Bouygues originally founded Bouygues as an industrial works and construction firm. Martin Bouygues grew the firm into a highly diversified conglomerate with interests in real estate, media, water treatment and telecommunications.

The self-made billionaire is not wholly missing from the French economic elite. Typically, they are found in the finance sector of France and is overall the most representative sector for France's billionaires. This is in stark contrast to Germany, where tight regulations appear to have reined in the potential for the amassment of great fortune. In finance and banking, self-made billionaires actually outnumber inheritances, albeit the difference is insignificant. Although their absolute numbers are small, there are some interesting phenomena at play. Table 5.2 shows that in finance (40), the first self-made billionaires appeared in 2007, a number of whose successes can be attributed to observing the potential to exploit the opportunities arising from deregulation of France's finance industry. Individuals such as Romain Zaleski and Marc Ladreit de Lacharrière managed to accumulate fortunes during the era of French financial deregulation. Melitz (1990) emphasises the dramatic scope of the reforms by arguing that the reforms in truth represented a significant reversal of the trend towards bank nationalisation and increased regulation. Instead, the reforms of the 1980s in particular gave a rapid rise to a liberal system with 'the only administered interest rates that remain concern bank deposits, a host of financial products has emerged, and there is no "*encadrement*"' (Melitz, 1990, p. 394). Perhaps most tellingly, Melitz (1990) views the shift as a move towards a financial system more modelled along the lines of the Anglo-Saxon world, as exemplified by the movement to financing of the business sector which was 'once exceptionally reliant on banking for finance… [to one that] now depends to a more conventional extent on internal finance and the capital market' (p. 398).

The UK: Europe's Odd One Out

On the surface, there is no a priori reason to suppose that the defining characteristic of continental economic elites, the ascendency of patrimony, should not apply to the UK, too. The UK shares much with both Germany and France in terms of social stratification, the existence of landed aristocracy, early industrialisation and significant human and capital losses in two world wars and being a former colonial power. If one were to turn to history, and to describe the defining characteristic of western European civilisation one of the major ideas would be the importance of imperial expansion. Britain and France expanded their colonial holdings throughout Africa, the Americas and

Asia during the 1700s and 1800s. The rise of colonialism is considered by some to be a defining characteristic of 1800s' capitalism. German colonialism, very much the latecomer in European affairs largely grew as a response to the British and French expansionism. For Marxists, colonialism, no matter where it took hold represented a common valve through which capitalism could flourish in these lands. On writing about the links between capitalism and slavery, Eric Williams (1944) famously stated, 'The colonial system was the spinal cord of the commercial capitalism of the mercantile epoch' (p. 142). In some regards, the spinal cord somewhat still manifests itself among the family dynasties observed in Germany. Families such as Krupp, Rochling, Merck and so forth laid the foundations for their descendants' successes between 1870s and 1945, for example.

Does the evolution of the economic elite of Great Britain, with all its colonial history, and still existent landed aristocracy reflect the experience of Europe? Or does Anglo Britain more closely resemble the Anglo US and Canada in the composition and evolution of their economic elites? Much work has already been produced examining the upper echelons of British society in economic history. Rubinstein (1980) notes that historically (at least when examining the historical record of the mid to late 1800s), although inherited wealth has always existed in British society, the degree of new wealth represented is surprising.

Today, a similar phenomenon can be observed. Turning once again back to Fig. 5.11, a striking trend is revealed. Between 1990 and 1999, the proportion of inherited wealth averaged 76% compared to 24% for self-made wealth among the wealthiest of Britons. For the period 2000–2013, the values reverse with approximately 31% of elites having inherited their fortunes, compared to 69% who made their wealth through their own means. The factors for the reversal tend to be many and varied within the industries of the British economy. A deep examination of the sectoral distribution, presented in Table 5.4, reveals that the growth in self-made fortunes tends to be concentrated in the finance and consumer discretionary sectors of the economy and more recently in materials. In the finance sector, the bulk of wealth has been generated in real estate, but there has been a robust representation from diversified financials too. The first financial billionaire appeared in 2000 and had by 2013 increased to 12. These 12 billionaires represent the bulk of the British ultra-rich.

Much like the US, the fortunes of these individuals is tightly bound to sweeping economic changes particularly brought upon by policy and regulatory change. For example, of the propertied rich, there were six individuals in 2013. The majority of the individuals first appeared relatively late in the

Table 5.4 British industrial distribution of billionaires, 1990–2013

	Self-made							Inherited				
Year	10	15	20	25	30	40	50	15	20	25	30	40
1990				3				1		1		1
1991				1				1		1		1
1992			1							2	1	1
1993			1							2	1	1
1994			1							2		1
1995			1							2	1	2
1996			1							2	1	2
1997			1						2	2	1	1
1998			1						1	1	1	2
1999			1	1		1			1	3	1	3
2000			1	1		1	1		2	3	1	3
2001			2	1				1	2	2		3
2002			1	1		1	1		2	3		3
2003			1	2		1	1		1	3		3
2004			1	3		1	2		1	3		3
2005		3	3	4		7	2			3		3
2006		4	3	5		7	1			2		3
2007		6	3	5		9	1			3		4
2008		6	3	5		11	4			3		4
2009		3	2	5		4	2			2		4
2010	3	6	4	4		12	2	2		2	1	3
2011	1	4	1	5	4	10	2			3		3
2012	1	5	2	4	4	13	3		1	1		4
2013	1	6	3	4	4	12	3		2	1		3

Source: Forbes (1990–2013), authors' compilation from various secondary sources
Note: The table provides a summary of the distribution of billionaires across the UK industries using the two-code GICS. The data is presented on a five-year interval basis. The number and associated sectors are: **10:** Energy, **15:** Materials, **20:** Industrials, **25:** Consumer Discretionary, **30:** Consumer Staple, **35:** Health Care, **40:** Financials, **45:** Information Technology, **50:** Telecommunications, **55:** Utilities

sample, at approximately 2007. In fact, in 2006, there was only one individual with a fortune in excess of $1 billion, that being Joseph Lewis. The lack of property moguls in Germany compared to Britain can be explained by a comparison of house prices in those countries. Knoll, Schularick and Steger (2017) found that over the period 1980–2012, UK property prices far outpaced those in Germany. On average, UK property prices rose by 7.10% per annum, compared to Germany which saw house prices decreasing by 1.68% per annum over the same period. In absolute terms, German house prices rose 59% over this period, compared to 616% for the UK. Although many factors could be cited for the rapid rise in house prices in the UK, one primary candidate must reside in the effective 'privatisation' of home ownership. In 1981, the Thatcher Government introduced the Right-to-Buy scheme where tenants of local authority housing were provided with a 60% discount to purchase the dwelling outright. According to King (2012), the effect of the Right-to-Buy was to shift 2.5 million dwellings in the less regulated private sector. The scheme along with liberalisation of the mortgage market effectively increased demand from the working-classes for owner-occupied housing.

The massive increase in the debt-to-income ratio of the UK described in Chap. 3 further provides an element of causality to this. The beginnings of the property boom in the 1980s, was also when individuals such as John Whittaker, and the Reuben brothers already possessed significant wealth holdings in property to benefit from the inevitable property price increases (Harper, 2013). Of Iraqi Jewish ancestry, and originally born in India, the brothers were brought up in relatively privileged surroundings. However, both of their fortunes were largely self-made. Simon Reuben originally started in real estate, whilst David Reuben engaged in metals trading in the 1970s. By the 1990s, the two brothers had combined their business interests and heavily invested in Russia's metals industry. After a legal dispute with their Russian partners, the brothers divested from their Russian and Kazakh holdings and heavily invested in real estate, predominantly in the United Kingdom (Lunn, 2014). The concomitant property boom of the 2000s in the United Kingdom, and particularly in London, ensured substantial gains for the brothers catapulting them into the billionaire club. Other beneficiaries of the 2000s property boom abound. One of the elder statesmen of the British propertied class, Yorkshire man John Whittaker, established investments across the north Eastern England. Whittaker joined the family business, Peel Holdings in the 1970s and successfully steered the company on a path of substantial growth. As has often been identified with property tycoons, the genesis of their wealth often resided in the investment and capitalisation of properties that would be under heavy demand. In the case of the Whittakers, this was exemplified by heavy investments in retail warehouse spaces, foreshadowing the rise of large shopping centres (Mathiason, 2009). Since then, Whittaker's Peel Holdings (that has remained majority family owned) has diversified into port holdings and large shopping centres. Most recently, the British Broadcasting Corporation moved to a new house to be located in Media City in Greater Manchester. Whittaker effectively assuming mantle of the BBC's landlord with the former renting 36 acres of buildings and several TV studios. Since the deal, he is reported to have amassed a wealth of $2.5 billion (Harper, 2013).

Despite a history of landed aristocracy, inherited wealth remains of relatively less import at least at the extreme end of the wealth distribution tail. Only two individuals appear in the list who are of British peerage ancestry. The wealthiest is Gerald Grosvenor with an estimated net worth of $11 billion. The modern heir has numerous holdings including 300 acres in Mayfair, 25,000 acreage grouse moor in Abbeystead, Lancashire, and an impressive 13,000 acres of farmland near the patrimonial home of Eaton Hall (Treneman, 1998). Unlike many of the British aristocracy whose position in the wealth ladder largely disappeared, Grosvenor very much views that the dynasty's inheritance is to be protected and grown for future generations rather than squandering the family's fortune through his own vices. A telling description the mindset that drives Gerald Grosvenor appears in the following quote:

> Yet he remains a paternalistic (some say feudal) landlord who is not above controlling his tenants and who is adamantly opposed to the right to roam. "Private" signs pepper his estates…. "I do not really feel that I own this land," he has said. "This land has been in our family for the last 900 years and it will, hopefully, continue to be in the family for the next 900 years. It would be inconceivable for me to dispose of it. I do not have a sense of ownership. It is a sense of duty and responsibility." (Treneman, 1998)

Beneficiary of the UK's peerage system, Gerald Grosvenor, Duke of Westminster, comes from a lineage that can be traced back to Sir Richard Grosvenor, 1st Baronet (born 1585). Peerage has been kind also to Charles Cadogan, the only other member of the British peerage system to be represented in the rich lists. With an estimated net worth in 2013 of $5.5 billion, much of Cadogan's wealth is tied up in extensive holdings in the exclusive and prestigious London suburbs of Chelsea and Knightsbridge.

Given the pre-eminence of London as a global financial centre one would be expected to find numerous individuals involved heavily in banking and finance-related activities. There is, however, a tendency for the success to have been attributable to the ballooning of asset prices in the 2000s. As with real estate, most of these individuals can be classified as self-made, the majority of these emerging during the 1990s and 2000s—with many employing a variety of strategies. A common element, between all, however, appears to be the rapid capitalisation of opportunities brought upon by the sudden financial deregulations, the 'Big Bang' during 1986 and 1987. A clear and direct instance of an individual capitalising on the deregulation was Peter Cruddas who made a fortune from financial spread-betting by founding CMC Markets in 1989. Spread-betting, the method of wagering on price movements, began in the 1960s and was regulated under the *Betting and Gaming Act 1960*. In 1986, the financial deregulations transformed futures contracts from a wager into an investment product enforceable under the *Financial Services Act*. This reform significantly increased the number of participants in the futures market (Loussouarn, 2013). Almost immediately, the spread-betting industry also managed to get the courts to rule that spread-betting, like futures contracts, were qualified as financial investments under the *Financial Services Act* 1986, thus opening CMC Market to a much wider market.

The Economic Elite in the Former Centrally Planned Economies

Thus far, the discussion has largely focused on the advanced capitalist economies of the western hemisphere. In this section, an exploration of the development and evolution of the economic elite amongst the three largest economies outside of the western bloc is discussed. Specifically, Russia, China and India are focused upon. The focus is on determining to what extent they share characteristics with the western elite, and how they can be differentiated.

Table 5.5 provides a sectoral breakdown across the three countries. Overall, both China and Russia exhibit very high growth rates in billionaire numbers, particularly after 2005. In Russia, the annual average growth rate is 44% since the first billionaire appeared in the list in 1997. In China, the average annual growth is higher at 77% although the first Chinese billionaire appears in 2001, a few years after the first Russians make an appearance.

Sector wise, there are certain differences worth noting. Russian billionaires are largely clustered around three industries: materials (GICS 10); industrials (GICS 20); and financials (GICS 40). In 2013, these three industries accounted for 77% of Russian billionaires. In monetary terms, the combined wealth of this 77% is at an estimated $321USD billion in 2013. Or approximately 10% of Russia's gross national income $3.1USD trillion in 2013.

By contrast, the sectoral breakdown of China's economic elite exhibits far more diversity in the number of individuals across industries. The largest represented industry is financials with 28 individuals appearing on the rich list in 2013. This is closely followed by industrials with 25 individuals, consumer discretionary with 21 billionaires, and materials and health care with 15 and 13 individuals, respectively. Jointly, these individuals constitute the bulk of China's billionaires as at 2013, contributing approximately 94% to China's elites. In monetary terms, the combined wealth of the individuals in these industries is at an estimated USD198 billion.

Table 5.5 Billionaire industrial distribution across Russia, China and India

	Russia										
	10	**15**	**20**	**25**	**30**	**35**	**40**	**45**	**50**		**Total**
1997	3			1							4
1998		1									1
2001	6	1	1								8
2002	4	1	1								6
2003	10	3	1				2		1		17
2004	12	5	3				4		1		25
2005	6	10	4				6		1		27
2006	5	14	6				8		1		34
2007	8	19	11	2	1		11		1		53
2008	9	22	17	5	4	1	29		1		88
2009	6	12	6	1			7		1		33
2010	7	22	14	1	1		13		1		59
2011	9	32	26	6	4	1	22	1	1		102
2012	9	29	27	2	3		25	1	1		97
2013	11	33	28	5	6	1	24	2	1		111
	China										
	10	**15**	**20**	**25**	**30**	**35**	**40**	**45**	**50**	**55**	**Total**
2001			1								1
2002					1						1
2004			1								1
2005			1	1							2
2006			2	1	2		2	1			8
2007		1	4	2	4	1	4	1			17
2008	3	4	9	4	5	1	12	4			42
2009	1	2	10	3	4		6	2			28
2010	1	9	13	12	9	2	20	6			72
2011	2	15	24	21	9	15	21	7	1		115
2012	2	11	21	20	0	8	18	6			86
2013	2	15	25	21	11	13	28	5		1	120
	India										
	10	**15**	**20**	**25**	**30**	**35**	**40**	**45**	**50**		**Total**
1990			1								1
1991			1								1
1992			1								1
1993			1								1
1994			2								2
1995			2								2
1996	1	1	1								3
1997	1	1	2								4
1998	1	1									2
1999	1	1	3					2			7
2000	1	1	3	1				3			9
2001	1		1					2			4
2002	1	1	1					2			5
2003	1	1	1		1		1	2			7
2004	1	2	1		1		1	2	1		9

(continued)

Table 5.5 (continued)

2005	1	3	2		1	1	1	2	1	12
2006	2	2	5	3	2	2	3	3	1	23
2007	2	3	8	6	2	3	6	5	1	36
2008	6	3	11	7	2	5	12	6	1	53
2009	1	3	3	5	1	3	5	2	1	24
2010	1	2	13	4	2	8	11	5	1	47
2011	2	6	10	7	2	8	11	7	2	55
2012	2	6	5	7	4	8	8	6	2	48
2013	2	6	6	11	4	10	10	5	1	55

Source: Forbes (1990–2013), authors' compilation from various secondary sources
Note: The table provides a summary of the distribution of billionaires across French industries using the two-code Global Industry Classification System (GICS). The data is presented on a five-year interval basis. The number and associated sectors are: **10:** Energy, **15:** Materials, **20:** Industrials, **25:** Consumer Discretionary, **30:** Consumer Staples, **35:** Health Care, **40:** Financials, **45:** Information Technology, **50:** Telecommunications, **55:** Utilities

In the case of both China and Russia, there is a total absence of inheritance. Given the relatively recent transition to market-based economies this is to be expected.

India's billionaire numbers in contrast demonstrate rather anaemic levels and growth, when juxtaposed against those of China and Russia. Despite possessing the second largest population in the world, India had by 2013 only 55 billionaires. The largest movement in billionaire numbers is apparent in the 2005–2006 period when the number doubled from 12 to 23 individuals. A similar and approximate doubling is observed from 2009 and 2010 when the number increased from 24 to 47, although this is largely attributable to the reappearance of billionaires who had fallen from the wealth lists due to the global financial crisis as was documented in Chap. 3. Table 5.5 presents a sectoral decomposition of India's economic elites. Similar to China, India's sectoral allocation of billionaires appears to be largely concentrated across five of the nine represented sectors, while the other four have five or less individuals. The industries with the greatest representation include consumer discretionary with 11, followed by financials and health care at 10.

Differentials in the sectoral composition across the three former centrally planned economies naturally lend itself to the question of what political processes were in play that caused such an outcome. For example, why are Russia's oligarchs concentrated in a few key industries whilst China and India appear to exhibit much more diversity in the composition of their sectoral billionaire allocation. Is it part of a natural market process or a conscious effort on the part of their respective governments?

Nefariously, the evolution of vast private wealth holdings in the former centrally planned economies have typically been closely tied to either public servant favour or to the former or current political elite rather than through the natural outcome of competition. In India, for example, the repeal of the Licence Raj, a system of elaborate licensing arrangements, reduced enterprise to just a few select large conglomerates. Indeed, the Licence Raj would entail acquiring up to 80 approvals from various governmental agencies, placing an effective stranglehold on fostering new enterprise, while protecting the commercial interests of the large conglomerates, where such family names such as Birla and Hinduja came to dominate. Once the Indian economy was liberalised with the dismantling of the Licence Raj system in 1991, the Indian industrial conglomerates were in the best position to attain scale and diversify into new business opportunities. (Hendrick-Wong, 2007). Economic reform, of course, did provide scope for new entrepreneurs. IT was largely ignored by India's central planners, enabling enterprising individuals to exploit a clear opportunity during the era of the Licence Raj. Even during this era, IT entrepreneurs not tied to conglomerates still faced potentially debilitating hurdles. For example:

> in the 1980s Narayana Murthy, the legendary founder of Infosys, one of India's leading IT companies and the first Indian firm to list on the US stock market, had to make 50 trips over a period of two years, traveling from Bangalore, ... to Delhi to meet with ... bureaucrats in order to get a permit to import a computer worth $1,500. (Hendrick-Wong, 2007, p. 67)

In China, the grip of the Communist Party since its takeover in 1949 meant that property rights were negligible until 1988. Indeed, during that era, there were no individual land rights and no private land ownership, but by 2013 25 Chinese billionaires had made their fortunes in property investments, excluding those from Hong Kong. A wave of reforms in the 1990s ensured that the road to rapid capitalisation would be open to Chinese entrepreneurs. Such laws included, for example, a 1997 constitutional amendment in which incomes from interest and dividends were sanctioned and, in 2006, it became possible for a private citizen to become the sole founding member of a limited liability entity (Clarke, Murrell & Whiting, 2008). Perhaps coincidently, during the same period, the number of Chinese billionaires increased from 2 in 2005 to 8 in 2006, before doubling to 17 by 2007. By 2013, there were 121 billionaires, second only to the US in terms of absolute numbers.

Has the transformation of the Chinese economy from a centrally planned regime to a market-based regime been wholly free from the past regime? That is, is China's new economic elite divorced of ties to the Communist Party (past and present), or is the economic and political elite effectively the same? A full analysis of this issue is beyond the scope of this chapter, but a number of basic facts provide a clue as to the composition and dynamics of China's economic elite. One journalistic wealth list, the *Hurun Report*, found that in 2011, for the 1000 richest people in China, 90% were either officials or founding members of the Chinese Communist Party. New officials often seek membership in the Communist Party to protect their wealth. For example:

> The top three richest members of the CPPCC [Chinese People's Political Consultative Conference] are all sons of Hong Kong tycoons, with Victor Li, the son of Asia's richest man Li Ka-shing, coming in first with an estimated family fortune of $32bn.
>
> Hong Kong's relatively smooth transition from a former British colony back to Chinese territory over the last 15 years has been helped by support from the territory's richest citizens, who were mostly co-opted by the Communist party in exchange for business opportunities on the mainland. (Anderlini, 2013, para. 11–12)

Numerous mechanisms are available to party insiders to protect their wealth, or to confer substantial competitive advantage vis-à-vis privately owned businesses. The close relationship between state and business affords numerous benefits to insiders. For example:

> The most important and lucrative sectors of the economy have been reserved for state-owned-enterprises (SOEs) through preferential policies and support that leaves private domestic firms at a heavy disadvantage. For example, during much of the past decade, around two-thirds of the country's formal finance (mainly bank loans) was reserved for SOEs at discounted rates, rising to an astounding 90% from 2008 to 2010 before settling back to its current 80%. (Lee, 2011, para. 3)

The family of China's former premier, Wen Jiabao, is believed to control assets worth approximately $2.7 billion. How the family achieved such prominence demonstrates the close nexus between political power and the generation and protection of vast wealth:

> Unlike most new businesses in China, the family's ventures sometimes received financial backing from state-owned companies, including China Mobile, one of the country's biggest phone operators….

> The holdings include a villa development project in Beijing; a tire factory in northern China; a company that helped build some of Beijing's Olympic stadiums, including the well-known 'Bird's Nest'; and Ping An Insurance, one of the world's biggest financial services companies. (Barboza, 2012, para. 6–7)

The apparent monopoly of economic advantage by Communist Party insiders echoes Figueroa's (2008) view that the rise of an economic elite first erects barriers to entry and Bodley's (1999) claim that any major growth policies are aimed to benefit the growth in the incumbent elite's wealth or economic power.

In the case of Eastern Europe, similar factors are at play, but there is some debate over the true reason for the number of billionaires. Corruption is the most often cited explanation for the size of the fortunes of some of Russia's billionaires, or the 'Russian oligarchs' as they are often labelled. Torgler and Piatti (2013) persuasively argue that much of the extraordinary wealth observed in former Communist states is generated from collusion between former Communist Party members of the Soviet Union, and the incumbent regime.

Alternatively, Kryshtanovskaya and White (2005) examine the evolution of Russia's oligarchy and find that there is increasing state interference and control over the oligarchs, resulting in fewer individuals presiding over vast conglomerates. Further, they document the increasing representation of wealthy individuals in many of Russia's decision-making institutions at both a federal and regional level. The interlocking relationships do not necessarily imply corruption. They conclude that Russia's oligarchy is most likely to follow the pattern of South Korea's *chaebols,* where a few wealthy families with close ties to government possess substantial control and ownership over the country's resources (Kryshtanovskaya & White, 2005).

How has Russia's wealth evolved under President Putin? Rutland (2009) argues that there has been a spreading of wealth from oil and gas to various other industries. The bulk emanates from banking, largely due to the recycling of the petrodollar earned during the 1990s. However, Rutland (2009) agrees with Kryshtanovskaya and White (2005) that the impact of Putin's policies has been to concentrate wealth into fewer hands, even if it is spread across more industries—this process, however, has been part of a conscious effort by the Russian government.

South Korea and Japan: Dominance of Family Dynasties?

Shifting focus to the East Asian region, specifically Japan and South Korea, there is substantial and readily available evidence that government policies constituted the key element in the growth of many of the fortunes. A priori, one could assume that the two countries would share many similarities that would filter through to the characteristics and composition of their wealthy. Both countries are viewed as the original Asian tigers and are often viewed as sharing a common ideological and cultural trajectory. After the Second World War, both countries embarked on a programme of orientating their respective economies to exporting, with Japan the pioneer throughout the 1950s and 1960s and Korea following suit throughout the 1970s.

From the perspective of the observer of the ultra-rich, the similarities stop there. An examination of the wealth sources, presented in Table 5.6, presents striking differences. Firstly, there is a divergence in the overall trends. As of 2013, the number of Korean billionaires has peaked at 25, whilst in Japan it fell to 22, one of the lowest recorded points. For Japan, the decrease is secular since the early 1990s when Japanese dominated the world rich lists. The main breaking point for Japan appears in 2001, when the number of billionaires fell from a high of 43 in 2000 to 29 in 2001 with further declines in subsequent years. Conversely, in South Korea it can be observed that the number of billionaires has historically remained low. On average, there were approximately 3 to 4 billionaires in Korea during the 1990s and first half of the 2000s. However, from 2007 there has been a clear increase in the number of known extreme wealthy. In 2007, the number of billionaires increased to 7, and by 2013 it had increased to 25, representing an increase of 300% since 2007.

Secondly, the trends in the two countries are being principally driven by divergent patterns in the dynamics of inherited wealth and the infusion of new wealth. Indeed, examining South Korea, the number of individuals with inherited wealth increased from 8 in 2007 to 19 by 2013, compared to 2 and 6 for those of self-made wealth. In Japan, the reverse is observed. Since a high of 22 in 1993, the number of Japanese inheritance beneficiaries has decreased to single digits hitting a low of 5 in 2011 before settling at 6 in 2012 and 2013. Instead, the bulk of Japanese wealth now comes from entrepreneurial initiatives.

Table 5.6 disaggregates the South Korean wealth ranks by sector, industry and inheritance. By far the majority of movement has been in the capital goods (20) and consumer discretionary (25) industries. In both, the number

Table 5.6 South Korean industrial distribution of billionaires, 1990–2013

	Self-made						Inherited			
Year	15	20	25	35	40	45	20	25	30	40
1990		2	2				1			
1991		2	2				1			
1992		1	2							
1993		1	2				1			
1994		1	2							
1995		3	3				1	1		
1996		2	3				1	1		
1997		1	1				1	1		
1998			1							
1999			1				1			
2000							1			
2001							2			
2002			1				1			
2003			1				1			
2004			1				1			
2005			1				1	1		
2006			1				2	1		
2007	1		1				2	5	1	
2008	1						3	7	1	
2009							1	3		
2010							3	6		1
2011			1			1	3	9	1	1
2012			1			1	7	9	1	1
2013		3	1	1	1		6	10	1	2

Source: Forbes (1990–2013), authors' compilation from various secondary sources

Note: The table provides a summary of the distribution of billionaires across South Korean industries using the two-code GICS. The data is presented on a five-year interval basis. The number and associated sectors are: **10:** Energy, **15:** Materials, **20:** Industrials, **25:** Consumer Discretionary, **30:** Consumer Staples, **35:** Health Care, **40:** Financials, **45:** Information Technology, **50:** Telecommunications, **55:** Utilities

of self-made has remained exceptionally low, and are often tied to the names of some of Korea's oldest entrepreneurs, such as the founder of Samsung, Lee Byung-chul. With the death of many of these individuals in the 1990s, there is a dramatic swelling of the ranks of Korea's inheritance billionaires to family members. For example, the Lee family accounts for five names at least, while the Koo family of Lucky Goldstar (LG) also show a similar dominance.

The families that dominate South Korea's industrial and commercial landscape have done so since the 1950s. Their transition to billionaire status in the 2000s followed the success of their respective commercial interests across the globe. The manner in which Korean families came to dominate Korea's economic life echoes that found in India, where the primary unit of Korea's industrial organisation, the conglomerates known as *chaebol* were central. The *chaebol* became the favoured vehicles for Korea's rapid industrialisation in the 1960s by the Park regime. For example, under Lee Byung-Chul's leadership, Samsung managed to develop a close and substantial commercial relationship with the Park military dictatorship during the 1960s.

Although state privilege and patrimony explain the initial success of the *chaebol* and their dynastic owners, the narrative of how they have maintained such commercial control shifts in the recent past. Kwon and O'Donnell (2001) argue that much of this narrative changes in examining the decades after the 1980s when state privilege largely disappeared. The response of the *chaebol* was to consolidate their economic power through rapid diversification and control throughout the Korean economy. By the 1990s, Samsung had diversified into electronics, engineering and construction. Today, such is the dominance of Samsung (and by extension the Lee family) in Korean society and economy that it has been estimated that Samsung's revenue equates to approximately 17% of South Korea's economic output. The Koo family, whose name is synonymous with LG, followed a very similar evolution. The process of diversification, however, does not necessarily involve majority ownership stakes in newly acquired firms. A distinct mechanism used is that of tunnelling. Johnson, La Porta, Lopez-de-Silanes, and Shleifer (2000) define tunnelling as 'the transfer of resources out of a company to its controlling shareholder (who is typically also a top manager)' (p. 3). These tactics allow a controlling shareholder to extend vast control over a network of enterprises often involving a degree of wealth transfer from smaller shareholders to the family dynasty (Baek, Kang, & Lee, 2006). As Moskalev and Park (2010) observe, despite the *chaebol* only claiming 10.96% of the cash flow generated by their firms, they paradoxically maintain full control over these firms—with most of the funds funnelled to the family dynasties. Baek et al. (2006) find that at least with private security offerings there is very strong evidence that the controlling interests of the *chaebol* typically accrue substantial and material private benefits at the expense of minority ownership.

If for Korean wealth the rise and dominance of *chaebol* characterises the ultra-wealthy, then for Japan, it is the fall of many of the dominant families and the rise of an entrepreneurial *nouveau riche*. The experience of Japan's wealthy is perhaps somewhat at odds with the story of stagnation that has beset Japan's economy since the early 1990s. As presented in Table 5.7, the degree of old or inherited wealth has shown a systematic decrease since the mid-1990s. In 1990, 22 individuals or families had inherited their wealth, and by 2013 the number had fallen to just 6. In contrast, the self-made billionaires, though initially decreasing from a high of 27 in 2007, have been in the mid-teens throughout the 2000s and in fact have slightly grown since

Table 5.7 Japanese industrial distribution of billionaires, 1990–2013

	Self-made								Inherited							
Year	15	20	25	30	35	40	45	50	0	10	15	20	30	35	40	45
1990	4	2	11		1	10	1					4	2	1	4	1
1991	4	2	12		1	10	1					4	2	1	3	1
1992	1	2	5			9	1					6	3	1	4	1
1993	1	1	6			9	1					8	3	1	5	2
1994	1		7			9	1					6	1	1	6	1
1995	1	2	10		1	10	2				1	4	1	1	4	1
1996		3	12		1	8	3				2	4	1		5	1
1997		1	5			3	2					0	0		2	1
1998			3			3	1					0	1		4	
1999		2	10		1	5	1	1			2	1	1		5	1
2000		3	11	1	2	5	6	1	2		2	3	1		4	2
2001		2	10		2	3	2				1	3	1		4	1
2002		1	9		1	3	1			1	1	2	1		4	1
2003			8			3	1					1	1		4	1
2004		1	9			3	1				1	1	1		4	1
2005		1	9			4	1	1			1	1	1		4	1
2006		1	9			4	2	1			1	1	1		6	1
2007		1	10			3	2	1			1	1	1		3	1
2008		1	9			3	3	1			1	1	1		3	1
2009		1	8			2	2					0	1		2	1
2010		1	11	1		2	3					1	1		2	1
2011		1	16			2	4					0	0		2	1
2012		1	13	1		2	4					0	0		2	1
2013		1	10	1		2	3	1	1			0	1		1	1

Source: Forbes (1990–2013), authors' compilation from various secondary sources
Note: The table provides a summary of the distribution of billionaires across Japanese industries using the two-code GICS. The data is presented on a five-year interval basis. The number and associated sectors are: **10:** Energy, **15:** Materials, **20:** Industrials, **25:** Consumer Discretionary, **30:** Consumer Staples, **35:** Health Care, **40:** Financials, **45:** Information Technology, **50:** Telecommunications, **55:** Utilities

2011. Across both the self-made and inherited groups, financials fell from 14 (10 self-made, 4 inherited) individuals in 1990 to 3 in 2013. The fall is in line with the significant fall in Japan's wealth-income ratio during the early 1990s, where the fall in the value of property prices played a central role, as discussed in Chap. 3.

Much of Japan's ultra-rich arose in the post-war era. Unlike Germany, the continuity from an earlier Japanese economic elite is absent. Even among the 'older' wealth in Japan, wealth generated in the vicinity of the Second World War, the linkages to the old *zaibatsu* are either non-existent, or they are of sufficiently different nature to not permit a historical lineage found in, for example, Germany. Compared to post-war Germany, many of the Japanese industrialists did not successfully navigate allied occupation. Rather, smaller, newer entrepreneurs arose in their place. In the early post-war period, the Allied General Command instituted policies to dissolve the *zaibatsu*, based on the rationale that they regarded the *zaibatsu* as an important mechanism in the creation of and maintenance of Japan's militaristic and imperialistic tendencies. Delving into the detail provided by the rich lists, the Allied policy generally appears to have succeeded in its endeavour of severing Japan's economic links to its imperialistic past. Among the inherited wealth group, the Matsushita family is the only one that can directly be associated with the older economic order. The Matsushita family name had, however, vanished from the *Forbes* list by 1996. Only for the Toyodas, founders and major shareholders in Toyota Motor Corporation (TMC), has allied occupation and the Korean War proved to be a boon. Unlike other *zaibatsu* and the associated controlling families, the Toyoda family emerged relatively unscathed from the war and the subsequent Allied occupation and have managed to maintain a presence (Bernstein, 1997).

In the absence of the *zaibatsu*, and with very little to tie them to Japan's imperial adventures, the small nascent enterprises being established in Japan were largely ignored by Allied occupying forces. The absence of the large *zaibatsu* provided a vacuum into which many entrepreneurs poured in. These entrepreneurs found wealth and fortune in industries that rode to prominence in the consumerism wave of the post-War globe which export orientated Japan could exploit. As Table 5.5 shows, the majority are concentrated in consumer discretionary sector, with most emanating from retail, electronics and gaming (be it casino or video game entertainment). Perhaps the most well-known Japanese electronics conglomerate is Sony. The founding of Sony in the immediate aftermath of the war exemplifies the success of the Japanese entrepreneur in developing new opportunities. Sony was founded in the immediate post-war period by Akio Morita and Masaru Ibuka. Early on both agreed to a corporate style that would be free of any *zaibatsu* influence. This freedom ensured that 'the founders were able to exercise real management in the establishment of Sony' (Lambert, 2001, p. 33). Approximately 67 years after the founding of Sony, many of Morita's relatives and offspring have morphed Sony into a conglomerate with businesses groups spanning home electronics, gaming, consumable entertainment and financial services. Once again, in a model seemingly replicated across time and space, when the original founder is no longer heavily involved or has passed away, there is a clear movement towards the diversification of business interests, often significantly expanding beyond original business lines. The associated concomitant increase in wealth perhaps attests to the success of such a strategy.

In gaming, names synonymous with businesses that have captured both the Japanese thirst for entertainment and gambling abound. Much of their initial success had almost wholly to do with pent up consumer demand but requiring circumventing government policies on gambling and gaming. The *pachinko* industry grew out of a means of negating the prohibition on gambling (Criminal Code, Chapter 23)—the *pachinko* slot machines involve getting a ball into a slot. Successfully doing so entails the user to a prize that often involves an avenue to exchanging the prize for a monetary reward (Kinder, 2014). The potential for arbitrage was not lost on Han Chang-Woo Han who became the biggest and wealthiest supplier of the slot machines (Whan-woo, 2014).

The obvious question is whether self-made wealth will continue to dominate in Japan. Given the low growth rates and high savings rates in Japan and slow population growth, one could argue that inheritance will invariably come to play a significant role in Japan. As Japan has the highest observed wealth-income ratios among the countries considered here (see Chap. 3), the possibility does certainly exist that inheritance will come to play a strong role.

Australia and New Zealand

Writing on the wealth of the Gilded Age, Rubinstein (1980) argued that the size of the observed riches in the US to Great Britain was very much a product of the large land mass of the US relative to Great Britain. Given the size of Australia, and the relatively small population density, one would expect Australia to have also produced substantial wealth. In the context of Australia, a similar set of forces seems to apply to the observed composition of ultra-rich. Table 5.8 presents the combined sectorial distribution of wealthy individuals for Australia and New Zealand.

A perusal of Australia's popular media would often suggest that the majority of Australia's economic elite come from the ranks of miners and media moguls. However, as Table 5.6 shows, most of the great fortunes come from finance in the form of diversified financials. The majority who appear in the list are relatively new entrants, with the number from financial services increasing from five in 2006 to 13 by 2013. Among the property magnates, there is a small increase from three in 2004 to 6 by 2013. In financial terms, aggregate wealth among this group increased from USD4.800 billion to USD17.6 billion over the course of the same period. In the diversified financials sector, the rise over the 2006–2013 period is just as impressive. In 2005,

Table 5.8 Australian and New Zealand industrial distribution of billionaires, 1990–2013

Year	10	15	20	25	30	35	40
1990				1			
1991				1			
1992				1			
1993				1			
1994				1			
1995				1			
1996				1			
1997				1			
1998				1			
1999		1		1			
2000		1		1			
2001	1	1		1			
2002				1	1		
2003		1		1			
2004		1		1			
2005		1		2			
2006	1	1		2			5
2007	1	3		4			7
2008	1	3	2	3			9
2009		3		2			7
2010		2		4			7
2011		3	2	4		1	10
2012		4	2	3		1	11
2013		2	2	6	1	1	13

Source: Forbes (1990–2013), authors' compilation from various secondary sources
Note: The table provides a summary of the distribution of billionaires across Australian and New Zealand industries using the two-code GICS. The data is presented on a five-year interval basis. The number and associated sectors are: **10:** Energy, **15:** Materials, **20:** Industrials, **25:** Consumer Discretionary, **30:** Consumer Staples, **35:** Health Care, **40:** Financials, **45:** Information Technology, **50:** Telecommunications, **55:** Utilities

there were no Australian or New Zealand investors that could claim a net worth in excess of $1 billion. In 2006, there were two, both from New Zealand, and by 2013 there were six from both Australia and New Zealand. Just like the property tycoons, their associated aggregate wealth holdings substantially increased over this period. In 2006, the New Zealanders Richard Chandler and Graeme Hart had a combined net worth of $3.7 billion. By 2013, a small increase in the Australian representative contingent had bolstered aggregate holdings to $20.2 billion. Among the Australians are Michael Hintze, Kerr Neilson and Ivan Glasenberg.

Much of the wealth generated by property investments are associated with property development rather than pure speculation, and very much follows the patterns of the US, whose government policies in the post-war era fuelled massive demographical changes and coincidently provided ample opportunity for expansion. Individuals such as Frank Lowy, John Gandel, Harry Triguboff and Langley Walker all benefited from these changes. For Frank Lowy, the longest-serving Australian billionaire, the path to great wealth resided in entrepreneurial alertness to the massive urbanisation across Australia's metropolitan cities. Mass immigration, growth in public housing and increasing industrial production provided the necessary catalyst to spur population increases from which Lowy was able to significantly capitalise. Similarly, John Gandel managed to exploit rising population and incomes in Melbourne's south-eastern suburbs to create one of the largest shopping centres. Gandel's road to riches started with the inheritance of his parents' successful Australian clothing business, Sussan, in the 1970s. A latecomer to property development, Gandel purchased Chadstone Shopping Centre in 1983 and has since expanded to other Australian cities.

The miners perhaps represent most accurately the Australian economic story over the past decade. The boom in the mining business has generated enormous levels of national income for Australia throughout the 1990s and 2000s. It is, therefore, startling that among Australia's wealthiest individuals, only two from mining are recorded by *Forbes*. Nevertheless, the combined wealth of those two, Gina Rinehart and Andrew Forrest, in 2013 was an estimated $22.7 billion compared to, for example, the $17.6 billion estimated for the property sector. Although a booming China represents the obvious reason for the wealth of the miners, the actual genesis often lies much earlier as is often the case. The genesis of the Rinehart fortune is largely found in a fierce political battle, in which Rinehart's father, Lang Hancock, managed to gain a virtual monopoly over the Pilbara region's iron ore deposits through a fierce campaign against the Western Australian government (Jamieson, 2011). Gina Rinehart has carried on her father's legacy in terms of both business ambition and political influence. The other titan of Australian mining, Andrew Forrest, founder of the mining company Fortescue Mining Ltd., demonstrated a keen sense of entrepreneurial awareness in extending the fortunes he has generated throughout the Pilbara region in Western Australia. A significant element of both individuals has been the propensity to enlarge the scope of their holdings, with both entering agriculture on an enormous scale, mainly in response to slowing demand from Asia for iron ore.

Media and entertainment, often considered the other great pillar of Australia's wealthy, has generally remained a small affair, with only a few making the list. When one considers the small size of the Australian market, this may not be surprising. Although the Murdoch family once resided in Australia, since Rupert Murdoch took up US citizenship, they no longer appear in

Australian wealth lists. Instead, Kerry Packer (deceased) and his son James Packer, and the part-time media mogul, Kerry Stokes, dominate the list. Kerry Packer's rise to wealth resides in the media empire first established by his grandfather, Sir Frank Packer. Kerry Packer significantly altered the family's business interests by shifting into gaming and film production. Given the exit of James Packer from Australia's media industry, in reality the only other wealthy individual now associated with media is Kerry Stokes. Stokes very much represents the romanticised rags-to riches-story that stands in stark contrast to the story of the Packers and other Australian wealth dynasties. Often forgotten, Stokes' diversified interests are such that, along with his holdings in WesTrac, he now largely controls the lucrative machinery hire sector in Australia.

Summary

This chapter analyses the major social and policy sources of great fortunes amongst many of the world's largest economies. The analysis at the national levels reveals striking differences in the source of wealth and how it is managed. The most significant finding pertains to the degree of differentiation between the relative proportions of inheritance and self-made wealth. North America (dominated by the US), the UK and Australia all exhibit a trend towards more self-made individuals appearing in the ranks of the economic elite. The rise of the self-made billionaire is only evident in Japan. The finding in Japan is somewhat counterintuitive given the significant element of state patrimony in the business affairs of Japan's corporations. By contrast, France, Germany and South Korea all exhibit greater representation of inherited wealth amongst their wealthiest.

For the self-made wealthy, amongst the Anglo-Saxon countries, in countries where self-made wealth dominates, much of the evidence suggests that fortuitous social and political developments played a substantial role. This is particularly prevalent amongst those industries which benefitted greatly by the changes in political landscape in the post-Second World War era. In Australia and the US, property interests benefited greatly from the great urbanisation and immigration developments of the era. Even amongst industries where direct state aid may have been absent, there still appear to be substantial government influence. Both the finance and information technology sectors benefitted substantially from deregulation in the case of finance, to public aid in research and development in the instance of information technology moguls.

The role of the state in great fortunes is far more evident in countries where inheritance dominates the wealth ranks. In Germany and South Korea, various governments and regimes throughout history have supported the rise of family dynasties. In Germany, the immediate post-war period saw many dynasties manage to maintain their control over vast swathes of Germany's industrial base despite close ties to the Nazi regime. In South Korea, certain dynasties were favoured to ensure rapid national growth.

The many ways in which the individuals managed their vast fortunes suggests that diversification plays an important role. Across most family dynasties, inheritance beneficiaries tend to form major conglomerates with commercial interests across various industries or through diversified financial holdings. Similarly, this strategy is reflected amongst the oldest self-made cohorts. Many individuals are observed to have divested their holdings in their original founding enterprises and subsequently moved into financial investments or property holdings. The consequent decline of overall entrepreneurial effort in some countries and the move into more rentier-based activities, particularly by inheritance beneficiaries, may be a response to the observation of declining real rates of return.

Finally, a significant finding is the extent to which finance dominates self-made wealth across the UK, the US, France and Australia compared to the other countries examined. Here, either financial deregulation or agreeable property-related dynamics have given rise to vast fortunes. This echoes one of the defining characteristics of the first Gilded Age, which was the prevalence of the financiers among the extremely wealthy (Rockoff, 2012).

References

Anderlini, J. (2013, March 7). Chinese parliament holds 83 billionaires. *Financial Times*. Retrieved from http://www.ft.com/

Backhaus, S., & Hanßler, B. (2014). An inventor with heart. *Be Top, 1*, 29–31.

Baek, S., Kang, J., & Lee, I. (2006). Business groups and tunneling: Evidence from private securities offerings by Korean chaebols. *The Journal of Finance, 61*(5), 2415–2449.

Bagdikian, B. H. (2000). *The media monopoly*. Boston: Beacon Press.

Barboza, D. (2012, October 26). Family of China's Wen worth billions. *Australian Financial Review*. Retrieved from http://www.afr.com

Berger, M. (2010, September 9). John W. Kluge, Metromedia's founder and a major philanthropist, dies at 95. *The New York Times*, p. A29.

Bernstein, J. R. (1997). Toyoda automatic looms and Toyota automobiles. In T. K. McCraw (Ed.), *Creating modern capitalism how entrepreneurs, companies, and countries triumphed in three industrial revolutions* (pp. 396–438). Cambridge, MA: Harvard University Press.

Bodley, J. H. (1999). Socioeconomic growth, culture scale, and household well-being: A test of the power-elite hypothesis. *Current Anthropology, 40*, 595–620.

Bourne, L. S. (2014). Urban geography in transition: A Canadian perspective on the 1980s and beyond. In B. J. L. Berry & J. O. Wheeler (Eds.), *Urban geography in America 1950–2000: Paradigms and personalities* (pp. 191–216). New York: Routledge.

Bryant, A. (1994, December 20). Edward J. DeBartolo, developer, 85, is dead. *The New York Times*, p. A17(N).

Canterbery, E. R., & Nosari, E. J. (1985). The Forbes four hundred: The determinants of super-wealth. *Southern Economic Journal, 5*, 1073–1083.

Ceruzzi, P. E. (2003). *A history of modern computing*. Cambridge, MA: MIT Press.

Chung, J. (2014, May 28). Ziffs shut down hedge fund, shift way wealth is managed. *The Wall Street Journal*. Retrieved from http://www.wsj.com/

Clark, A. (2000). The first PC. *Wired, 8*(12). Retrieved from http://archive.wired.com/

Clarke, D., Murrell, P., & Whiting, S. (2008). The role of law in China's economic development. In T. Rawski & L. Brandt (Eds.), *China's great economic transformation* (pp. 375–427). Cambridge, UK: Cambridge University Press.

Committee on Innovations in Computing and Communications: Lessons from History. (1999). *Funding a revolution: Government support for computing research*. Washington, DC: National Academy Press.

Daumard, A. (1980). Wealth and affluence in France since the beginning of the nineteenth century. In W. D. Rubinstein (Ed.), *Wealth and the wealthy in the modern world* (pp. 90–121). London: Croom Helm.

Demirgruc-Kunt, A., & Levine, R. (1999). *Bank-based and market-based financial systems: Cross-country comparisons*. World Bank Policy Research Working Paper. Retrieved from http://elibrary.worldbank.org/

Dolan, K. A., & Kroll, L. (2001, June 21). Billionaire dynasties. *Forbes*. Retrieved from http://www.forbes.com/

Feldman, G. D. (2001). *Allianz and the German insurance business, 1933–1945*. Cambridge, UK: Cambridge University Press.

Figueroa, A. (2008). Competition and circulation of economic elites: Theory and application to the case of Peru. *The Quarterly Review of Economics and Finance, 48*, 263–273.

Fohlin, C. (2005). The history of corporate ownership and control in Germany. In R. K. Morck (Ed.), *A history of corporate governance around the world family business groups to professional managers*. Lake Louise, AB: NBER.

Forbes. (1990–2013). *The world's billionaires*. Retrieved from http://www.forbes.com/lists

Forsyth, A. (2005). *Reforming suburbia. The planned communities of Irvine, Columbia, and the Woodlands*. Berkeley, CA: University of California Press.

Frieden, B. J., & Sagalyn, L. B. (1991). *Downtown, Inc., how America rebuilds cities*. Cambridge, MA: MIT Press.

Gerschenkron, A. (1998). *Economic backwardness in historical perspective*. London: Routledge.

Goldsmith, R. W. (1969). *Financial structure and development*. New Haven, CT: Yale University Press.

Harper, T. (2013, October 18). The biggest company you've never heard of: Lifting the lid on Peel Group – The property firm owned by reclusive tax exile John Whittaker. *The Independent*. Retrieved from http://www.independent.co.uk/

Hendrick-Wong, Y. (2007). *Succeeding like success: The affluent consumers of Asia*. Singapore, Singapore: Wiley.

Hevesi, D. (2011, September 11). Frank Batten Sr., media executive and founder of Weather Channel, dies at 82. *The New York Times*, p. A17.

Hillman, K. (2001). Die 100 reichsten DeutschenGespür für "Leichen im Keller". *SpiegelOnline*. Retrieved from http://www.spiegel.de/

Hirsch, M. (1911). *The problem of wealth (an open letter to Andrew Carnegie) and other essays*. Melbourne, VIC: Renwick, Pride, Nuttall Pty. Ltd..

Hobbs, S., & Toscano, P. (2014, January). Four-year boom expected for the US hotel industry. *CNBC*. Retrieved from http://www.cnbc.com/

Jamieson, R. (2011). *Charles Court: I love this place*. Adelaide, SA: St George Books.

Jeidels, O. (1905). *Das verhältnis der Deutschen großbanken zur industrie*. Leipzig, Germany: Duncker und Humblot.

Johnson, S., La Porta, R., Lopez-de-Silanes, F., & Shleifer, A. (2000). Tunneling. *The American Economic Review, 90*(2), 22–27.

Jones, R. (1831). *An essay on the distribution of wealth. Part 1: Rent*. London: John Murray.

Kahn, J. (2011). Billionaire Nicolas Berggruen is always on the move, looking for the next deal. *The Washington Post*. Retrieved from http://www.washingtonpost.com/

Kaplan, S. N., & Rauh, J. D. (2013). Family, education, and sources of wealth among the richest Americans, 1982–2012. *The American Economic Review, 103*(3), 158–162.

Kinder, T. (2014, October 21). Popularity of pachinko proves Japanese gambling is the world's most lucrative untapped market. *The International Business Times*. Retrieved from http://www.ibtimes.co.uk/

King, P. (2012). Financial deregulation. In S. J. Smith, L. F. O'Mahony, O. S. Eng, S. Watcher, & A. Sanders (Eds.), *International encyclopaedia of housing and home* (pp. 176–180). Oxford, UK: Elsevier.

Knoll, K., Schularick, M., & Steger, T. (2017). No price like home: Global house prices, 1870–2012. *American Economic Review, 107*, 331–353.

Kryshtanovskaya, O., & White, S. (2005). The rise of the Russian business elite. *Communist and Post-Communist Studies, 38*, 293–307.

Kwon, S., & O'Donnell, M. (2001). *The chaebol and labour in Korea: The development of management strategy in Hyundai*. London/New York: Routledge.
Lambert, R. (2001). Sony's Morita: A visionary leader. *Asia Pacific Perspectives, 1*(1), 32–38.
Lee, J. (2011, September 14). China's rich lists riddled with Communist Party members. *Forbes*. Retrieved from http://www.forbes.com/
Loussouarn, C. (2013). Spread betting. *Risk & Regulation, 26*(2), 10–11.
Lunn, E. (2014, March 12). *How Britain's richest brothers made billions from nothing*. Retrieved from https://uk.finance.yahoo.com/
Mankiw, N. G. (2013). Defending the one percent. *Journal of Economic Perspectives, 27*(3), 21–34.
Martel, J. (2014, December 28). 5 once-wealthy families who lost their fortunes. *Business Insider*. Retrieved from http://www.businessinsider.com/
Mathiason, N. (2009, October 18). Glasgow Harbour development poised to boost tycoon's property fortune. *The Guardian*. Retrieved from http://www.theguardian.com/
Mazzeo, T. J. (2010). *The secret of Chanel no. 5: The intimate history of the world's most famous perfume*. New York: Harper Collins.
McFadden, R. D. (2009, March 12). Leonore Annenberg, doyenne of protocol, dies at 91. *International Herald Tribune*. Retrieved from http://www.iht.com/
McFadden, R. D. (2015, April 20). A. Alfred Taubman, former Sotheby's owner and mall developer, Dies at 91. *The New York Times*, p. D8(L).
Medeiros, M., & de Souza, P. H. G. F. (2014). *The rich, the affluent and the top incomes: A literature review*. IRLE Working Paper Series, Berkeley.
Melitz, J. (1990). Financial deregulation in France. *European Economic Review, 34*, 394–402.
Melvin, D., & Sutton, J. (2015, April 18). Alfred Taubman, pioneer of indoor malls, dies at 91. *CNN*. Retrieved from http://edition.cnn.com/
Merck. (2013). *Exploring new horizons*. Darmstadt: Group Communications Merck. Retrieved 15 January, 2014, from http://www.merckgroup.com/company.merck.de/en/images/Merck_History_EN_2013_tcm1612_105832.pdf
Merck. (2014). *Merck annual report 2014*. Frankfurt, Germany: Merck KGaA, Group Communications.
Moskalev, S., & Park, S. C. (2010). South Korean chaebols and value-based management. *Journal of Business Ethics, 92*, 49–62.
Nullen, N. (1970). Gesellschaft/August von Finck. *Der Spiegel, 21*, 66–84.
Packard, D. (1995). *The HP way: How Bill Hewlett and I built our company*. New York: Harper Business.
Piketty, T. (2014a). *Capital in the twenty-first century*. Cambridge, MA: The Belknap Press of Harvard University Press.
Piketty, T. (2014b). Capital in the twenty-first century: A multidimensional approach to the history of capital and social classes. *The British Journal of Sociology, 65*, 736–747.

Preqin. (2014). *Investing in hedge funds: All about returns? The real drivers for institutional investor allocation.* Retrieved from https://www.preqin.com/docs/reports/Preqin_Special_Report_Investing_in_Hedge_Funds_June_14.pdf

RetroIndy. (2014, December 15). RetroIndy: Mel and Herb Simon. *Indy Star.* Retrieved from http://www.indystar.com/

Rocha, E. (2015, April 16). Calloway to acquire SmartCentres in C$1.16 bln deal. *Reuters.* Retrieved from http://www.reuters.com/

Rockoff, H. (2012). The great fortunes of the Gilded Age and the crisis of 1893. *Research in Economic History, 28*, 233–262.

Rosen, S. (1981). The economics of superstars. *The American Economic Review, 71*, 845–858.

Rubinstein, W. D. (1980). Modern Britain. In W. D. Rubinstein (Ed.), *Wealth and the wealthy in the modern world* (pp. 46–89). London: Croom Helm.

Rutland, P. (2009). The oligarchs and economic development. In S. K. Wegren & D. R. Herspring (Eds.), *After Putin's Russia: Past imperfect, future uncertain* (4th ed., pp. 159–182). Lanham, MD: Rowman & Littlefield Publishers.

Schwinn, W. K. (1944). *Intelligence report no. EW-Pa 128.* London: US Department of Defence.

Sherman, M. (2009). *A short history of financial regulation in the United States.* CEPR Working Paper. Retrieved from http://www.cepr.net/documents/publications/dereg-timeline-2009-07.pdf

Shorrocks, A. F. (1988). Wealth holdings and entrepreneurial activity. In D. Kessler & A. Masson (Eds.), *Modelling the accumulation and distribution of wealth.* Oxford, UK: Clarendon Press.

Solow, R. M. (2014, April 22). Piketty is right. *New Republic.* Retrieved from http://www.newrepublic.com/

Sorkin, A. R. (2003, April 22). Goldman bought questions along with Spear, Leeds. *The New York Times*, p. C1.

Spanier, G. (2012, October 12). A closer look at the Bauer media family. *The Independent.* Retrieved from http://www.independent.co.uk/

Stulz, R. M. (2007). Hedge funds: Past, present, and future. *Journal of Economic Perspectives, 21*(2), 175–194.

Swedin, E. G., & Ferro, D. L. (2005). *Computers: The life story of a technology.* Westport, CT: Greenwood Press.

Tamarkin, B. (1986, December 7). The ordeal of Lester Crown. (Pentagon challenges security clearance, cost overruns for General Dynamics). *The New York Times Magazine, 136*, S40.

The West 100. (2006, August 13). The west 100. *Los Angeles Times.* Retrieved 19 May, 2014, from http://articles.latimes.com/2006/aug/13/magazine/tm-toppower33

Thurow, L. (1975). *Generating inequality.* New York: Basic Books, Inc..

Torgler, B., & Piatti, M. (2013). Extraordinary wealth, globalization, and corruption. *Review of Income and Wealth, 59*, 341–359.

Treneman, A. (1998, March 1). Profile: The Duke of Westminster – Private property: Keep out. *The Independent*. Retrieved from http://www.independent.co.uk/
van Praet, N. (2014, March 4). 93-year-old Canadian real estate mogul makes Forbes billionaires list for first time. *Financial Post*. Retrieved from http://business.financialpost.com/
Watkins, G. P. (1907). The growth of large fortunes. *Publications of the American Economic Association, 8*(4), 1–170.
Whan-woo, Y. (2014, February 5). Big leisure center planned on Yeongjong. *The Korea Times*. Retrieved from http://www2.koreatimes.co.kr/
Williams, E. (1944). *Capitalism & slavery*. Chapel Hill, NC: The University of North Carolina Press.
Willoughby, J. (1994, December 12). A modern-day Rockefeller. *Investment Dealers' Digest*, 12–19.

6

Conclusion

The global economic system has generated substantial upsurges in prosperity since the conclusion of the Second World War. An outcome of this process has been a concomitant increase in high wealth accumulation. Globally, the extremely wealthy have attained levels of wealth that closely resemble those of the Gilded Age of the late nineteenth and early twentieth centuries in the US. This New Gilded Age not only represents a global historical phenomenon but potentially has enormous implications with regard to economic growth policy and policies that seek to lift individuals out of poverty through redistributive mechanisms. The purpose of this book was to document and analyse the rise of this new economic elite as a section of society worthy of study, and to explore how its wealth has been generated and sustained across the globe since the 1990s. By utilising a comprehensive database on the globe's wealthiest individuals, this book has sought to shed light on the degree to which entrepreneurial effort and inherited wealth have played their part across various advanced economies.

This chapter is structured as follows. The first section summarises the main findings of this study. The second section explores the possible policy implications of the findings, with attention to calls for wealth taxes and the potential impact on economic growth. Lastly, we provide some thoughts on future research avenues.

S. Tsigos, K. Daly, *The Wealth of the Elite*, https://doi.org/10.1007/978-981-15-2148-5_6

Summary of Findings

Although wealth accumulation, particularly as represented by the ultra-rich, often receives substantial attention from popular media, as well as from policy makers in the context of taxation, economists on the whole have shied away from exploring the ultra-rich. This lack of research output can be contrasted against the vast poverty focused literature. The reasons for this are a confluence of factors. Firstly, there has been a relative dearth of easily accessible data on the ultra-rich, and the data that is available is often criticised for its potential inaccuracies. Secondly, the bifurcation of the definitions of wealth and capital has resulted in discussions of vast wealth accumulation being jettisoned in favour of notions of human capital, for example.

Although lacking in quantity, the extent to which economists have explored patterns of extreme wealth accumulation in the modern era can be divided into three approaches. The first approach focused on the associated industrial structure where wealthy individuals found success. Generally, the wealthiest are found in industries in which intense competition is the norm, but this is to be expected given the stochastic nature of free enterprise success. Secondly, the ability of skills and education, under the umbrella of human capital, has been espoused to support the existence of the extreme wealthy, such as computer scientists who became billionaires owing to returns on human capital. Thirdly, institutional approaches have sought to place the rise of extreme wealth accumulation in the context of significant technological, legal or financial changes. However, the problem with these approaches is that they do not necessarily take into account the broader macroeconomic trends that have led to the overall wealth distribution observed across the advanced economies.

The extent to which modern wealth has accrued to an extraordinary degree to the highest echelons of society was explored in Chap. 3. The global nature of the New Gilded Age is clearly delineated, with much of the growth in billionaires arising due to the influx of individuals from the developing world and the re-emergence of new entrepreneurs in North America, particularly in finance and IT. Since 1990, the number of billionaires has increased from approximately 200 to nearly 1500 in 2013. The growth in the number of ultra-rich is also reflected in the growth of the number of countries represented in the sample. The growth in billionaires has seen a commensurate stabilisation of the average wealth of billionaires across the globe at approximately USD4 billion throughout the 2000s. Much has been made of the impact of crises on the wealth of the ultra-rich. The GFC only had a transitory impact on the extremely wealthy, as many of those who fell out of the wealth lists eventually reappeared a year or two afterwards. A global sectoral decomposition of the data reveals that wealth is predominantly concentrated in the finance and consumer discretionary industries, reflecting the increasing consumerism and financialisation of the global economy. Although all industries have exhibited growth in billionaire numbers, IT has demonstrated the greatest increases, closely followed by financial services. Old established industries such as energy, despite being popularly perceived as the means to riches, have not had dramatic representation in the wealth rankings since the 1990s.

The influx of new billionaires has emanated from across both the developed and developing world. In the latter, China, India and Russia have demonstrated significant growth, which can be tied just as much to political favouritism as to economic growth by itself. Indeed, many of the billionaires from Russia and China had, or have, meaningful or material ties to the governing powers of their country. In India, where private enterprise has maintained a degree of freedom, the stringent controls or regulations imposed by the government largely ensured the rise of large conglomerates and the families that dominate them. The relation between former (or current) authoritarian regimes and an economic elite is observed in South Korea and Germany too.

Perhaps the most striking differences across the globe are the patterns of old wealth versus new wealth. Here, old wealth refers to family dynasties or the incidence of inheritance, whereas new wealth refers to wealth generated from entrepreneurial effort. The proportion of old wealth is much lower in the developing world than in the developed world, although this is mainly driven by the influx of billionaires from Russia, Eastern Europe and China. In the developed world, there are substantially different inheritance patterns. North America demonstrates the lowest propensity towards inheritance, and this has consistently decreased over the sample period. In contrast, Western Europe has consistently shown a propensity for majority inheritance.

Chapter 4 examined the nexus between wealth accumulation, inequality and the various macroeconomic forces governing them. It adopted the general frameworks of Piketty (2014), Piketty and Zucman (2014) and Saez and Zucman (2014), considering the relations underpinning the aggregate wealth-income ratio across seven advanced economies and how they have evolved over the past 40 years. A significant element in the rise of wealth-income ratios has been the high rates of return relative to national income growth, which were observed to be associated with progressively lower real returns since at least the 1960s. The reasons for the inverse relationship between rates of return and the wealth-income ratio were explored in Chap. 5. Initial entrepreneurial effort in the 1960s and before were viewed as a potential catalyst for this phenomenon, while subsequent decades have witnessed a decrease in entrepreneurial effort and a concomitant increase of more rentier-based approaches to wealth accumulation.

While wealth accumulation has substantially increased since the 1960s, as evidenced by increasing wealth-income ratios, the nature of the accumulation has been highly inequitable. The process of inequality appears to be tied to the processes of consumerism and financialisation. Both processes have ensured little upward mobility for the low to middle classes, while maintaining the upward trajectory of the wealthiest individuals and households. In Chap. 4, various economic forces were shown to have given rise to the aforementioned social changes. Consumption is undertaken by poorer households in greater proportion to their wealth or income compared to wealthy households. In addition, given the low rates of income growth among poorer households, the manner in which they have sought to maintain their consumption has had a further deleterious impact on their potential for wealth accumulation and upward mobility. The increasing financialisation of households results in greater debt levels and supresses the potential for upward mobility. In contrast, rather than assume greater levels of liability, wealthier households have typically increased their holdings of savings and investment, with the latter becoming more significant as one moves up the wealth ladder, as these households derive a greater proportion of their income from capital investments.

Although the reappearance of the ultra-rich is a global phenomenon, the possibility of heterogeneity in the patterns of ultra-rich development across countries was explored in Chap. 5. Overall, there are substantial similarities in the degree to which certain sectors generate vast fortunes across the seven developed countries. In Chap. 4, it was suggested that financialisation and consumerism are two of the major forces that have shaped the distribution of wealth in advanced economies. Consequently, it is not surprising perhaps to find that industries at the cutting edge of these phenomena tend to dominate wealth lists. This was evident in the US and the UK, where the financial services and consumer discretionary sectors have represented a robust source of growth particularly over the past ten years. However, continental Europe shows significant divergence from such patterns, as inherited wealth plays a far more dominant role. In both France and Germany, most extreme wealth is held by inheritors, and, although the proportion has decreased, inheritance is still highly represented in the wealth stakes. Given the destruction that both nations experienced in the Second World War, this is surprising. Particularly in Germany, many of the individuals on the wealth lists are associated with families whose heritage stretches back to periods before the war. Whereas entrepreneurial success was the key in the Anglo world, the Germanic model very much followed a pattern of solidifying and tying business interests with political interests.

The Far East also shows contrasting patterns of development. Japan and South Korea demonstrated dramatic variations in the degree to which old wealth dominates. The immediate post-war era saw a dramatic reduction in the role of Imperial Japan's economic elite due to the occupying forces' economic policies. This created a vacuum in which new entrepreneurs emerged and propelled Japan to the forefront of, for example, the electronics industry. In contrast, South Korea adopted an approach in which political and business interests largely intersected, particularly in the 1960s, allowing five or so key families to dominate the economy. Since the 1990s, the Korean families at the head of *chaebol* have come to extend their corporate holdings and wealth without direct state preference and through the exploitation of the corporate governance structures, such as by tunnelling.

A further finding of Chap. 5 was the substantial role played by diversification in the business affairs of extremely wealthy individuals across all countries and sectors. Here diversification refers to the expanding sphere of business holdings and activities beyond the individual's or family's originating point. This phenomenon cuts across the old and new rich and industries. The conglomeration of business interests among the ultra-rich originating in advanced economies suggests a tendency to seek out new business opportunities. Theoretically, in periods of low returns, one may expect a degree of diversification to emerge as individuals try their hand at different business opportunities. At a macro level, real rates of returns demonstrate secular decreases across all economies since the 1960s and 1970s, which appears to have increased the degree of diversification by billionaires. Although inherited wealth tends to exhibit this trend more strongly, similar behaviour is observed among self-made entrepreneurs, even among the new breed of Internet entrepreneurs.

Policy Implications

The extent of extreme wealth accumulation in the contemporary era is clearly being grappled by policy makers, as outlined in Chap. 1. Broadly speaking, policy discourse has centred on creating tax regimes to reduce tax avoidance or evasion or to implement a progressive taxation regime. The most visible manifestation of the former arose from the G20 summit of April 2009, where G20 countries sought treaties with tax havens under the threat of sanctions. Between the G20 summit in April 2009 and December 2009, more than 300 treaties had been signed by the world's tax havens (Johannesen & Zucman, 2014).

On implementing progressive wealth tax regimes, an argument can be mounted that it would not have a deleterious impact on entrepreneurialism and economic growth. The evidence accumulated in Chap. 5 suggests that much of the extreme wealth today emerged in the post-war era when wealth-income ratios were at their lowest point. Indeed, many of today's billionaires made their initial fortunes amid high taxation and high government spending. The majority of North America's property tycoons, for example, required the massive highway infrastructure being developed in the 1960s. In South Korea, government contracts and a penchant for rapid development policies help to explain the emergence of that country's economic elite. Entrepreneurial effort is unlikely to be blunted by greater incidence of wealth taxation. Of all the industries considered, only IT has shown a degree of natural competitive evolution, although its beginnings too were associated with large government spending in research and development. The individuals at the forefront of the central processing unit (CPU) revolution managed their initial seismic innovations in this climate. Even among the fashion houses of France, entrepreneurialism was not dented by higher taxes.

Although a global wealth taxation system would provide a rapid mechanism through which wealth inequality might be reduced, the political realities are likely to make this an ineffective approach. Even tentative steps to reduce the incidence of tax avoidance through 'treasure island' tax havens have not been effective. Johannesen and Zucman (2014) provide a convincing account of how the wealthy simply reorganise their financial affairs, negating the impact of bilateral or multilateral policies aimed at increasing tax revenues. Shaxson and Christensen (2011) argue that the moves by policy makers, particularly at the G20 level, were shambolic and not likely to result in any significant reversal of the conjoint issues of tax evasion and avoidance, and financial secrecy. The political realities between nation-states are also likely to sound a death knell for a global wealth tax, despite evidence of the effectiveness of wealth taxes in the past (Piketty, 2014).

An alternative approach to reducing the inequality of wealth accumulation is to view it within the context of how households deal with their financial holdings. The increasing household financialisation has so far appeared to have an asymmetric impact on households, depending on which side of the wealth distribution one examines. The extent to which household risk-taking in financial matters is a function of wealth was analysed in this study. The results suggest that wealth is the largest element driving the propensity to save and invest. A policy implication that naturally emerges from this is to consider the adoption of policies that incentivise savings and investment by all. The potential of utilising finance to increase the probability of upward mobility regardless of classes was well recognised by Watkins (1907) and more recently by Saez and Zucman (2014).

In addition, the extent of the representation of inheritance in the wealth lists requires some attention. Setting aside the moral issue of whether such vast inheritances should be under the examination of policy makers and society for the moment, the issue of how one should lessen the effectiveness of family dynasties needs to be considered. Wealth taxes in themselves are not likely to have a dramatic impact given the formidable international issues that would emerge. Instead, large wealth accumulation by these dynasties may perhaps be blunted by restricting the span and sphere of business interests in which these families engage.

Avenues for Future Research

Any study that seeks to investigate issues associated with wealth accumulation utilising micro data is invariably confronted with problems of the accessibility and quality of data, particularly when focusing on the ultra-rich. Despite the limitations of the data used in this book, several fruitful research avenues have been identified.

The existence of substantial heterogeneity in the proportion of inherited versus self-made wealth across countries warrants further research. The acute differences observed even among countries in relatively close geographical and cultural proximity, as in the cases of Germany, France and the UK or Japan and South Korea, suggests that minor legal or historical developments can have a profound impact on the degree to which patrimony dominates a society. An underexplored element in this book (Chap. 5) is the extent to which differing patterns of inheritance across countries is a function of alternative corporate governance institutions. In South Korea, for example, legal forms of tunnelling have ensured that the wealthiest families are easily able to extend their sphere of control through their country's business landscape. Similarly, for Germany, the prevalence of dynastic wealth may in part be explained by the realm of corporate governance, where stakeholders have a rational interest in maintaining the *status quo*. In the future, a natural experiment may be found in comparing China and Russia as their first billionaires make way for new entrepreneurs or their families assume the dynastic dynamic observed in some advanced economies over the past 60 years.

A further potential research avenue revolves around the issue of wealth diversification by the ultra-rich, which can be explored along two lines. Firstly, Chap. 5 noted the propensity of the ultra-rich, be they inherited or self-made groups, to expand the sphere of their business holdings. This is particularly the case in Anglo economies where the general pattern appears to be one of entrepreneurial activity followed by the proliferation of holdings across a range of business activities and investments. In contrast, less-developed economies appear to forgo this pattern and typically rapidly establish large conglomerates and holding companies from the outset. In Germany, the pattern appears to be one of acquiring companies within the same or similar sectors. The issue is why this should arise in the first place. A potential key element in this regard is the empirical regularity of the existence of lower rates of return since the 1960s. Could the secular decline in rates of return potentially explain the rise of highly diversified business interests? Watkins (1907) once argued that during periods of low interest rates, speculative activity becomes an attractive option for the ultra-rich. Alternatively, with the lower cost of capital in recent years, the ultra-rich may just be seeking to diversify their holdings, rationally responding to changed market conditions. Secondly, diversification can be explored from the perspective of how it is attained. In the developing world, for example, much of the industrial diversification arises within the confines of large conglomerates. In the West, this does not appear to universally hold, with the ultra-rich's business interests not being necessarily tied under the umbrella of a single holding company.

In addition, the issue of how the wealth of the ultra-rich is secured during economic or financial crises warrants further consideration. Chapter 4 touched upon this and found that the impact of the GFC was not as pronounced as one may have previously thought. Many billionaires were able to rapidly reassert their wealth in subsequent years, with those from the financial sector demonstrating a particularly robust survival rate. A systematic analysis should be undertaken of the determinants of dramatic reversals in fortune during these periods and of those factors that ensure the security of wealth.

Finally, one consequence of both the rise of an ultra-rich, greater returns to capital and depressed wage growth of workers has not been considered. That is, the possibility of an upper bound to the accumulation and concentration of wealth being achieved. 'Trickle down economics' has in contemporary times not been as effective as hoped. Conversely, the ultra-rich can only maintain their position through a 'trickle up', but invariably this process can only plateau or even decline in the future. Taxation and transfer policies can all assist in reducing further accumulation but, in the very long term wealth accumulation will plateau. So how much of a concern is this for the wealthy themselves?

References

Johannesen, N., & Zucman, G. (2014). The end of bank secrecy? An evaluation of the G20 tax haven crackdown. *American Economic Journal, 6*, 65–91.

Piketty, T. (2014). *Capital in the twenty-first century*. Cambridge, MA: The Belknap Press of Harvard University Press.

Piketty, T., & Zucman, G. (2014). Capital is back: Wealth-income ratios in rich countries 1700–2010. *The Quarterly Journal of Economics, 129*, 1155–1210.

Saez, E., & Zucman, G. (2014). *Wealth inequality in the United States Since 1913: Evidence from capitalized income tax data* (NBER Working Paper No. 20625). Retrieved from National Bureau of Economic Research website http://www.nber.org/papers/w20625

Shaxson, N., & Christensen, J. (2011). *The finance curse*. Chesham, UK: Tax Justice Network.

Watkins, G. P. (1907). The growth of large fortunes. *Publications of the American Economic Association, 8*(4), 1–170.

References

Allen, E. (2002, December 31). In the shadow of a grocery giant: A thrifty strategy La Fiesta caters to Hispanic market and keeps overhead to a minimum. *San Antonio News Express*. Retrieved from http://nl.newsbank.com

Almond, S. (1994, December 1). Citizen Wayne – The unauthorized biography. *Miami New Times, 9*(33).

Alvaredo, F., Atkinson, A. B., Piketty, T., & Saez, E. (2013). The top 1 percent in international and historical perspective. *Journal of Economic Perspectives, 27*(3), 3–20.

Amoils, A., & Read, N. (2015). *Second citizenship & the migration of HNWIs 2000–2014*. New World Wealth. Retrieved from http://nebula.wsimg.com/

Anderlini, J. (2013, March 7). Chinese parliament holds 83 billionaires. *Financial Times*. Retrieved from http://www.ft.com/

Arrow, K. (1971). *Essays in the theory of risk bearing*. New York: Markham.

Ashby, R. (2002). *Steve Case: America Online pioneer*. Brookfield, CT: Twenty-First Century Books.

Atkinson, A. B. (2006). *Concentration among the rich*. World Institute for Development Economic Research RP2006/151. Retrieved from http://www.wider.unu.edu/sites/default/files/rp2006-151.pdf

Atkinson, A. B. (2012). *Wealth and inheritance in Britain from 1896 to the present*. Retrieved from http://piketty.pse.ens.fr/files/Atkinson2012.pdf

Atkinson, A. B., & Leigh, A. (2013). The distribution of top incomes in five Anglo-Saxon countries over the long run. *Economic Record, 89*, 31–47.

Atkinson, A. B., & Salverda, W. (2005). Top incomes in the Netherlands and the United Kingdom over the 20th century. *Journal of the European Economic Association, 3*(4), 883–913.

Austin, M. M., & Vidal-Naquet, P. V. (1977). *Economic and social history of ancient Greece: An introduction*. Berkeley, CA: University of California Press.

S. Tsigos, K. Daly, *The Wealth of the Elite*, https://doi.org/10.1007/978-981-15-2148-5

Australian Bureau of Statistics. (2013). *Managed Funds, Australia Dec, 2013* (cat. no. 5655.0). Retrieved 10 January, 2014, from http://www.abs.gov.au/

Australian Bureau of Statistics. (2014). *Australian National Accounts: Distribution of Household Income, Consumption and Wealth, 2003–04 to 2011–12*. Retrieved 20 February, 2015, from http://www.abs.gov.au/

Backhaus, S., & Hanßler, B. (2014). An inventor with heart. *Be Top, 1*, 29–31.

Baek, S., Kang, J., & Lee, I. (2006). Business groups and tunneling: Evidence from private securities offerings by Korean chaebols. *The Journal of Finance, 61*(5), 2415–2449.

Baer, D. (2014, September 30). 14 billionaires who started with nothing – Including Jack Ma and Larry Ellison. *Business Insider*. Retrieved from http://www.businessinsider.com.au/

Bagdikian, B. H. (2000). *The media monopoly*. Boston: Beacon Press.

Baranzini, M. (1991). *A theory of wealth distribution and accumulation*. Oxford, UK: Clarendon Press.

Barboza, D. (2012, October 26). Family of China's Wen worth billions. *Australian Financial Review*. Retrieved from http://www.afr.com

Barr, A. (2009, March 25). *Top managers' pay dropped 48% last year*. Retrieved from http://www.marketwatch.com/

Bauman, Z. (2007). *Work, consumerism and the new poor*. Maidenhead, UK: Open University Press.

Beaverstock, J. V., Hubbard, P., & Short, J. R. (2004). Getting away with it? (Exposing) the geographies of the super-rich. *Geoforum, 35*, 401–407.

Belson, K. (2003, July 29). With sun on roof, more Yen in the pocket. *The New York Times*, p. C1.

Benhabib, J., Bisin, A., & Zhu, S. (2013). *The wealth distribution in Bewley models with investment risk*. Working Paper, New York University, New York.

Berger, M. (2010, September 9). John W. Kluge, Metromedia's founder and a major philanthropist, dies at 95. *The New York Times*, p. A29.

Bernstein, J. R. (1997). Toyoda automatic looms and Toyota automobiles. In T. K. McCraw (Ed.), *Creating modern capitalism how entrepreneurs, companies, and countries triumphed in three industrial revolutions* (pp. 396–438). Cambridge, MA: Harvard University Press.

Bertrand, M., & Morse, A. (2013). *Trickle-down consumption* (NBER Working Paper No. 18883). Retrieved from National Bureau of Economic Research website https://www.nber.org/papers/w18883.pdf

Bertrand, M., & Mullainathan, S. (2001). Are CEOs reward for luck? The ones without principals are. *The Quarterly Journal of Economics, 116*, 901–932.

Bird, R. M. (1978). Canada's vanishing death taxes. *Osgoode Hall Law Journal, 16*(1), 133–145.

Birmingham, J. (2006, April 1). Now who's "the one?" Kerry Stokes: The fun begins at Seven. *The Monthly*, 40–46.

Blainey, G., & Jamieson, R. (1995). *Charles Court, the early years: An autobiography*. Perth, WA: Fremantle Arts Centre Press.

Blinder, A. S. (1976). Intergenerational transfers and life cycle consumption. *American Economic Association, 66*, 87–93.

Blitz, R. C., & Siegfried, J. J. (1992). How did the wealthiest Americans get so rich? *The Quarterly Review of Economics and Finance, 32*, 5–26.

Blume, L. E., & Durlauf, S. N. (2015). Capital in the twenty-first century: A review essay. *Journal of Political Economy, 123*, 749–777.

Bodley, J. H. (1999). Socioeconomic growth, culture scale, and household well-being: A test of the power-elite hypothesis. *Current Anthropology, 40*, 595–620.

Bonnet, F., & Théry, C. (2014). *Sociology and political science in the patrimonial society: Implications of Piketty's Capital.* Retrieved from https://halshs.archives-ouvertes.fr/halshs-01060570/document, <halshs-01060570>.

Booth, W. J. (1993). *Households: On the moral architecture of the economy*. New York: Cornell University Press.

Bourne, L. S. (2014). Urban geography in transition: A Canadian perspective on the 1980s and beyond. In B. J. L. Berry & J. O. Wheeler (Eds.), *Urban geography in America 1950–2000: Paradigms and personalities* (pp. 191–216). New York: Routledge.

Bradley, B. H. (1999). *The works: The industrial architecture of the United States*. New York: Oxford University Press.

Bridge, B. (1999). Europe and the Asian financial crisis: Coping with contagion. *Asian Survey, 39*, 456–467.

Bronars, S. (2013). How Margaret Thatcher Tuned Great Britain's Labor Markets Around. *Forbes*. Retrieved from http://www.forbes.com/

Bryant, A. (1994, December 20). Edward J. DeBartolo, developer, 85, is dead. *The New York Times*, p. A17(N).

Burrell, A. (2013). *Twiggy: The high-stakes life of Andrew Forrest*. Melbourne, VIC: Black Inc..

Burrell, A. (2014, March 1). Andrew Forrest buys up Pilbara stations in Stowe sale. *The Australian*. Retrieved from http://www.theaustralian.com.au/

Byford, S. (2012, November 30). King of Samsung: A chairman's reign of cunning and corruption. *The Verge*. Retrieved from http://www.theverge.com/

Cagetti, M., & De Nardi, M. (2006). Entrepreneurship, frictions, and wealth. *Journal of Political Economy, 114*, 835–870.

Canterbery, E. R., & Nosari, E. J. (1985). The Forbes four hundred: The determinants of super-wealth. *Southern Economic Journal, 5*, 1073–1083.

Carnegie, A. (1900). *The gospel of wealth and other timely essays*. New York: Century.

Carnevale, D. (2007). Pearson's purchase of eCollege signals publishers' interest in online education. *The Chronicle of Higher Education, 53*(38), 37–37.

Carroll, C. D., Slacalek, J., & Tokuoka, K. (2014). *The distribution of wealth and the marginal propensity to consume* (No. 1655). European Central Bank Working Paper Series. Retrieved from https://www.ecb.europa.eu/

Castañeda, A., Diaz-Gimenez, J., & Rios-Rull, J. (2003). Accounting for the U.S. earnings and wealth inequality. *Journal of Political Economy, 111*, 818–857.

Ceruzzi, P. E. (2003). *A history of modern computing*. Cambridge, MA: MIT Press.
Chung, J. (2014, May 28). Ziffs shut down hedge fund, shift way wealth is managed. *The Wall Street Journal*. Retrieved from http://www.wsj.com/
Clark, A. (2000). The first PC. *Wired, 8*(12). Retrieved from http://archive.wired.com/
Clarke, C. (2016). What are tax havens and why are they bad? *Texas Law Review, 95*(1), 59-79.
Clarke, D., Murrell, P., & Whiting, S. (2008). The role of law in China's economic development. In T. Rawski & L. Brandt (Eds.), *China's great economic transformation* (pp. 375–427). Cambridge, UK: Cambridge University Press.
Cohen, R. (1991, 20 December). Maxwell's empire: How it grew, how it fell – A special report; Charming the Big Bankers Out of Billions. *The New York Times*. Retrieved from http://www.nytimes.com/
Committee on Innovations in Computing and Communications: Lessons from History. (1999). *Funding a revolution: Government support for computing research*. Washington, DC: National Academy Press.
Commons, J. R. (1893). *The distribution of wealth*. New York: Macmillan and Co..
Costa-Santos, C., Antunes, L., Souto, A., & Bernardes, J. (2010). Assessment of disagreement: A new information-based approach. *Annals of Epidemiology, 20*(7), 555–561.
CQS Seeks. (2010, March 24). CQS seeks to open Australia office. *FINalternatives*. Retrieved from http://www.finalternatives.com/
Cynamon, B. Z., & Fazzari, M. (2013). *Inequality and household finance during the consumer age* (No. 752). Levy Economics Institute Economics Working Paper Archive. Retrieved from http://www.levyinstitute.org/
Dabla-Norris, E., Kochhar, K., Suphaphiphat, N., Ricka, F., & Tsounta, E. (2015). *Causes and consequences of income inequality: A global perspective* (No. 15/13). IMF Staff Discussion Notes. Retrieved from https://www.imf.org/
Datastream. (2015). *MSCI World index data 1996–2013*. Retrieved from Datastream.
Daumard, A. (1980). Wealth and affluence in France since the beginning of the nineteenth century. In W. D. Rubinstein (Ed.), *Wealth and the wealthy in the modern world* (pp. 90–121). London: Croom Helm.
Davies, J. B., & Shorrocks, A. F. (2000). The distribution of wealth. In A. B. Atkinson & F. Bourguignon (Eds.), *Handbook of income distribution* (Vol. 1, pp. 605–675). Amsterdam: North-Holland.
de Foville, M. A. (1893). The wealth of France and of other countries. *Journal of the Royal Statistical Society, 56*, 597–626.
Delanglade, S. (2007, October 5). Finance et culture sont complémentaires. *L'Expansion*. Retrieved from http://lexpansion.lexpress.fr/
DeLong, J. B. (1998). *Robber barons*. Retrieved from http://www.uni-muenster.de/PeaCon/dgs-mills/mills-texte/RobberBarons.htm
DeLong, J. B. (2015). Mr. Piketty and the "Neoclassics": A suggested interpretation. *National Tax Journal, 68*, 393–408.

Demirgruc-Kunt, A., & Levine, R. (1999). *Bank-based and market-based financial systems: Cross-country comparisons.* World Bank Policy Research Working Paper. Retrieved from http://elibrary.worldbank.org/

Desai, M. A., Foley, F. C., & Hines, J. R. (2004). *Economic effects of regional tax havens* (NBER Working Paper No. 10806). Retrieved from National Bureau of Economic Research website https://www.nber.org/papers/w10806.pdf

Di Nicola, A. (2006). Offshore financial centres and corruption: A toolkit for KNAB investigators. *Transcrime.* Retrieved from http://www.knab.gov.lv/

Dilnot, A., Kell, M., & Webb, S. (1988). The 1988 Budget and the structure of personal taxation. *Fiscal Studies, 9,* 38–47.

Disraeli, B. (1845). *Sybil or the two nations.* London: Henry Colburn.

Dolan, K. A., & Kroll, L. (2001, June 21). Billionaire dynasties. *Forbes.* Retrieved from http://www.forbes.com/

Domhoff, G. W. (1967). *Who rules America?* Englewood Cliffs, NJ: Prentice Hall.

Downer, L. (1994). *The brothers: The hidden world of Japan's richest family.* New York: Random House.

Dunn, A. (1999, April 1). Internet: Huge transaction underscores feverish buying spree by web firms seeking to dominate in cyberspace. (Yahoo, Broadcast.com Merging in a $5.7-Billion Stock Deal). *Los Angeles Times,* p. 1.

Dunn, J. (2013, June 12). New wealthy investors courted by private banking sector. *Australian Financial Review.* Retrieved from http://www.afr.com/

Dynan, K. E., Skinner, J., & Zeldes, S. P. (2004). Do the rich save more? *Journal of Political Economy, 112,* 397–444.

Epstein, G. (2002). *Financialization, rentier interests, and central bank policy.* Paper presented at the PERI conference on Financialization of the World Economy, University of Massachusetts, Amherst. Retrieved from http://www.peri.umass.edu/fileadmin/pdf/financial/fin_Epstein.pdf

Evans, L. (2016). *And justice for all … even teamsters.* Morrisville, NC: Lulu Publishing.

Ewen, S. (1976). *Captains of consciousness: Advertising and the social roots of the consumer culture.* New York: McGraw Hill.

Fama, E. F. (1970). Efficient capital markets: A review of theory and empirical work. *The Journal of Finance, 25,* 383–417.

Feldman, G. D. (2001). *Allianz and the German insurance business, 1933–1945.* Cambridge, UK: Cambridge University Press.

Feller, W. (1971). *An introduction to probability theory and its applications 2.* New York: Wiley.

Fesseau, M., & Mattonetti, M. L. (2013). *Distributional measures across household groups in a national accounts framework* (No. 2013/04). OECD Statistics Working Papers..

Fetter, F. A. (1930). Capital. In E. R. A. Seligman & A. Johnson (Eds.), *Encyclopaedia of the social sciences* (Vol. 3, pp. 187–190). New York: Macmillan.

Figueroa, A. (2008). Competition and circulation of economic elites: Theory and application to the case of Peru. *The Quarterly Review of Economics and Finance, 48,* 263–273.

Fisher, I. (1906). *The nature of capital and income*. New York: Macmillan.

Fligstein, N. (1990). *The transformation of corporate control*. Cambridge, MA: Harvard University Press.

Fligstein, N., & Goldstein, A. (2015). The emergence of a finance culture in American households. *Socio-Economic Review, 3*, 575–601.

Fohlin, C. (2005). The history of corporate ownership and control in Germany. In R. K. Morck (Ed.), *A history of corporate governance around the world family business groups to professional managers*. Lake Louise, AB: NBER.

Foley, S. (2002, October 4). Paul Singer, the hedge fund holdout. *Financial Times*, p. C4.

Forbes. (1990–2013). *The world's billionaires*. Retrieved from http://www.forbes.com/lists

Forsyth, A. (2005). *Reforming suburbia. The planned communities of Irvine, Columbia, and the Woodlands*. Berkeley, CA: University of California Press.

Frieden, B. J., & Sagalyn, L. B. (1991). *Downtown, Inc., how America rebuilds cities*. Cambridge, MA: MIT Press.

Fulford, B. (2000). Japan's last electronics tycoon. *Forbes, 166*(1), 166–167.

Galbraith, J. K. (1958). *The affluent society*. New York: Houghton Mifflin Company.

Galbraith, J. K. (2014). Kapital for the twenty-first century?. *Dissent*. Retrieved on 15 September, 2015, from https://www.dissentmagazine.org/

Gaynor, B. (2012, February 18). Oz deal brings Chandler closer to home. *The New Zealand Herald*. Retrieved from http://www.nzherald.co.nz/

Gentry, W. M., & Hubbard, R. G. (2004). Entrepreneurship and household saving. *Advances in Economic Analysis & Policy, 4*(1), 1–55.

Gerschenkron, A. (1998). *Economic backwardness in historical perspective*. London: Routledge.

Giang, V., & Goudreau, J. (2014, February 21). 16 billionaires who started with nothing – Including WhatsApp's cofounder. *Business Insider*. Retrieved from http://www.businessinsider.com.au/

Giffen, R. (1889). *The growth of capital*. London: G. Bell.

Goff, S. (2010, March 25). The Rothschilds' family fortune. *Financial Times*. Retrieved from http://www.ft.com/

Goldin, C., & Margo, R. A. (1992). The great compression: The wage structure in the United States at mid-century. *The Quarterly Journal of Economics, 107*, 1–34.

Goldsmith, R. W. (1969). *Financial structure and development*. New Haven, CT: Yale University Press.

Gordon, R., & Slemrod, J. (2000). Are 'Real' Responses to Taxes Simply Income Shifting between Corporate and Personal Tax Bases?. In J. Slemrod (Ed.), *Does Atlas Shrug: The Economic Consequences of Taxing the Rich* (pp. 240–279). New York: Russell Sage Foundation.

Gorea, D. (2015). *Catch me if you can: U.S. Tax Treaties and Shifts in Offshore Investments*. Working Paper, European University Institute.

Gottfried, P., & Schellhorn, H. (2004). *Empirical evidence on the effects of marginal tax rates on income – The German case* (No. 15). IAW Discussion Papers Institut für Angewandte Wirschaftsforschung.

Hanlon, M., Maydew, E. L., & Thornock, J. R. (2015). Taking the long way home: U.S. tax evasion and offshore investments in U.S. equity and debt markets. *Journal of Finance, 70*, 257–287.

Häring, N., & Douglas, N. (2012). *Economists and the powerful: Convenient theories, distorted facts, ample rewards*. London: Anthem Press.

Harper, T. (2013, October 18). The biggest company you've never heard of: Lifting the lid on Peel Group – The property firm owned by reclusive tax exile John Whittaker. *The Independent*. Retrieved from http://www.independent.co.uk/

Hassler, S. (1999). *The super-rich*. London: Macmillan.

Hazledine, T., & Siegfried, J. J. (1997). How did the wealthiest New Zealanders get so rich? *New Zealand Economic Papers, 31*, 35–47.

Heilbroner, R. L. (1987). Wealth. In J. Eatwell, M. Milgate, & P. Newman (Eds.), *The new Palgrave: A dictionary of economics* (1st ed.). London: Macmillan.

Hemingway, E. (1936). The Snows of Kilimanjaro. *Esquire, 27*, 194–201.

Hendrick-Wong, Y. (2007). *Succeeding like success: The affluent consumers of Asia*. Singapore, Singapore: Wiley.

Henry, J. S. (2012). The price of offshore revisited. *Tax Justice Network*. Retrieved from http://www.taxjustice.net/

Henry, J. S. (2016). More than $12 trillion stuffed offshore, from developing countries alone. *Tax Justice Network*. Retrieved from http://www.taxjustice.net/

Herschel, J. F. (1841). Review of Whewell's history of the inductive sciences from the earliest to the present times (1837) and the philosophy of the inductive sciences founded upon their history. *The London Quarterly Review, 68*, 177–238.

Hevesi, D. (2011, September 11). Frank Batten Sr., media executive and founder of Weather Channel, dies at 82. *The New York Times*, p. A17.

Hillman, K. (2011). Die 100 reichsten DeutschenGespür für "Leichen im Keller". *SpiegelOnline*. Retrieved from http://www.spiegel.de/

Hirsch, M. (1911). *The problem of wealth (an open letter to Andrew Carnegie) and other essays*. Melbourne, VIC: Renwick, Pride, Nuttall Pty. Ltd..

Hobbs, S., & Toscano, P. (2014, January). Four-year boom expected for the US hotel industry. *CNBC*. Retrieved from http://www.cnbc.com/

Hodgson, G. M. (2014). What is capital? Economists and sociologists have changed its meaning: Should it be changed back? *Cambridge Journal of Economics, 38*, 1063–1086.

Hosking, G. (1985). *A history of the Soviet Union*. London: Fontana Press.

Hubert Burda Media. (2015). *100 years on*. Retrieved May 18, 2015, from http://www.hubert-burda-media.com/company/history/

Hurst, E., & Lusardi, A. (2004). Liquidity constraints, household wealth, and entrepreneurship. *Journal of Political Economy, 112*, 319–347.

Idato. (2014, October 29). James Packer's RatPac to back Warner Bros films with $254 million purse. *Sydney Morning Herald*. Retrieved from http://www.smh.com.au/

Investment Company Institute. (2015). *2015 Investment company fact book*. Retrieved on 15 August 2015, from http://www.icifactbook.org/fb_data.html

Irvine Company. (n.d.). *Donald Bren*. Retrieved August 30, 2014, from https://www.irvinecompany.com/donald-bren

Jaher, F. C. (1980). The gilded elite: American multimillionaires, 1865 to the present. In W. D. Rubinstein (Ed.), *Wealth and the wealthy in the modern world*. London: Croom Helm.

Jamieson, R. (2011). *Charles Court: I love this place*. Adelaide, SA: St George Books.

Jaumotte, F., & Buitron, C. O. (2015). Inequality and Labor Market Institutions. *IMF Staff Discussion Note*, SDN/15/14.

Jeidels, O. (1905). *Das verhältnis der Deutschen großbanken zur industrie*. Leipzig, Germany: Duncker und Humblot.

Johannesen, N., & Zucman, G. (2014). The end of bank secrecy? An evaluation of the G20 tax haven crackdown. *American Economic Journal, 6*, 65–91.

Johnson, D. (2005, September 25). Sheila Johnson, marrying very well. *Washington Post*. Retrieved from http://www.washingtonpost.com/

Johnson, S., La Porta, R., Lopez-de-Silanes, F., & Shleifer, A. (2000). Tunneling. *The American Economic Review, 90*(2), 22–27.

Jones, R. (1831). *An essay on the distribution of wealth. Part 1: Rent*. London: John Murray.

Josephson, M. (2013). *The robber barons*. Piscataway, NY: Transaction Publishers.

Joumard, I., Pisu, M., & Bloch, D. (2012). Tackling income inequality: The role of taxes and transfers. *OECD Journal: Economic Studies*. Published online first. https://doi.org/10.1787/eco_studies-2012-5k95xd6l65lt

Kahn, J. (2011). Billionaire Nicolas Berggruen is always on the move, looking for the next deal. *The Washington Post*. Retrieved from http://www.washingtonpost.com/

Kakwani, N. C. (1977). Measurement of tax progressivity: An international comparison. *The Economic Journal, 87*, 71–80.

Kaldor, N. (1960). *Essays on value and distribution*. Glencoe, UK: Free Press.

Kalleberg, A. (2011). *Good jobs, bad jobs: The rise of polarized and precarious employment systems in the United, 1970s–2000s*. New York: Russell Sage Foundation, American Sociological Association Rose Series in Sociology.

Kanbur, R., & Stiglitz, J. (2015). *Wealth and income distribution: New theories needed for a new era*. VOX CEPR Policy Portal. Retrieved from http://voxeu.org/article/wealth-and-income-distribution-new-theories-needed-new-era

Kaplan, S. N., & Rauh, J. D. (2013). Family, education, and sources of wealth among the richest Americans, 1982–2012. *The American Economic Review, 103*(3), 158–162.

Keen, M., & Ligthart, J. E. (2006). Information sharing and international taxation: A primer. *International Tax and Public Finance, 13*(1), 81–110.

Kerry Packer; Obituary. (2005, December 28). Kerry Packer; Obituary. *Times*, p. 48.

Kinder, T. (2014, October 21). Popularity of pachinko proves Japanese gambling is the world's most lucrative untapped market. *The International Business Times*. Retrieved from http://www.ibtimes.co.uk/

King, P. (2012). Financial deregulation. In S. J. Smith, L. F. O'Mahony, O. S. Eng, S. Watcher, & A. Sanders (Eds.), *International encyclopaedia of housing and home* (pp. 176–180). Oxford, UK: Elsevier.

King, W. I. (1915). *The wealth and income of the people of the United States*. New York: Macmillan.

Klevmarken, N. A., Lupton, J. P., & Stafford, F. P. (2003). Wealth dynamics in the 1980s and 1990s: Sweden and the United States. *The Journal of Human Resources, 38*, 322–353.

Knaus, C. (2019). Tax office may apply 40% tax against multinationals for diverting profits. *The Guardian*. Retrieved from https://www.theguardian.com/australia-news/2019/apr/05/tax-office-may-apply-40-tax-against-multinationals-for-diverting-profits

Knoll, K., Schularick, M., & Steger, T. (2017). No price like home: Global house prices, 1870–2012. *American Economic Review, 107*, 331–353.

Koh, S. Y., Wissink, B., & Forrest, R. (2016). Reconsidering the super-rich: Variations, structural conditions and urban consequences. In I. Hay & J. V. Beaverstock (Eds.), *Handbook on wealth and the super-rich* (pp. 18–42). Cheltenham: Cheltenham Edward Elgar Publishing.

Kopczuk, W. (2013). Taxation of intergenerational transfer and wealth. In A. J. Auerbach, R. Chetty, M. Feldstein, & E. Saez (Eds.), *Handbook of public economics, volume 5*. Amsterdam: Elsevier.

Kopczuk, W., & Saez, E. (2004). Top wealth shares in the United States, 1916–2000: Evidence from estate tax returns. *National Tax Journal, 57*(2), 445–487.

Krippner, G. R. (2005). The financialization of the American economy. *Socio-Economic Review, 3*, 173–208.

Kroll, L. (2014, September). Methodology. *Forbes*. Retrieved 30 September, 2014, from http://www.forbes.com/sites/luisakroll/2014/03/03/inside-the-2014-forbes-billionaires-list-facts-and-figures/

Kruger, C. (2013, October 30). James Packer's Macau gamble pays off. *Sydney Morning Herald*. Retrieved from http://www.smh.com.au/

Krugman, P. (2014a, January 18). The myth of the deserving rich. *The New York Times*. Retrieved from http://krugman.blogs.nytimes.com/2014/01/18/the-myth-of-the-deserving-rich

Krugman, P. (2014b. May 8). Why we're in a new Gilded Age. *The New Review of Books*. Retrieved from http://www.nybooks.com/articles/2014/05/08/thomas-piketty-new-gilded-age/

Krugman, P. (2015. March 2). Walmart's visible hand. *The New York Times*. Retrieved from http://nyti.ms/18DFTRd

Kryshtanovskaya, O., & White, S. (2005). The rise of the Russian business elite. *Communist and Post-Communist Studies, 38*, 293–307.

Kuehn, D. (2015). *Human capital in the twenty first century*. Retrieved from http://ssrn.com/abstract=2605840

Kwon, S., & O'Donnell, M. (2001). *The chaebol and labour in Korea: The development of management strategy in Hyundai*. London/New York: Routledge.

La Roche, J. (2012, January 11). The fabulous life of Chase Coleman: The world's most profitable hedge funder in 2011. *Business Insider*. Retrieved from http://www.businessinsider.com.au/

Labaton, S. (2000, December 15). AOL and Time Warner gain approval for huge merger, but with strict conditions. *The New York Times*, p. A1.

Lambert, R. (2001). Sony's Morita: A visionary leader. *Asia Pacific Perspectives, 1*(1), 32–38.

Landais, C. (2007). *Les hauts revenus en France (1998–2006): Une explosion de inégalités?*. Working Paper, Paris School of Economics.

Lane, R. E. (1962). *Political ideology: Why the American common man believes what he does*. New York: The Free Press.

Lee, J. (2011, September 14). China's rich lists riddled with Communist Party members. *Forbes*. Retrieved from http://www.forbes.com/

Leigh, A. (2005). Deriving long-run inequality series from tax data. *The Economic Record, 81*, S58–S70.

Leigh, A. (2009). Top incomes. In W. Salverda, B. Nolvan, & T. M. Smeeding (Eds.), *The Oxford handbook of economic inequality*. Oxford, UK: Oxford University Press.

Leigh, A. (2013). *Battlers & billionaires: The story of inequality in Australia*. Melbourne, VIC: Black, Inc..

Lewis, R. (2014, November 14). G20 to launch 'aggressive' attack on tax avoidance among multinationals. *The Australian*. Retrieved from http://www.theaustralian.com.au/

López, M. (2013). Elite theory. *Sociopedia.isa*.https://doi.org/10.1177/2056846013112.

Loussouarn, C. (2013). Spread betting. *Risk & Regulation, 26*(2), 10–11.

Low profile city. (2006, September 15). Low profile city financier to join dollar billionaire club. *London Evening Standard*. Retrieved from http://www.standard.co.uk/

Lundberg, F. (1969). *The rich & the super rich: A study in the power of money today*. London: Nelson.

Lunn, E. (2014, March 12). *How Britain's richest brothers made billions from nothing*. Retrieved from https://uk.finance.yahoo.com/

Luxembourg Income Study. (n.d.). *LIS Web Tabulator*. Retrieved on 10 June, 2015, from http://www.lisdatacenter.org/

Maney, K. (2005, March 22). 10 years ago, eBay changed the world, sort of by accident. *USA Today*, p. 01B.

Mankiw, N. G. (2013). Defending the one percent. *Journal of Economic Perspectives, 27*(3), 21–34.

Martel, J. (2014, December 28). 5 once-wealthy families who lost their fortunes. *Business Insider*. Retrieved from http://www.businessinsider.com/

Marx, K. (1981). *Capital, vol. 3*. Harmondsworth, UK: Pelican.

Mathiason, N. (2009, October 18). Glasgow Harbour development poised to boost tycoon's property fortune. *The Guardian*. Retrieved from http://www.theguardian.com/

Maxwell, K. (2012, July 30). "Mikoshi" management: How Kazuo Inamori lifted Japan Airlines. *The Wall Street Journal*. Retrieved 15 August, 2014, from http://blogs.wsj.com/japanrealtime/2012/07/30/mikoshi-management-how-kazuo-inamori-lifted-japan-airlines/

Mazzeo, T. J. (2010). *The secret of Chanel no. 5: The intimate history of the world's most famous perfume*. New York: Harper Collins.

McCrann, T. (2012, May 5). Packer to close media chapter. *The Australian*. Retrieved from http://www.theaustralian.com.au/business/

McFadden, R. D. (2009, March 12). Leonore Annenberg, doyenne of protocol, dies at 91. *International Herald Tribune*. Retrieved from http://www.iht.com/

McFadden, R. D. (2015, April 20). A. Alfred Taubman, former Sotheby's owner and mall developer, Dies at 91. *The New York Times*, p. D8(L).

Meade, J. E. (1964). *Efficiency, equality, and the ownership of property*. London: George Allen & Unwin.

Meade, J. E. (1975). *The just economy*. London: George Allen & Unwin.

Medeiros, M., & de Souza, P. H. G. F. (2014). *The rich, the affluent and the top incomes: A literature review*. IRLE Working Paper Series, Berkeley.

Melitz, J. (1990). Financial deregulation in France. *European Economic Review, 34*, 394–402.

Melvin, D., & Sutton, J. (2015, April 18). Alfred Taubman, pioneer of indoor malls, dies at 91. *CNN*. Retrieved from http://edition.cnn.com/

Merck. (2013). *Exploring new horizons*. Darmstadt: Group Communications Merck. Retrieved 15 January, 2014, from http://www.merckgroup.com/company.merck.de/en/images/Merck_History_EN_2013_tcm1612_105832.pdf

Merck. (2014). *Merck annual report 2014*. Frankfurt, Germany: Merck KGaA, Group Communications.

Milanovic, B. (2014). The return of "Patrimonial Capitalism": A review of Thomas Piketty's capital in the twenty-first century. *Journal of Economic Literature, 52*, 519–534.

Mill, J. S. (1929). *Principles of economics*. London: Longman Company.

Mills, C. W. (1956). *The power elite*. New York: Oxford University Press.

Modigliani, F., & Brumberg, R. (1954). Utility analysis and the consumption function: An interpretation of cross-section data. In K. K. Kurihara (Ed.), *Post Keynesian economics*. New York: Rutgers University Press.

Moran, J. (1996). *Jim Moran, the courtesy man*. Los Angeles: Bonus Books.

Morelli, S., Smeeding, T., & Thompson, J. (2014). *Post-1970 trends within-country and poverty: Rich and middle income countries* (No. 356). CSED Working Papers, Centre for Studies in Economics and Finance, University of Naples, Italy.

Moriguchi, C., & Saez, E. (2008). The evolution of income concentration in Japan, 1886–2005: Evidence from income statistics. *The Review of Economics and Statistics, 90*, 713–734.

Morita, A., Reginold, E., & Shimomura, S. (1986). *Made in Japan*. New York: E.P. Dutton.

Moskalev, S., & Park, S. C. (2010). South Korean chaebols and value-based management. *Journal of Business Ethics, 92*, 49–62.

Murtin, F., & d'Ercole, M. M. (2015). *Household wealth inequality across OECD countries: New OECD evidence*. OECD Statistics Brief, No. 21.

Net Applications. (n.d.). *Desktop search engine market share*. Retrieved 10 January, 2015, from https://www.netmarketshare.com/

North, D. (1907). *Discourses upon trade*. Baltimore: The John Hopkins Press. Retrieved on 10 June, 2016, from http://lf-oll.s3.amazonaws.com/titles/299/North_0446_EBk_v6.0.pdf

Nullen, N. (1970). Gesellschaft/August von Finck. *Der Spiegel, 21*, 66–84.

OECD. (1998). *Harmful tax competition: An emerging global issue*. Retrieved from http://www.oecd.org/tax/transparency/44430243.pdf

Oxfam. (2014). *Working for the few. Political capture and economic inequality* (No. 178). Oxfam Briefing Paper. Retrieved from http://www.oxfam.org/en/research/working-few

Pace of consolidation. (1996). Pace of consolidation in the industry accelerates. *Chain Drug Review, 18*(9), 106.

Packard, D. (1995). *The HP way: How Bill Hewlett and I built our company*. New York: Harper Business.

Parkinson, S., Searle, B. A., Smith, S. J., & Wood, G. (2009). Mortgage equity withdrawal in Australia and Britain: Towards a wealth-fare state? *European Journal of Housing Policy, 9*, 365–389.

Pasinetti, L. (1962). Rate of profit and income distribution in relation to the rate of economic growth. *Review of Economic Studies, 29*, 267–279.

Passmore, D. (2014, September 12). The Sunday Mail Queensland's top 150 rich list: John Van Lieshout is new No. 1. *The Courier-Mail*. Retrieved from http://www.couriermail.com.au/

Pedrick, W. H. (1982). Oh, to die down under!: Abolition of death and gift duties in Australia. *Western Australian Law Review, 14*, 438–468.

Petras, J. (2008). Global ruling class: Billionaires and how they "make it". *Journal of Contemporary Asia, 38*, 319–329.

Piketty, T. (1998). Les hauts revenus face aux modifications des taux marginaux supérieurs de l'impôt sur le revenu en france, 1970–1996. *Economie et prévision, 138–139*, 25–60.

Piketty, T. (2014a). *Capital in the twenty-first century*. Cambridge, MA: The Belknap Press of Harvard University Press.

Piketty, T. (2014b). Capital in the twenty-first century: A multidimensional approach to the history of capital and social classes. *The British Journal of Sociology, 65*, 736–747.

Piketty, T. (2015). About capital in the twenty-first century. *American Economic Review: Papers & Proceedings, 105*(5), 48–53.

Piketty, T., & Saez, E. (2006). The evolution of top incomes: A historical and international perspective. *American Economic Review, 96*, 200–205.

Piketty, T., & Saez, E. (2014). Inequality in the long run. *Science, 344*(6186), 838–843.

Piketty, T., Saez, E., & Stantcheva, S. (2014). Optimal taxation of top labor incomes: A tale of three elasticities. *American Economic Journal: Economic Policy, 6*, 230–271.

Piketty, T., Saez, E., & Zucman, G. (2013). *Rethinking capital and wealth taxation.* Working Paper. Retrieved from http://piketty.pse.ens.fr/files/PikettySaezZucman2013RKT.pdf

Piketty, T., & Zucman, G. (2014a). Capital is back: Wealth-income ratios in rich countries 1700–2010. *The Quarterly Journal of Economics, 129*, 1155–1210.

Piketty, T., & Zucman, G. (2014b). *Appendix of Capital is back: Wealth-income ratios in rich countries 1700–2010.* Retrieved on 10 June, 2015, from http://gabriel-zucman.eu/files/PikettyZucman2013Data.zip

Piketty, T., & Zucman, G. (2015). Wealth and inheritance in the long run. In A. B. Atkinson & F. Bourguignon (Eds.), *Handbook of income distribution* (pp. 1303–1368). Oxford, UK: Elsevier.

Plagge, A., Scheve, K., & Stasavage, D. (2010). *Comparative inheritance taxation database.* ISPS Data Archive, http://hdl.handle.net/10079/dz08kx8

Poulantzas, N., & Miliband, R. (1972). The problem of the capitalist state. In R. Blackburn (Ed.), *Ideology in social science: Readings in critical social theory* (pp. 238–262). New York: Pantheon Books.

Preqin. (2014). *Investing in hedge funds: All about returns? The real drivers for institutional investor allocation.* Retrieved from https://www.preqin.com/docs/reports/Preqin_Special_Report_Investing_in_Hedge_Funds_June_14.pdf

Pressman, S. (2015). *Understanding Piketty's capital in the twenty-first century.* London: Routledge.

Price, R. W., & Dang, T. (2011). *Adjusting fiscal balances for asset price cycles* (No. 868). OECD Economics Department Working Papers, OECD Publishing. https://doi.org/10.1787/5kgc42t3zqkl-en

Quadrini, V. (1999). The importance of entrepreneurship for wealth concentration and mobility. *Review of Income and Wealth, 45*, 1–19.

Quadrini, V. (2000). Entrepreneurship, saving and social mobility. *Review of Economic Dynamics, 3*, 1–40.

Quinn, R. (2010, March 10). Why Stan Perron's oresome at 89. *Perth Now*. Retrieved from http://www.perthnow.com.au/

Rashid, S. (1979). Richard Jones and Baconian historicism at Cambridge. *Journal of Economic Issues, 13*, 159–173.

Reserve Bank of Australia. (2012). *Household Debt – Distribution – E7*. Retrieved on 20 February, 2015, from http://www.rba.gov.au/

RetroIndy. (2014, December 15). RetroIndy: Mel and Herb Simon. *Indy Star.* Retrieved from http://www.indystar.com/

Reynolds, A. (2007). *Has U.S. income inequality really increased?* (No. 586). Cato Institute Policy Analysis Series.

Reynolds, M., & Smolensky, E. (1977). *Public expenditures, taxes, and the distribution of income: The United States, 1950, 1961, 1970*. New York: Academic Press.

Ricardo, D. (1821). *On the principles of political economy and taxation*. London: John Murray.

Roach, B. (2003). *Progressive and regressive taxation in the United States: Who's really paying (and not paying) their fair share?* (No. 03-10). Global Development and Environment Institute Working Paper.

Rocha, E. (2015, April 16). Calloway to acquire SmartCentres in C$1.16 bln deal. *Reuters*. Retrieved from http://www.reuters.com/

Rockoff, H. (2012). The great fortunes of the Gilded Age and the crisis of 1893. *Research in Economic History, 28*, 233–262.

Rognlie, M. (2015). *Deciphering the fall and rise in the net capital share: Accumulation, or scarcity?* Retrieved from http://economics.mit.edu/files/10924

Roine, J., Vlachos, J., & Waldenström, D. (2008). *The long-run determinants of inequality: What can we learn from top income data?*. Working Paper, Stockholm University.

Roine, J., & Walenström, D. (2008). The evolution of top incomes in an egalitarian society: Sweden, 1903–2004. *Journal of Public Economics, 92*, 366–387.

Rosen, S. (1981). The economics of superstars. *The American Economic Review, 71*, 845–858.

Roush, C. (1999). *Inside home depot: How one company revolutionized an industry through the relentless pursuit of growth*. New York: McGraw-Hill.

Rubinstein, W. D. (1980). Modern Britain. In W. D. Rubinstein (Ed.), *Wealth and the wealthy in the modern world* (pp. 46–89). London: Croom Helm.

Rutland, P. (2009). The oligarchs and economic development. In S. K. Wegren & D. R. Herspring (Eds.), *After Putin's Russia: Past imperfect, future uncertain* (4th ed., pp. 159–182). Lanham, MD: Rowman & Littlefield Publishers.

Saez, E. (2006). Income and wealth concentration in a historical and international perspective. In A. J. Auerbach, D. Card, & J. M. Quigley (Eds.), *Public policy and the income distribution*. New York: Russell Sage Foundation.

Saez, E., & Veall, M. R. (2005). The evolution of high incomes in Northern America: Lessons from Canadian evidence. *American Economic Review, 95*, 831–849.

Saez, E., & Zucman, G. (2014). *Wealth inequality in the United States Since 1913: Evidence from capitalized income tax data* (NBER Working Paper No. 20625). Retrieved from National Bureau of Economic Research website http://www.nber.org/papers/w20625

Samuelson, P. A. (1969). Lifetime portfolio selection by dynamic stochastic programming. *The Review of Economics and Statistics, 51*, 239–249.

Sanandaji, T., & Leeson, P. T. (2013). Billionaires. *Industrial and Corporate Change, 22*, 313–337.

Sanders, K. (2015, January 20). Obama wants higher tax rate on capital gains and tax rates. *Politifact.* Retrieved on 15 June, 2015, from http://www.politifact.com/
Scherer, F. M. (1980). *Industrial market structure and economic performance.* Boston: Houghton Mifflin Company.
Schumpeter, J. A. (1954). *History of economic analysis.* Oxford, UK: Oxford University Press.
Schumpeter, J. A. (2003). *Capitalism, socialism and democracy* (6th ed.). London: Routledge.
Schwinn, W. K. (1944). *Intelligence report no. EW-Pa 128.* London: US Department of Defence.
Shaxson, N., & Christensen, J. (2011). *The finance curse.* Chesham, UK: Tax Justice Network.
Sheppard, L. (2009). Don't ask, don't tell, part 4: Ineffectual information sharing. *Tax Notes*, 1411–1418.
Sherman, M. (2009). *A short history of financial regulation in the United States.* CEPR Working Paper. Retrieved from http://www.cepr.net/documents/publications/dereg-timeline-2009-07.pdf
Shorrocks, A. F. (1988). Wealth holdings and entrepreneurial activity. In D. Kessler & A. Masson (Eds.), *Modelling the accumulation and distribution of wealth.* Oxford, UK: Clarendon Press.
Siegfried, J. J., & Roberts, A. (1991). How did the wealthiest Britons get so rich? *Review of Industrial Organization, 6*, 19–32.
Siegfried, J. J., & Round, D. K. (1994). How did the wealthiest Australians get so rich? *Review of Income and Wealth, 40*, 191–204.
Skinner, J. (1988). Risky income, life cycle consumption, and precautionary saving. *Journal of Monetary Economics, 22*, 14–35.
Slemrod, J. (2000). The economics of taxing the rich. In J. Slemrod (Ed.), *Does atlas shrug? The economic consequences of taxing the rich* (pp. 2–28). Cambridge, MA: Harvard University Press.
Smith, A. (1952). *An inquiry into the nature and causes of the wealth of nations.* Chicago: William Benton.
Solow, R. M. (2014, April 22). Piketty is right. *New Republic.* Retrieved from http://www.newrepublic.com/
Sorkin, A. R. (2003, April 22). Goldman bought questions along with Spear, Leeds. *The New York Times*, p. C1.
Spanier, G. (2012, October 12). A closer look at the Bauer media family. *The Independent.* Retrieved from http://www.independent.co.uk/
Spånt, R. (1987). Wealth distribution in Sweden: 1920–1983. In E. Wolff (Ed.), *International comparisons of the distribution of household wealth.* Oxford, UK: Oxford University Press.
Spengler, J. J. (1984). Boisguilbert's economic views vis-à-vis those of contemporary *reformateurs. History of Political Economy, 16*, 69–88.
Stensholt. (2004, May 20). The mall master. *Business Review Weekly*, p. 46.

Stiglitz, J. E. (1969). Distribution of income and wealth among individuals. *Econometrica, 37*, 382–397.

Stiglitz, J. E. (1978). Notes on estate taxes, redistribution, and the concept of balanced growth path incidence. *Journal of Political Economy, 86*, S137–S150.

Stilwell, F., & Ansari, M. (2003). Wealthy Australians. *Journal of Australian Political Economy, 52*, 143–157.

Stilwell, F., & Jordan, K. (2007). *Who gets what?: Analysing economic inequality in Australia*. Cambridge, UK: Cambridge University Press.

Stockhammer, E., & Wildauer, R. (2015). *Debt-driven growth? Wealth, distribution and demand in OECD countries* (No. 1503). Post Keynesian Economics Study Group.

Stokes, Carlyle buy Coates Hire. (2007, October 3). Stokes, Carlyle buy Coates Hire. *The Australian*. Retrieved from http://www.theaustralian.com.au/

Stonington, J. (2010, December 6). Twenty billionaires who started with nothing. *Bloomberg*. Retrieved from http://www.bloomberg.com/

Stulz, R. M. (2007). Hedge funds: Past, present, and future. *Journal of Economic Perspectives, 21*(2), 175–194.

Sullivan, M. A. (2009). Proposals to fight offshore tax evasion. *Tax Notes*, 264–268.

Summers, L. H. (2014). The inequality puzzle. *Democracy Journal*. Retrieved from http://www.democracyjournal.org/

Swan, T. W. (1956). Economic growth and capital accumulation. *Economic Record, 32*, 334–361.

Swedin, E. G., & Ferro, D. L. (2005). *Computers: The life story of a technology*. Westport, CT: Greenwood Press.

Tamarkin, B. (1986, December 7). The ordeal of Lester Crown. (Pentagon challenges security clearance, cost overruns for General Dynamics). *The New York Times Magazine, 136*, S40.

The Economist. (2015, October 7). Global house prices. Retrieved from http://www.economist.com/blogs/dailychart/2011/11/global-house-prices

The West 100. (2006, August 13). The west 100. *Los Angeles Times*. Retrieved 19 May, 2014, from http://articles.latimes.com/2006/aug/13/magazine/tm-toppower33

Thurow, L. (1975). *Generating inequality*. New York: Basic Books, Inc..

Tinbergen, J. (1975). Substitution of academically trained by other manpower. *Review of World Economics, 111*, 466–479.

Torgler, B., & Piatti, M. (2013). Extraordinary wealth, globalization, and corruption. *Review of Income and Wealth, 59*, 341–359.

Treneman, A. (1998, March 1). Profile: The Duke of Westminster – Private property: Keep out. *The Independent*. Retrieved from http://www.independent.co.uk/

Trumbull, G. (2012). Credit access and social welfare: The rise of consumer lending in the United States and France. *Politics and Society, 40*, 9–34.

Tsigos, S., & Daly, K. (2016). "Fair go" for all? Wealth and risk aversion of Australian households. *Australian Economic Papers, 55*, 274–300.

Tuckman, E. (1973). *The economics of the rich*. New York: Random House.

Umfairteilung. (2012, September 8). *The Economist*. Retrieved from http://www.economist.com/

van Praet, N. (2014, March 4). 93-year-old Canadian real estate mogul makes Forbes billionaires list for first time. *Financial Post*. Retrieved from http://business.financialpost.com/

Veall, M. R. (2012). Top income shares in Canada: Recent trends and policy implications. *Canadian Journal of Economics, 45*, 1247–1272.

Verbit, G. P. (1978). Do estate and gift taxes affect wealth distribution? *Trusts & Estates, 117*, 598–616.

Vissing-Jørgensen, A. (2003). Perspectives on behavioral finance: Does irrationality disappear with wealth? Evidence from expectations and actions. In M. Gertler & K. Rogoff (Eds.), *NBER macroeconomics annual 2003*. Cambridge, MA: MIT Press.

von Neumayer, E. (2004). The super-rich in global perspective: a quantitative analysis of the Forbes list of billionaires. *Applied Economics Letters, 11*(13), 793–796.

Wachter, J. A., & Yogo, M. (2010). Why do household portfolio shares rise in wealth? *The Review of Financial Studies, 23*, 3929–3965.

Wai, J. (2014). Investigating the world's rich and powerful: Education, cognitive ability, and sex differences. *Intelligence, 46*, 54–72.

Waldman, D. E. (1991). How did the wealthiest Britons get so rich?: A comment. *Review of Industrial Organization, 6*, 291–294.

Watkins, G. P. (1907). The growth of large fortunes. *Publications of the American Economic Association, 8*(4), 1–170.

Wearing, R. (2005). *Cases in corporate governance*. London: Sage Publications.

Weber, M. (1958). *The Protestant ethic and the spirit of capitalism*. New York: Cambridge University Press.

Weil, D. N. (2014). *Capital and wealth in the 21st century*. Working Paper, Brown University.

Welbes, J., & Brewer, J. (2013, June 13). Dwight Opperman, former West Publishing chief, dies at 89. *TwinCities*. Retrieved from http://www.twincities.com/

Werdigier, J. (2011, July 15). Leo Kirch, media giant in Germany, dies at 84. *The New York Times*, p. B10(L).

Whan-woo, Y. (2014, February 5). Big leisure center planned on Yeongjong. *The Korea Times*. Retrieved from http://www2.koreatimes.co.kr/

Williams, E. (1944). *Capitalism & slavery*. Chapel Hill, NC: The University of North Carolina Press.

Willoughby, J. (1994, December 12). A modern-day Rockefeller. *Investment Dealers' Digest*, 12–19.

Yamashita, T. (2003). Owner-occupied housing and investment in stocks: An empirical test. *Journal of Urban Economics, 53*, 220–237.

Yamokoski, A., & Dubrow, J. K. (2008). How do elites define influence? Personality and respect as sources of social power. *Sociological Focus, 41*(4), 319–336.

Zaun, T. (2004, May 19). Technology briefing software: Sammy to acquire Sega for $1.45 billion. *The New York Times*, p. C3.

Zoromé, A. (2007). *Concept of offshore financial centers: In search of an operational definition* (WP/07/87). IMF Working Paper.

Zucman, G. (2014). *The hidden wealth of nations: The scourge of tax havens*. Chicago: The University of Chicago Press.

Index

S. Tsigos, K. Daly, *The Wealth of the Elite*, https://doi.org/10.1007/978-981-15-2148-5

The manufacturer's authorised representative in the EU is Springer Nature Customer Service Centre GmbH, Europaplatz 3, 69115 Heidelberg, Germany. If you have any concerns regarding our products, please contact ProductSafety@springernature.com

Printed and bound by CPI Group (UK) Ltd, Croydon, CR0 4YY
25/09/2026
02222898-0006